BOB NGUYEN

Midlife Crisis: Adapt, Evolve, Survive

I dedicate this book to my mom and dad because that's what you do, and my daughter, my light who never fails to give it back to me.

Contents

Preface   iii

Acknowledgement   iv

I   THE ROAD TOWARD CRISIS, MIDLIFE OR
OTHERWISE

1   Introduction   3

2   Saying F*ck It! When You're 50   9

3   The Midlife Crisis Pandemic   19

4   This is my story, and I'm sticking to it.   29

5   Your 20s: On Your Marks...   33

6   Your 30s: The Hedonic Treadmill and Happi-
    ness Set Point   42

7   Your 40s: Wait For It...   54

II   ADAPT

8   Emotional Well-Being: The Lay of the Land   65

9   Do Not Pursue Happiness   70

10 Winning the Expectations Game   87

11 Awareness and Self-Care   98

12 Kindness, Gratefulness and Awe   125

III   EVOLVE

13   Before You Wreck Yourself, Repurpose Yourself.   145
14   Break Out of Your Comfort Zone: Finding
     Optimal Anxiety   162
15   Laugh and Have Fun. But Don't Die.   179
16   It's Your Relationships, Stupid.   194

IV   SURVIVE

17   What Does a Body Good? It's Your DNA.   213
18   What Does Your DNA Good? Surprise, it's
     Exercise and Diet...   240
19   I'll Take Immortality Please.   266
20   You Might Want a Death Plan   282

21   Conclusion   297
Notes   300

Preface

We're all just walking each other home.
—Ram Dass

I wrote this book in the hopes of retiring early. Failing that, my other intention is to share some collective human wisdom and a bit of myself. Happy reading.

—b

Acknowledgement

With gratitude to friends who listened and spurred me on. Special thanks to Virginija Gecaite and Irad Eyal for their editorial support and Mary Hollendoner for her technical advice. Additional dope cover credits go to Mr. Eyal, co-creator of *Floor is Lava*.

I

THE ROAD TOWARD CRISIS, MIDLIFE OR OTHERWISE

There's 106 miles to Chicago, we've got a full tank of gas, half a pack of cigarettes, it's dark, and we're wearing sunglasses.
—*Elwood Blues*

Hit it.
—*Jake Blues*

1

Introduction

The aim of life is to live...No why or wherefore...
—Henry Miller

During a heated discussion with Albert Einstein, Nobel Prize winning Danish physicist Niels Bohr is purported to have proclaimed that a deep truth is one whose opposite is also a deep truth. Stated a different way, profound truths are recognized by the fact that their opposite is also a profound truth. But physicists talking about truth? Perhaps he and Albert had a few too many *akvavit* shots that evening. Be that as it may, it is an insight that applies to much more than physics. For instance, while we staunchly value our independence, we simultaneously derive meaning from our community. While we admire people with strong convictions, we also praise open-minded folk. While we must strive to be efficient in all things, we also need to make time for play. While we should love ourselves, we must always endeavor to become our best versions.

Similarly, the opposite great truth to crises such as midlife is that they can be equally transformative, paving the way for growth, with our lives often taking a remarkable upturn following them. With regard specifically to midlife crisis, happiness has been shown to initially bottom at midlife, then rise in the years to follow, sometimes surpassing the joy we experience in early adulthood. For many of us, however, hitting rock bottom is a necessary inflection point before we can turn it around. In this book, I will make the case that if this turn-around is executed properly, it can put us on the path to both emotional well-being and longevity.

In exploring this path, I will give multiple examples of psychological and scientific truths that are contrasted by equal and opposite truths. As we will see, there is complexity to the way our minds, bodies and cellular processes work, and when we try to oversimplify them, we often trip over our own cognitive feet.

** * **

The U-Shaped Curve of Happiness

An often-cited study originally published in 2008 by David G. Blanchflower and Andrew J. Oswald and later confirmed in other research shows that happiness follows a predictable U-shaped curve,[1] with peaks early and late in life. Midlife was noted to be the time when happiness was at its lowest, being defined as falling between 40-50 years. Fortunately, the curve consistently turns back up in the 50s, and people were found to achieve the same or even greater level of happiness in their 70s than they had in their 20s.

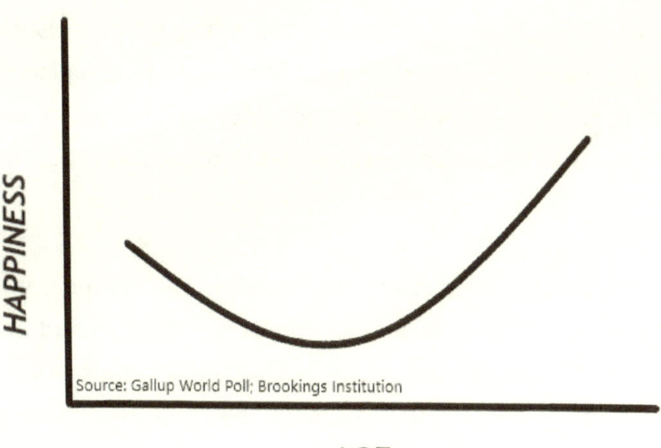

Knowing this is a natural phenomenon allows us to more gracefully experience this impermanent phase in our lives and mindfully prepare for our second act. Realizing this is normal, you can remind yourself and your friends that you are not alone and that there is nothing wrong with you. In his book, *The Happiness Curve: Why Life Gets Better After 50*,[2] Jonathan Rauch writes that "The curve seems to be imprinted on us in a way to repurpose us for a changing role in society as we age." This is an inviting way of thinking about midlife. Wisdom teaches us to reframe life events in a way as to derive meaning from things that are out of our control and may otherwise seem random or cruel.

Rather than a crisis, one could think of the events around midlife as a slowly progressive epiphany. This puts the emphasis on the end result rather than the beginning turmoil. Instead of neurotically fixating on our perceived failures and the reality that we have less life in front of us than behind us, we realize that the competitiveness and comparisons that incessantly occupied and partially served our lives up to that point no longer benefit us. It dawns on us at midlife that this is not the beginning of the end but rather the end of the beginning. Our early adult behavioral patterns fade away and are replaced with greater appreciation and more connectedness. Moreover, as we learn to be happy with who we are, we also learn to receive others as they are.

Though not everyone experiences a midlife crisis, for those who do, if they are successful in reframing this challenging period in their lives, it sets them up to maintain the strong relationships and healthy lifestyles that are essential to fulfillment and longevity in the second half of their lives.

I have organized this book into four sections. The first part will define the scope of the issue by exploring the phenomenon of midlife crisis and explain how data took it out of the realm of being a social peculiarity and showed that it is in fact a biologic commonality across nationalities and even primate species. In addition, I will describe how COVID took the crisis out of midlife, making it a trans-generational pandemic that afflicted adults of all decades. I will argue that despite the turmoil, the pandemic provided an opportunity for adults to reassess their choices and in many cases make changes that improved their quality of life.

In the second section, we will examine the adaptive processes possible following crisis. By taking a deep dive into mechanisms for emotional well-being, we can explore the potential for transformational growth. In order to do so, we must bring awareness to our individual behavioral tendencies, then turn this awareness outward.

In Part III, we will learn how to use the tools gained from our psychological adaptations to evolve our social behaviors. Starting from how we define ourselves and proceeding to how we interact with others, we can begin to move forward following our emotional reshuffling.

What will become clear following Parts II and III is the codependent relationship of social well-being with neurologic and overall physical health. This understanding and framework are useful at any point and not just at midlife. Often though, it takes a crisis for us to reassess where we are at and how to move forward. So whether it is due to age, COVID, another looming black swan event or just the cumulative stress of life, developing self-awareness and healthy coping tools will serve adults in any decade of life well.

In Part IV, I will explore how we optimize our physical bodies. Once we have adapted and evolved our psychosocial health following our personal crises, we can turn back to ourselves. I will address means of maximizing our healthy years and our lifespans. Not just a metaphoric inquiry, I offer answers to the question of how do we survive better and live longer? In this era of discovery, the quest for eternal life and the science to make it feasible seem on the cusp of converging. Research is rife with interventions to make the vision of radically expanded healthspans and lifespans a possible reality. As such, we will take another deep dive, this time inward to the DNA and cellular level. With the information I present, my hope is to provide a data-driven framework for readers to make longevity-promoting individual biohacking choices. This section represents the last arena in which we can transform crisis into growth.

Finally, I will fittingly close the book with a short discussion of the end of our days. Unlike other stages of our lives, for now death is a certainty for all of us, and I believe it can be mindfully anticipated rather than ignored or fretted over.

The chapters to follow will include incursions into psychology, philosophy, physics, politics, history, life science, molecular biology, statistics, economics, religion, pop culture and my life. Be warned, it will sometimes be tough sledding, as I will make frequent efforts to summarize topics that entire books have been based on. However, for the reader who values content and data over opinion, this is your book.

2

Saying F*ck It! When You're 50

And so it goes.
—*Kurt Vonnegut*

This section will first explore the makings of a crisis. While COVID-19 was the recent global turmoil du jour, any forthcoming catastrophic event could be substituted in its stead. Whether the crisis is due to approaching midlife or the result of existential mayhem, how we respond is everything. Do we choose the path of least resistance, not deviating from the status quo, and simply try to survive until the storm passes? Or do we right the ship and turn it into the wave? Chess masters will tell you that even in retreat, you can attack. I vote for the latter.

During our adult lives, circumstances will sometimes come to a head without reaching the level of a crisis. Although most of us probably like to believe that we possess full agency when reacting to them, psychological research has shown that our genetic makeup exerts a significant and consistent influence, oftentimes without our

9

awareness. Elements such as optimism bias, the hedonic treadmill, our happiness set point and intrinsic expectations all conspire to lean each of us in an emotional direction.

In conjunction with reviewing these psychological tendencies, this section will summarize the pandemic's influence on decade-specific situations. And after I have firmly established the case that we are unknowingly at the mercy of our inborn predispositions, I will review how we may be able to out-maneuver them in Parts II and III of the book.

* * *

At the time I started writing this book, I was within sniffing distance of being 50 years old. The idea for it came as a result of a surprising revelation I had, a classic *A-ha!* moment. I was at work, walking out of the preoperative holding area. I had just greeted my next surgical patient, initialed the operative site and answered their last-minute questions about if I had a good night's sleep and something to eat this morning, to which I answered yes and of course not (called caloric restriction, I will expand on this later).

I love my job for many reasons, but it is due in large part to the great relationships I have there. With one colleague, I have discussed many a life and relationship issue. We are of similar age, both divorcees and fathers to one daughter. This is a fellow that I had originally gotten to know well through the low-risk pastime of downhill mountain biking. Over the years, I have managed to break my face, wrist and hand all in the pursuit of finding flow in dirt, loam and rock. Keeping the rubber side down is sometimes an elusive goal.

The appeal of mountain biking is many-fold, with aerobic exercise serving as the entry fee for flying downhill at white-knuckle speeds. Après with high-fives and IPAs follow in the parking lot. I got indoctrinated in this faith starting in my mid-30s, and I have no doubt it has changed my life for the better.

During a period spanning years and as a result of multiple smaller, then progressively larger setbacks, my colleague developed refractory, disabling back problems. Before he was done with his 40s, he had the gamut of failed conservative treatments, culminating in multiple spine surgeries. After all that, he did experience relief, albeit still incomplete and intermittent.

During this extended period, he was unable to ride with us consistently, and as a result, I rarely saw him outside of work. And when I did run into him on the job, it was often an awkward balancing act between showing concern and just making casual conversation.

After putting initials on my patient's extremity in preparation for the time-out procedure,* I passed my friend and colleague in the hallway this particular day. I asked him how he was, and he casually mentioned that he had just spent a five-figure sum of money on a full suspension electric mountain bike. I was floored. A few years ago during a low back pain period, he had purchased a new four-figure mountain bike, only to be forced to sell it after realizing he could not ride it regularly due to recurring discomfort. We had not ridden together or even talked about biking much since then, and then he dropped this news. Sensing my confusion, he expressed that he was just past midlife, and though he may pay for it with a return of his back problems, he loved mountain biking, and this was possibly his last chance to enjoy it in this life. I interpreted this as his *f*ck it!* moment.

> **A time-out, which The Joint Commission on Accreditation of Healthcare Organizations defines as "an immediate pause by the entire surgical team to confirm the correct patient, procedure, and site," was introduced in 2003. This hospital checklist approach was adopted from a similar process that airline pilots have employed in their pre-flight procedures since 1935.*

As I went through my day and during the period that followed, I reflected on the state of mind that allowed my former riding companion to not only throw caution to the wind regarding a serious chronic ailment but to moreover double down and throw his wallet at it as well. Walking toward the operating room, I reflected on my own life. What lingering hesitations could I say *f*ck it!* to? What was I not saying yes to? And if not now, when?

* * *

I experienced my own midlife crisis at age 42 that was precipitated by my divorce. At 30, I had gotten married in City Hall on a Monday to a Russian woman I dared speak with while crashing a party in the trendy South End neighborhood of Boston. Twelve years later, with minimal drama and having produced a then 3-year-old girl, we parted ways because we had had stopped growing together. Despite that, as I neared midlife, I noticed a distinct upturn in my life outlook. The manner in which I experienced events suddenly took on a much lighter weight. I made decisions without worrying so much about how others would judge me and stopped viewing myself through the presumed lens of the world. This is precisely when my friend told me about his e-bike purchase, and this is when things clicked. I realized that I too felt footloose and fancy-free, despite having a seven-figure mortgage, an expanding forehead line and being a single dad and a health care worker in the eye of a pandemic. Unwittingly, I had also officially entered the *f*ck it* point of my life. Like falling in love and falling asleep, arriving at this stage happened slowly at first, then all at once.

Since 2005, I have lived in the Silicon Valley, the birthplace of the modern American Dream, where billion-dollar companies are given birth to in mom and dad's garage. For all the beauty and benefits of living in the San Francisco Bay Area, there are of course Bohr-downsides: anxiety, uncertainty, competition. Despite being immersed in this milieu, there was a return to happiness and easygoingness that I experienced as I approached midlife. As I explored this feeling more and researched it, I realized that I was not alone in having it. Finding out that people become happier as they approach and surpass 50 was shocking and exciting. This was not what I expected, and I wanted to learn more and share it.

Youth is wasted on the young, who rightly are too busy having fun to worry about health and their future. However, as a result of the COVID pandemic in the U.S., many adults in their 20s and 30s have gone through a version of their own midlife crisis while those in their 40s and 50s who were already on schedule for theirs had magnified experiences.[3,4,5] Older adults who had already experienced their crises just shook their heads. The confluence of uncertainty about health and employment combined with social isolation and time to reassess life goals resulted in this pan-generational phenomenon. As a result, I believe the content I present here is applicable to adults of any age. As COVID has reminded us, you don't have to be at midlife to have a crisis.

Approaches for Change

Before we begin this journey, how might you make it more likely you will follow the path of your choosing? In one of his skits, Jerry Seinfeld talks about how he never gets enough sleep because he likes to stay up late. He calls this person "Night Guy." What about his 5am wakeups? Oh that's "Morning Guy's" problem. That's not Night Guy's problem. In our everyday lives, we have conflicting interests. There are the wants of the present moment, and then there are the necessities of our future selves. How can we be good to morning guy and at the same time not rain on night guy's parade? One technique is a *commitment device*.

A commitment device is a means of future-proofing.[6] In essence, it is a voluntary act you make in the present to try to ensure that your future self sticks to a plan of action that your present self knows is good for you. Importantly, there is a tangible and punitive consequence should you deviate from this plan.

For instance, while drafting this book, I informed friends early on about my intentions, knowing that failure to complete the writing would be inconsistent with my self-perception of being true to my word. In so doing, I twisted my psychological arm and coerced myself to follow through. This takes advantage of the phenomenon of *cognitive dissonance,* where we try to minimize the degree to which our actions are in conflict with our core values. Though we most commonly attempt to reduce dissonance by rationalizing bad behavior that clashes with our positive principles—e.g., smoking, lying, cheating—in Bohr fashion, it is possible to exploit this human tendency for our own benefit. Instead of making a bad decision feel *less* uncomfortable, we can make *not* doing something good feel *more* uncomfortable.

An unexpected source of motivation for change came from my own espousal of the emotional and physical health hacks I researched. The more I tried to convince others of their merits, the more unwittingly committed I became to them. This has been described as the *hypocrisy paradigm* and represents another psychological manipulation of cognitive dissonance theory.[7] In this situation, people are enlisted to promote a socially beneficial behavior and in turn adopt that very behavior in order to not experience dissonance and appear hypocritical. Try it out on yourself!

Other commitment devices may take the form of prepaid gym memberships, not having junk food or alcohol in the house or having automatic 401k deductions. Indeed, a 401k in and of itself is a commitment device.

Temptation bundling is a similar type of strategy whereby one only participates in an enjoyable activity –such as bingeing a show—when it is bundled with a less enjoyable but healthier activity, such as exercise. As an incentive to write, I bundled it with drinking a warm cup of green tea in the morning or a glass of red wine paired with dark chocolate in the evening (more about this in the *What Does Your DNA Good?* chapter).

Another pro-tip about finding success when committing to change is to make short-term goals linked with some type of indulgence. It is similar to temptation bundling, but in some instances it may only be feasible to obtain your reward after the task has been completed. The key is to morselize the larger objective into smaller bite-size tasks, building up your task-endurance, and when they are accomplished, treat yourself to a carrot of your liking—perhaps to 30 minutes of you-time in which you are free to luxuriate in a mindless activity of your choosing.

Another approach to effect change is described by management and strategy professors Nordgren and Schonthal. In their book, *The Human Element: Overcoming Resistance That Awaits New Ideas* (2021),[8] they describe the influences of fuel versus friction to facilitate individual and group change. They point out that fuel is the often the first and only way we try to motivate a shift in behavior or thinking. Fuel is embodied by actions that heighten the appeal or "sizzle" of an idea, product or action by adding effort, features or incentives. This is the *Go Big or Go Home* mentality.

What is often neglected and underestimated in this "fuel-based mindset" is the power that psychological friction has to oppose change. Reducing friction requires knowing your audience, knowing yourself. To glean your personal friction, you need to ask what it is that resists change. For instance, is it related to lack of clarity or confidence, your life situation or specific emotional triggers?

Consider the tangible example of horsepower versus wind resistance in determining an object's top speed. Adding fuel in the form of power is intuitive and effective, but after a certain point, it is a much less efficient way to increase speed because friction in the form of wind resistance increases as the square of velocity. This is why all falling objects have a terminal velocity. Ultimately, when we try to modify behavior to increase our own well-being, there is typically the right individual combination of increasing fuel versus decreasing friction that will be effective, and recognition of these two different factors is a key step.

Perhaps the biggest psychological friction we all experience that slows down our adoption of any change is time itself. We innately recognize that every choice we make comes at the price of not making a different choice, and time is the unreplenishable currency we spend. Referred to as *opportunity cost*, it represents a significant source of resistance that we all contend with when making decisions. We will discuss it in detail in the Repurposing chapter.

In all the above examples, the change process begins as an internal acknowledgment of its need, an *awareness* of it (to be explored in a later chapter). Wharton Business School professor Katy Milkman has devoted her career to the study of behavior change. Her book, *How to Change: The Science of Getting from Where You Are to Where You Want to Be (2021)*,[9] is a clear and insightful manual on how to bring positive changes to your life. She reminds us that accomplishing our goals is easier when we make it pleasurable and that "most goals are just a means to a greater end." She emphasizes the importance of identifying our individual obstacles getting in the way of change (friction), being consistent with the approaches we choose to circumvent those obstacles and being adaptable if those obstacles fluctuate.

* * *

With these approaches for change in our repertoire, we might more consistently adopt a behavior that is both beneficial individually and brings us closer to others. For the remainder of Part I, I will survey the related elements of midlife and pandemic-induced crises. In Parts II and III, I will detail a number of adaptations for transforming crisis into growth while maximizing emotional health and evolving social connections. In Part IV, having adapted and evolved to the crisis, we can turn our focus to our physical bodies, where ageing, DNA and the pursuit of radical life extension take center stage. The scope of this book has been ambitiously exhaustive. In so being, I hope to provide an all-inclusive road map for how to travel from turmoil to well-being.

3

The Midlife Crisis Pandemic

Never let a good crisis go to waste.
—Winston Churchill

There has been plenty written about the midlife crisis phenomenon. However, I believe evaluating this experience deserves a revisiting in the context of the COVID-19 pandemic. No degree of superlatives can adequately describe the magnitude of the impact it had on all of our lives.

Overnight, adults used to spending 40+ hours a week at work were now stuck at home. Leaving the house occurred out of necessity only, and normal social outlets were unavailable. Seeing family members took on a life-or-death context, and with more than 6 million deaths worldwide, all of us suddenly came face to face with mortality. Add into all this the perception that the world is spinning out of control with climate change, social injustice and the specter of war once again upon Europe, and it makes for a potent midlife crisis concoction.

As a result of COVID, adults in all decades of their lives were given compelling reasons and a bunch of time to consider their choices in life up to that point and their path going forward, typical for someone going through midlife. For instance, more than 30 million U.S. workers quit their jobs in the second half of 2021, resulting in the so-called "great resignation."[10,11]

A line of thinking as to why COVID brought about a global midlife crisis is the increased occurrence of what psychologists call *counterfactual thinking*.[12] This refers to the "What if?" thoughts that we naturally ask, typically in the context of contemplating a less than ideal life circumstance. This type of rationale is central to human emotion and is divided into upward and downward counterfactual thinking.

In upward counterfactual thinking, people imagine how things could have been better if they had only made different decisions earlier. This often results in regret and feeling worse about their present scenario. For instance, imagining how a relationship might be more satisfying or a career better paying are examples of upward counterfactual thinking. In downward counterfactual thinking, people imagine how things might have been worse, typically in an attempt to reframe a negative life occurrence. Counting your blessings, as it were.

In the context of the pandemic, as a result of working from home or being laid off, millions of people collectively asked, "What if I didn't work so much, or what if I didn't work at all?" Sitting at home with a ton of time on their hands, people had plenty of opportunity to experience their own degree of counterfactual thinking. Counterfactual thinking influences our behavior both directly and indirectly. At times, it leads to a specific action while other times, it simply changes people's affect or mindset. In both instances, most psychologists believe it is an adaptive process and perhaps even an essential aspect of intelligence. Imagining how life circumstances could always be worse can be a productive means of reexamining unfortunate life circumstances.[13,14] However, excessively ruminating* on how things could be better can become maladaptive and is a risk factor for depression.[15]

> *The word ruminate has an interesting etymology. A ruminant is an animal such as a cow or sheep that chews things, then passes this chewed material down into a specialized stomach called a rumen, where it is fermented, brought back up into their mouths, now called cud, rechewed, then swallowed and fully digested. So when someone ruminates, they are continually regurgitating the same, typically negative thoughts from their psychological gut.*

All in all, COVID has sparked a global reevaluation of priorities. With this reevaluation, many people may now be living lives they believe more fulfilling and less stressful, but as Professor Bohr opined, this likely comes with an equal and opposite reality. For instance, in addition to less pay, part-time positions typically do not come with incentives such as health insurance or retirement benefits and are often unstable and less desirable positions.

A Brief History of Midlife Crisis

Before I launch into how life can be better after midlife crisis, let's touch on how the expression came into existence and whether a midlife crisis actually occurs. The first use of the phrase was by Canadian psychoanalyst Elliot Jaques in 1965.[16] "Death," he wrote, "instead of being a general conception, or an event experienced in terms of the loss of someone else, becomes a personal matter." The source of his insights is fascinating and came from studying some artistic giants of Western history.

From Beethoven to Voltaire to Chopin, he found that a creative crisis consistently occurred in these artists in their mid to late 30s. At that point, their work invariably underwent a decisive change. They emerged from this period in their 40s either markedly transformed or dead. For instance, Gauguin left his banking career at age 35 and became a preeminent post-impressionist painter at age 41. Shakespeare's early plays were comedies and written in his 20s, while in his 30s and 40s he wrote his most tragic pieces. Jaques purported that this process that he described in these artists in fact plays itself out in all of us. By studying the well-documented lives of these historical figures, he formed a theory that he felt applied to many of us.

Over time, reactions to the idea of a midlife crisis took on a stereotyped and negative social narrative. The notion became an excuse for people in their 40s and 50s to make impulsive decisions and justify whatever rash choices they made. And as is the American way, this trope has been taken to extremes in countless fictional depictions.

The midlife crisis became a perfect example of art copying life, then life copying the art that copied life in the first place. Yet just because it became farcical in some ways does not mean it is not true in others. Perhaps though, the idea of a *crisis* is overblown. The flaw with the idea of a crisis is that it implies that this midlife event occurs suddenly, quickly and with little time for adjustment or planned response. However, with an adequate understanding, a healthy mindset and a supportive community, this midlife turning point can be weathered with aplomb.

In Blanchflower and Oswald's study, they looked at 2 million people from 80 countries and found the consistent U-shaped curve described earlier. The same study also showed that this midlife low in happiness is not a strictly Western society phenomenon. Prior to the results of this study, there existed the notion that wealth and prosperity were strongly associated with midlife crisis, and that in more primitive and less affluent cultures, no such event occurs. However, when the researchers of this study adjusted for gender, income, marital status, presence of children, employment and other sociodemographic variables, that is when the U-shaped curve appeared, suggesting that age alone is the cause. In other words, the shape of the happiness U-curve is not a cultural or situational phenomenon but rather a biological one.

It bears noting that the bottoming of the happiness curve does *not* equate with having a midlife crisis. However, the occurrence of a crisis, though not a certainty, is a commonality that is temporally related to the bottoming of the U-curve.

It is also worth pointing out that culturally and historically, midlife crisis has been thought of as a "decidedly male" phenomenon.[17] Although women still experience the midlife low in happiness, they are not believed to experience midlife crisis as frequently as men, with perhaps only one-third of women having it.[18] Psychologists suggest that for men, the crisis is one centered around losing virility and youth, which serve as the primary motivations for their midlife antics. By contrast, in a study of 3,044 premenopausal women aged 42-52, they were found to consider midlife a critical point for "re-discovering self."[19] Thank god our species has women, most of whom understand how to productively channel their midlife issues.

The upturn in the U-shaped curve might be considered the *f*ck it inflection point*. As will be described later in the chapter on "Your 40s," a combination of high expectations early in life coupled with declining satisfaction and a peaking of regret are thought to lead us to the bottom of our happiness curve. After the inflection point, regret starts to decline at the same time our expectations level out and our life satisfaction increases.

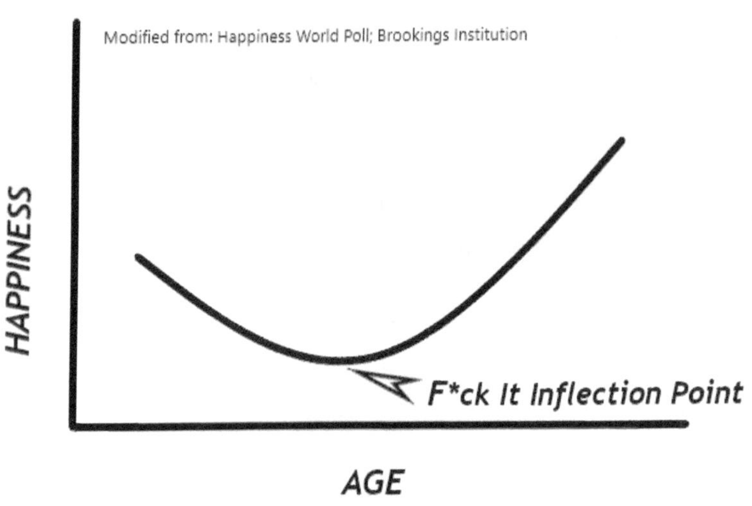

This U-shaped happiness relationship has been confirmed by more data that came out of the Brookings Institute from the 2010-2012 Gallup World Poll. Economists Graham and Pozuelo analyzed a survey set that included more than 160 countries and covers 99% of the world's population.[20] What they found is there is international consistency in the relative U-shape of the happiness curve. They also found that when data for stress level was available, the curve tracking it was predictably the opposite of the happiness curve, demonstrating a consistent hump-shaped pattern.

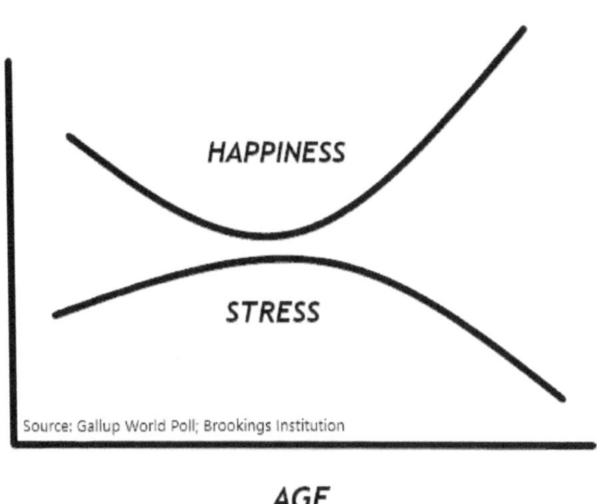

Where it is interesting is that the data showed that the curve turns upward earlier on average for happier people and for people in happier places. In those same places, when tracking stress levels, they were noted to decrease earlier in life. In effect, these people have longer periods of happiness and higher levels of happiness and concomitantly lower levels of stress. Also of note is the difference in the slope of the curves seen from one country to the next. For instance, the Indian happiness and stress curves trace much flatter lines, suggesting that they experience lower highs of happiness but higher lows of stress. Unfortunately, if you are Russian, you will have to wait until after you die to be happier, as the average age of death is 71 years, and their happiness curve does not project to turn up until 81.

Although the relationship between happiness and age is remarkably consistent in humans, it is obvious not everyone's life follows the same trajectory. In addition to the international differences in happiness U-curves, Graham and Pozuelo showed that people within the same country experience different shapes of their U-curves, with both different ages of transition and varying lows in their level of happiness.

And now, fascinating information from the primate kingdom. Not only is the happiness curve a collective human occurrence, but it is also not even strictly isolated to humans. In a study from Weiss et al. from 2012,[21] researchers found that great apes—which include gorillas, orangutans and chimpanzees—also suffered a midlife low in happiness at a chronologically equivalent point in their lives. The study showed that during this time period, these primates had the lowest mood, the least pleasure in social activities and the poorest capacity to achieve their goals. In other words, there seems to be a biological basis for this nadir in happiness across not only cultures, but also species.

As seen in the happiness curves, there is not an abrupt transition as we reach midlife. Perhaps then it might be better to think of this phase more as a rite of passage rather than a crisis. Arnold van Gennep is a French anthropologist who wrote that all rites of passage are characterized by three distinct phases: separation (leaving the familiar), transition (a time of testing, learning and growth), and return (incorporation and reintegration).[22] Breaking down the midlife transition in this way may help make it more manageable. At some point during our 40s to 50s, we will leave behind some of our hopes and dreams and dramatically shift our trajectory. As written in Joseph Campbell's hero saga which gave birth to the *Star Wars* series, "We must be willing to let go of the life we planned so as to have the life that is waiting for us…"[23] In a way, crises due to midlife or COVID have put us all on our own individual hero's journeys. At some point on this path, we will experience the death of a version of ourselves; and only from that death can we be reborn into our new lives.

Marie Kondo writes, "Your past will become a weight that holds you back and keeps you from living in the here and now."[24] With the simple philosophy that what we choose to keep in our lives should "spark joy," Ms. Kondo built a decluttering empire. Both literal and metaphoric, this approach to life has inspired millions globally and is equally suited to all adults. And like the pandemic-induced midlife crisis, one need not wait until 50 to start assessing, decluttering and making choices that spark joy. To be fully present in the second half of our lives, we need to tidy up and move on from much of the stuff we have collected in the first half. Only by cleaning out the Old Us can we make more space for New Us.

* * *

Stepping back a bit, it's important to realize that in the greater perspective of human evolution, living to a ripe old age beyond 50 is an extremely modern phenomenon for humans. The maximum lifespan in 1800 globally ranged from 28-35. By 1950, that increased to 72. In other words, over the span of homo sapiens' 300,000-year existence, we have only had to deal with midlife and its crisis for about 0.02 % of that time. Therefore, the whole process of experiencing it, recognizing it and then finally learning how to deal with it is relatively new territory for us as a species.

In the next chapter, I will briefly describe my family's immigrant beginnings and my parents' transformation of crisis into well-being.

4

This is my story, and I'm sticking to it.

All great deeds and all great thoughts have a ridiculous beginning.
—Albert Camus

Like many Vietnamese of my generation, I came to the United States as a result of the Vietnam War. I was one and a half and the youngest of four children aged 8 and under who my parents had in tow as they fled a falling Saigon in the spring of 1975.

My father was from Hanoi, North Vietnam, and at age 18, he went to Saigon, South Vietnam to go to college and eventually become a physician. He would never return home after that, because in Saigon he met my mother, who was a pharmacist and a beauty queen. She had many suitors, and my father was not the tallest of them by a long shot. He would come calling on her, be sat in the foyer, wait for hours, chatting with her sisters, and would often finally fall asleep. More times than he would like to admit, my mom never came down to greet him. That process repeated enough times for my mom to get the hint he was not going away. So they got married.

For many years, life was good for them, and they spawned 4 children. When the war that was simmering for some time finally broke out, my father held a position in the Saigon military police. There, he worked alongside American troops, and although he never talked about the war much, he did regale us with stories of offering the American soldiers "chicken" when in fact it was dog.

When Saigon fell, circumstances necessitated that my father leave separately from my mother and we children. Without the benefit of cell phones or instant messaging, it took my parents some time and emotional turmoil before reuniting in beautiful Salinas, California. After settling into a small home loaned to us by the local pastor, mom and dad began from scratch and restarted their educational processes. So while my dad took orders from residents half his age, my mom made my 8-year-old brother watch over the 3 of us in a park across the street from the university she was examining in.

Despite our best efforts to derail them, my father and mother completed their medical and pharmaceutical retraining. Tired of California climate and natural beauty, my parents moved to slightly less lovely Flint, Michigan. There, we learned about crawdads, grasshoppers and dented canned food that could kill you. As stipulated in his first hospital contract, my father purchased an icon of American motoring, a diarrhea-brown Chevrolet Impala full-size station wagon, coming standard with rear-facing child third row suicide seats. The year was 1980, and our house had orange shag carpeting, linoleum floors and clashing wallpaper.* We were rocking out to Hall and Oates, had snow days and Huffy bikes with banana seats. Five years after arriving in a foreign country, my parents had achieved the American dream.

> *The reader may note my inconsistent use of the Oxford comma, and I make no apologies about it. While it is sometimes required for clarity, most times, it's just an unnecessary keystroke. For a hilarious read on the Oxford comma, check out https://www.gq.com/story/oxford-comma-enthusiasts-unite*

Fresh out of residency and in his mid-40s now, my dad took the job he could get, which was working ER shifts out of a hospital in downtown Detroit. One night as he walked from the parking lot to the hospital, he was held-up at knife point. He told the assailant he could stab him, but he had no money in his wallet, which he showed him. The man let my dad go to work. Word. Wanting to share these fun experiences with him, I would manifest go-to-work-with-your-dad evenings, feasting on unlimited chocolate milk and re-heated mystery meat while watching late night television in his call room. Anything can become an adventure for a kid, and just spending time with my dad those few nights was probably the highlight of my entire relationship with him.

When my dad turned 50, my parents decided that there was no sustainable future with his current shift work ER employment. The job would not get any easier; the city was not getting any safer; my dad was not getting any younger. This was their *f*ck it!* moment when they packed up and left the first home they owned in this country. Ten years after their arrival to the United States, they came to their senses and headed back to California with the hope for something better. One year later, my mom and dad set up a private practice family medicine clinic in the San Fernando Valley. They enjoyed a 15-minute commute while serving the local population and transformed our family crisis into a successful business that allowed for lunchtime *phở* soup as well.

In the following chapters we will explore pivotal moments occurring in the decades preceding midlife that happened more frequently as a result of the pandemic. Like my parents, many people made career and life altering decisions because of their own personal crises.

5

Your 20s: On Your Marks…

Simple it's not, I'm afraid you will find, for a mind maker-upper to make up his mind.
—Dr. Seuss, Oh, The Places You'll Go!

I'm just drifting.
—Benjamin Braddock (Dustin Hoffman), The Graduate

Let's take a stroll down memory lane into your roaring twenties, in which you are wrapping up young adulthood and perhaps your higher education and subsequently ask, "Now what?" It is a decade of seemingly unlimited time, energy, and possibilities, with equally unlimited anxiety for choosing the right direction. This is also the period in your life for whatever grunt work is necessary.

In her book, *Passages: Predictable Crises of Adult Life,*[25] Gail Sheehy refers to this decade as "The Trying 20s." She writes, "Incandescent with {their} molten energies…{they} are not only trying to prove ourselves competent in the larger society but intensely aware of being on trial…".

Mark Manson advocates that we fail early and often in our 20s.[26] Roger that. I failed two of my undergraduate mandatory classes, one on purpose. Notable other failures range from Oprah Winfrey who was fired from a news anchor position, J.K. Rowling who was on welfare (more on her later!), and Steve Jobs who got sacked by the company he founded.

Meg Jay calls the 20s, *The Defining Decade*, and her 2012 book entitled as such speaks to the urgency of this time in our lives.[27] She states, "The one thing I have learned is that you can't think your way through life. The only way to figure out what to do is to do—something."

In my early twenties, I was a medical student, and in my mid-twenties, an orthopedic surgical resident. As was the time-honored tradition, we were chewed up and spit out to make us better, more compassionate doctors. As an intern at age 25 and throughout my residency, we worked up to 120 hours a week (for math fans, there are 168 hours in a week), before the current era when oversight and limits of an 80-hour work week for residents were installed. Whether or not you agree with this approach—be it in medicine or any other field—you cannot deny that you are much more able to withstand any manner of physical torture in your twenties than any other decade.

As a case in point, one evening around midnight after I had completed my intern laundry list of drawing blood, placing central venous lines, eyeballing postop incisions, checking labs and writing medication orders, I was paged because an elderly patient who had been given the whole gamut of defecation-inducing interventions had still not pooped. The night nurse informed me that there was only one other option: disimpaction. Webster's defines this process as the following:

A lubricated, gloved index finger is inserted into the rectum and the hardened stool is gently broken up using a scissoring motion.

Let's take a moment to disimpact this definition. Does the finger actually need to be lubricated and gloved? Furthermore, does it need to be the index finger? And finally, I think we would all agree that the image of scissoring someone's rectum is a bit disconcerting.

So I arrived at the patient's bedside shortly after the strike of midnight. I was in Boston, and while most other twenty-somethings were enjoying 10-cent wing night at Whiskey's or watching "Scrubs" that evening, here I was, living "Scrubs." I introduced myself to this gentleman, poised on the porcelain throne, sweating and clearly exhausted from bearing down to no effect. I described the procedure, as Webster did, and he nodded his consent to it. Not having ever read about let alone perform this procedure, I still instinctively just knew what to do. Oh the treasures I unearthed. Chocolate-chip-cookie-dough-like stuff. Whole undigested capsules. As I was gently scissoring, I tried to become one with the poop, willing it out, trying to find the Buddhist state of *no self* (described in detail in the Awareness chapter). In the end, I concluded that the only person other than me that this was more awkward for was him. These and other thoughts crossed my mind during the fifteen minutes or so I was in gentle action. Having completed my mission, the man thanked me, and we shook ungloved, unlubricated hands.

The problem that many twenty-somethings have is they fail to grasp the finiteness of their decade and its concomitant health and time surplus. They often squander this period in ambivalence.

Compounding this lackadaisical approach, they believe the choices they make in their career direction, relationship status and geographic location are irrevocable, which leads to indecision.

In addition to their failure to be decisive, people in their 20s are often paradoxically optimistic. Perhaps more so than in any other decade, they like to believe they are special, that they will succeed in the end. Interestingly but perhaps not surprisingly, this tendency, referred to as *optimism bias*,[28] follows a similar course as the U-shaped joy curve. It is high in our early lives, reaches a nadir in our 40s, then rises again afterwards.

With optimism bias, also referred to as *superiority illusion*, the individual believes their likelihood of positive outcomes is higher and/or their chance for a negative outcomes is lower than the "average" person. To be sure, optimism bias is very common and likely an important evolutionary trait. It is estimated that 80% of humans display this type of bias. In fact, according to Tali Sharot, a preeminent researcher on optimism bias, it is "one of the most consistent, prevalent, and robust biases documented in psychology and behavioral economics."[29] And for good reason. Optimism represents hopefulness and confidence that the future holds a positive outcome. One can see how believing in yourself to this degree can motivate action and courageousness with subsequent advantages for the individual and collectively for the human species. Optimism bias has even been shown to exist in birds and mice![30]

In her research into optimism bias, Sharot and her co-researchers found that different brain areas lit up during functional MRI* when humans receive positive data and when they receive negative data. In one study, they were able to temporarily and selectively shut down the positive data response center in the brain, which eliminated optimism bias. In general, she found people are better able to incorporate and learn from positive data than negative data. This is the basis of optimism bias and accounts for the phenomenon that we hear what we want to hear.

**Functional Magnetic Resonance Imaging (fMRI) is an imaging study devised in 1990 that can track small changes in blood flow to specific areas of the brain in response to whatever is being researched. Basically, specific areas of the brain "light up" in response to specific stimuli. Researchers use this information to assess the effect of stimuli on specific parts of the brain, such as in conditions as diverse as drug addiction, Alzheimer's Disease and sarcasm. In Sharot's research, adults with a larger orbitofrontal cortex were found to be more optimistic and less anxious. One intriguing use of fMRI involved tracking famous rock climber Alex Hannold's fear center in the brain. The amygdala is known to be the brain's fear center, the place where threats are interpreted and responded to. Among other accomplishments, Hannold was the first climber to "free-solo" El Capitan, Yosemite's 3000-foot granite cliff. This means he climbed without the use of aids or ropes. Researchers found that his fear center was completely cold when his brain was presented with any manner of fear-inducing imagery.*

In clinically depressed individuals, the centers correlating with optimistic responses were equally active when presented with the same positive data but the centers taking in negative data were more responsive. In other words, when depressed people received negative data, their brains were more receptive to it and therefore more realistic about it. By contrast, when non-depressed people were presented with the same negative data, they cognitively blew it off. "{Depressed people} see the world as it is," says Sharot. But is that good? The default pattern it seems leans toward optimism in ours and other species. Sharot writes, "…in the absence of a neural mechanism that generates unrealistic optimism, it is possible all humans would be mildly depressed."

Despite the intuitive advantages of being optimistic, the great truth of optimism bias has an opposite great truth. Its downside is it can lead to a failure to accurately assess risk in any particular situation. For instance, in one study, 93% of drivers believe they are better than average, leading to more accident-causing behaviors. In another example, a survey by two Ohio researchers found that 25% of respondents said they were in the top 1% for getting along well with others. Optimism bias is commonly observed in newlyweds who underestimate their chances for divorce, financial analysts who overestimate their profit margins and medical professionals who underestimate risks of treatments. Optimism bias in the workplace leads to failing to take measures to adequately mitigate risk on the individual level. For instance, optimism bias in firefighters has been shown to be a causative factor in firefighter death. On the organizational level, optimism bias is believed to be the cause for cost overruns in big budget projects such as the Olympics.[31]

But here's where it gets interesting. Sharot reports that although optimism bias is not founded in known statistics and has its downsides, it still has demonstrable health benefits. Overall, optimists live longer and are healthier. They have lower anxiety levels which in and of itself decreases levels of the stress hormone cortisol, a known detriment to brain health and even life expectancy when excessively elevated (more on this in the chapter on What Does a Body Good?).[32],[33] Optimists also tend to demonstrate healthier behaviors in eating and exercise. In the end, it may be a wash between the upsides and downsides of this bias if looking at individual examples.

However, evolutionary biologists have argued that optimism bias is in fact not just important, but actually necessary for the survival of the human species. They cite one factor that may tip the scale in favor of this bias. And it is the following: while our big brains allow us to do big things—plan ahead and see our future selves—this amazing sentience also comes with the burden of recognizing our own mortality. This is known as the *mortality paradox* (discussed in the Immortality chapter). Without optimism to counter this paradox, humans might become psychologically crippled, too depressed to leave the cave or get off the couch.

COVID's effect on 20-somethings

In the COVID era, optimism bias likely led individuals to believe they are less likely to become infected or severely affected by the condition. In a study by Kim,[34] both young and old people in the U.S. who initially mitigated their risk-taking behavior at the onset of COVID, subsequently increased their risk-taking behavior as the pandemic progressed. However, because optimism bias runs hotter in young adults, coupled with the reality that they are scientifically less likely to be stricken with significant disease, younger people tended to display a proportionately higher degree of risk-taking behavior as the pandemic progressed.

This tendency for higher risk-taking in younger people has been noted in previous work that pre-dates COVID. In a multi-national study looking at risk-taking behavior in 11 Western and non-Western countries,[35] propensity toward risk-taking consistently peaked across cultures in late adolescence. However, the researchers found that health risk-taking peaked during the mid or late 20s. Their explanation for this was that although *inclination* for risk was highest during adolescence, *opportunities* to act on those inclinations were more available in young adulthood.

During the pandemic, adults in their 20s continued to live with their parents, postponing marriage and the decision to have children.[36] Employment during the pandemic in the younger population showed a disproportionately higher job loss with correspondingly higher job insecurity.[37] Possibly as a result of all of these factors, young adults were hit hardest by loneliness during the pandemic.[38]

The birth rate during the pandemic demonstrates a mixed picture.[39] For the first few months of the pandemic in the Spring of 2020, births were down when extrapolating data nine months out. However, that trend reversed itself quickly, and by the summer and fall of 2020, the conception rate dramatically increased. When broken down into age groups, births dropped in older women and those with greater education and resources.[40] Instead, it was found that a greater proportion of babies born during late 2020 and early 2021 were born to younger people with fewer resources. As noted before, risk-taking behavior increased relatively more in younger people as the pandemic wore on, and this may just be an extension of that mentality of optimism bias.

Overall, because of the postponement of pivotal life decisions inherent to this decade, it is possible that adults in their 20s suffered the greatest proportion of personal crises due to the pandemic, with far-reaching consequences yet to be realized. That said, they do have health and time on their side along with the resilience and optimism bias of youth. As a result, they possess the opportunity to reassess and adjust their life trajectory, perhaps with a renewed sense of self and purpose they might not otherwise have gained without crisis.

* * *

During my 20s, I finished college, medical school and four of my five years of orthopedic surgical residency. To limit my life choice anxiety, I kept my focus on the next checkpoint—whether it be an exam, the completion of a rotation or the end of a night on call. For those 10 years, I did the necessary grunt work, and at age 30, I had an annual income of $40,000 and was living on the 21st floor of a studio apartment that overlooked the Charles River. The western-facing views of sunsets over the water made up for the drafts so wicked in my apartment in the winter that I could see my breath. I saved money by not using the heater, and though this residence demanded more than half my monthly paycheck, I was ecstatic, as medical training had ground my expectations for comfort down to bare minimums (much more on Expectations in a separate chapter). Despite frequent existential moments and what amounted to less than minimum wage for the hours I worked, I still felt fortunate in having chosen medicine because it truly did feel like my calling. Happily, my feeling did not lie. For many others in their 20s, this may not be the case, and finding a balance between sticking things out and reassessing choices is perhaps the biggest challenge of this decade.

6

Your 30s: The Hedonic Treadmill and Happiness Set Point

I just read that men reach their sexual peak at 18. Women reach their sexual peak at 35. Do you get the feeling that God is into practical jokes? We're reaching our sexual peak right around the same time they're discovering they have a favorite chair.
—Rita Rudner

In this world there are only two tragedies. One is not getting what one wants, and the other is getting it.
—Oscar Wilde

So you've survived your 20s and although your adulting timeline might have been delayed in some aspects due to crisis, hopefully you have something to show for it. In that decade, there was a flurry of change and upheaval, and you gave yourself little time to ponder the consequences of the choices you made, but you absolutely knew they had to be made. Some important boxes may have been checked, and as you near 30 you again ask yourself, *Now what?* We question whether that dream we had in our 20s is the same dream we should have in our 30s. At the same time we are told we need to have figured our path out by now, there is often a nagging but unfocused drive for more. More of what, we do not know.

Gail Sheehy writes, "A restless vitality wells up as we approach 30…the impulse to broaden often leads us to action even before we know what we are missing." She reminds us that "growth demands a temporary surrender of security…"[41]

In our 30s, we start to question what we have achieved and acquired. We may not regret the choices we made in our 20s, but there is a growing sense that there is more to life. The questioning may even lead to major changes in our career paths and relationships. We must choose to acknowledge and act on these swelling inclinations or to double down and settle even more deeply into the life we have thus far worked so hard to create for ourselves. Unfortunately, both options are justifiable, and both are deeply disruptive.

The 30s have been described as the decade when your friends disappear. A Finnish study in 2016 analyzing mobile phone com-munications concluded that friend generation peaks around age 25 and following that, to different degrees in women and men, begins to decline until around 45.[42] From 45 to 55, it stabilizes, then starts to decline again afterwards.

Several factors are thought to account for this shrinking of our friend count in our 30s.[43] First, our social circles simply become smaller. Instead of a massive student body, we have the break room. In addition, with career and family development under way, we have greatly reduced disposable time and energy to dedicate to maintaining outside relationships. Finally, another friend-depleting factor is the geographic mobility intrinsic to this decade. Of college-educated millennials, it is estimated that about a million cross state lines each year in the U.S.[44]

William Rawlins, an Ohio University professor who has been researching friendship for nearly 40 years, states, "There's a certain kind of poignancy in young adulthood, when we've come to develop a mature regard for friends at the very same time that somehow they've started slipping away."[45] One of life's ironies is that the friends that were there for us when we made our big career and relationship decisions in our 20s are the very ones that we lose touch with in our 30s because of those decisions.[46,47]

Though there is value and nostalgia in retaining friends *who knew us when,* it is equally true that creating new social circles and friendships are beneficial in that they allow us to reinvent ourselves and not be confined to the box in which our old friends lovingly imprison us. In our 30s we are often faced with these two social paths, and choose we must. If possible, one can strike a balance between these opposing types of social tendencies –referred to as homophily and heterophily. I will delve more deeply into these two polar phenomena in the chapter, "Break out of Your Comfort Zone: Finding Optimal Anxiety."

Although the plans we make in our 30s may be well laid-out and properly executed, that does not ensure happiness at the end of it all. A defining trait of human cognition and higher intelligence is the ability to foresee our future selves and plan for that. We are remarkably adept at this. However, foreseeing ourselves does not necessarily mean foreseeing ourselves *accurately.* Even when we achieve a goal, the extent and duration of our fulfillment is often not what we anticipated.

Conversely, when life throws body blow after body blow at us, we often get right back up as if we have emotional amnesia. It is perhaps in our 30s that this human peculiarity first dawns on many of us. Despite working hard to get to where we got to in our careers and lives, we still can't get no satisfaction. Let's explore this.

The Hedonic Treadmill

One significant purported cause of our tolerance to both sustained happiness and resilience to intermittent hardship is a phenomenon called *Hedonic Adaptation* or the *Hedonic Treadmill.* This phrase was coined by psychologists Philip Brickman and Donald Campbell in their essay "Hedonic Relativism and Planning the Good Society" (1971).[48] Hedonic adaptation is a phrase used to describe the observed tendency that we demonstrate to return to the same relative level of happiness or satisfaction, despite whatever positive or negative events befall us. On a neural level, the receptors and neurochemicals that control the happiness switch in our brains are thought to naturally adapt to increased or decreased stimuli and return to an individual intrinsic baseline. This will be described in more detail in the chapter, "Winning the Expectations Game."

Though hedonic adaptation may seem paradoxically counterproductive to staying happy, the thought is that it developed in order for humans to adjust to recurrent life events, positive or negative.[49] It is an automatic habituation process that adapts humans to respond less to constant stimuli in order to preserve their biological resources to respond to newer changes, which are more likely to require immediate attention.

Although hedonic adaptation makes sense from an evolutionary standpoint, it becomes a demotivating factor in the modern age when achievement is valued so highly. Ed Diener, one of the lead researchers in the field of subjective well-being, AKA Dr. Happiness, glumly summarizes it thus:[50]

"...imagine that no matter how much effort and care someone put into being happy, the long-term effects were no different than if he or she lived a profligate and dissolute life."

In their seminal study, Brickman and Campbell suggested that hedonic adaptation is explained by an individual's *happiness set point* that is genetically predetermined and that remains fairly fixed throughout someone's lifetime.[51] In spite of the ebb and flow of fortune and misfortune, people eventually return to their own happiness set point.

To look more deeply into the possibility that one's happiness set point is inherited, psychologists Lykken and Tellegen (1996) conducted a study following a thousand set of twins** for more than ten years.[52] In the end, after adjusting for other variables, they concluded that the happiness set point is close to 80% heritable. By contrast, they found that other variables such as socioeconomic status, educational attainment, family income, marital status and religion could not account for more than about 3% of the variance in well-being. Again, this is demotivating data for ambitious or hopelessly romantic people. This disparity of genetic influence on our happiness set point has been questioned in later research, and we will explore this and more in the chapter, "Do Not Pursue Happiness."

Brickman's* most well-known contribution to the study of happiness might have been his sexily titled article, "Lottery winners and accident victims: Is happiness relative?" (1978)[53] In this study, the researchers interviewed lottery winners and traumatic quadriplegics and paraplegics to determine their change in happiness levels following their respective life-changing events. For the lottery winners, though the winning event elevated their happiness levels initially, it eventually returned to a level not significantly different than people who had not won the lottery. Moreover, the lottery winners found less joy in "mundane" activities of life than controls. In the trauma group, their happiness level was below the controls, but what was surprising is that they still considered themselves above average in happiness.

> *Philip Brickman was 34 years old when he published this article and was thought to be an up-and-coming expert in the field of happiness. Tragically, he chose to take his own life at age 38. He jumped from the roof of the 26th floor of the tallest building in Ann Arbor, where he was just made director for a prestigious institute for social research. Despite his extensive work in human happiness, he failed to find his own. He wrote, "Happiness involves the enthusiastic and unambivalent acceptance of activities or relationships that are not the best that might possibly be obtained...There may be no way to permanently increase the total of one's pleasure except by getting off the hedonic treadmill entirely." And that is what he did.*

Though this study had significant design flaws, it is often cited as the source of the cliché that money does not buy happiness. More recent studies done on the relationship between the two has shown more nuanced results. For instance, research by Harvard Business School professor Jon Jachimowicz showed how money can indirectly increase well-being.[54] In his research, he found that money reduced the intensity of stressful events, brought greater control for people when negative events occurred and also resulted in higher life satisfaction. Thus, it is not what money gets you, it is what money allows you to avoid that is relevant. He states, "While money may not necessarily buy happiness, it reduces the intensity of stressors experienced in daily life—and thereby increase life satisfaction."

In another study, Jachimowicz and researchers found that "higher income is more consistently linked to how *frequently* individuals experience happiness than to how *intensely* happy each episode is."[55] They suggested that the frequency of happy events may be due to the amount of time people are engaged in leisure activities. They went on to further differentiate between active and passive leisure. They defined active leisure to include praying, socializing, exercise, hobbies and volunteering. They defined passive leisure as watching TV, relaxing, and sleeping.

They found that lower levels of income were related to higher levels of passive leisure time use, which in turn predicted lower happiness frequency. Interestingly, there was *not* a significant correlation between higher income and higher active leisure activities. In other words, the mechanism behind income's influence on happiness frequency may be that lower income leads to activities that generate less happiness rather than higher income leading to activities that generate more happiness. Higher income leads to fewer passive leisure activities, which in turn leads to greater happiness frequency. An intervention they suggest based on their findings was to "nudge low-income individuals away from passive leisure activities and toward uses of time that yield greater meaning." In modern times, scrolling social media on a smartphone might be considered passive leisure and therefore be associated with lower well-being.

*** A Brief Primer on Scientific Study Types: When studying human conditions, twins come in real handy. Why? Identical twins have identical DNA. So if researchers can gather enough twins and follow them long enough over time and ask the right questions, they can determine with good accuracy to what degree certain behaviors and traits are genetically influenced and to what extent they are the result of that person's environment (or study intervention).*

For instance, twin studies have estimated that height is 80% related to genetics, and intelligence is 75% related. Though there have been critics of the validity of twin studies, it is one of the oldest and accepted means of scientific research. Before people knew what genes were and how traits were passed on, scientists recognized the utility of twin studies.

Without twins, doing scientific studies is much more challenging. In general, there are two main types of scientific studies. First, there are studies in which a particular outcome or disease is looked at, and the researcher goes backwards and tries to determine what factors may have caused that outcome. For instance, in studying lung cancer, a researcher will ask what factors might have caused it. Looking at things such as behavior – i.e., smoking— or race/gender/age, the researcher can draw conclusions about tendencies by doing statistical analyses. Though this type of study is very useful because researchers can choose the specific disease or outcome they want to study, its main drawback is that trying to work in reverse to determine a reason for a disease can lead to any number of conclusion errors due to factors the researcher did not or could not account for. This is known as bias and is the most significant factor affecting the validity of these types of studies.

In the other type of study, researchers choose subjects who have not yet experienced a particular outcome. To do this study, researchers must subject participants to a specific "exposure" and determine its effects. This exposure can come in the form of a new medication, surgical treatment or psychological intervention. To make the results of the study as accurate as possible, researchers will try to control for as many factors as they can in the participants such as gender, age, ethnicity and other health and demographic variables. (With twin studies, everything except environmental factors is theoretically controlled for.)

This type of study of course has limitations as well. The main limitations are time, rarity of the condition and ethics. For diseases that take years or a lifetime to develop or conditions that are uncommon, it is often not possible to keep track of all the subjects over the entire course of the study. This is called loss to follow up. As a result, over time researchers will inevitably lose more and more data points. This will detract from the validity of any conclusions because had those subjects stayed in the study, they might have unequally affected the results in one direction or the other and this direction cannot be determined without their data.

The other downside to this type of study is there are only so many exposures you can ethically impose on subjects. That said, history provides many examples of ethical workarounds. Nazis would deliberately infect Jews with pus from another human and treat half of them with antibiotics and half with placebo. In another example, the American physician and eugenicist Leo Stanley experimented on inmates at San Quentin by implanting other inmates' testicles to determine if he could normalize their behavior. And when supply was low, he used deer and goat testicles. Of course. Another notorious example is the United States Public Health Service's Tuskegee experiments on syphilis in black men that continued to be run up until 1972. In this study, black men who had syphilis were lied to about the condition they were being treated for and what they were being treated with, in exchange for being given free medical care, meals and burial insurance. The study started in 1932 and even though by 1942 the standard treatment for syphilis was penicillin, the participants were not given this. Instead, researchers wanted to follow the progressive effects of untreated syphilis over time, which included blindness, brain damage and death. Of the 399 black men who had known syphilis at the beginning of the study, 128 of them died of the disease or its complications. In addition, 40 wives were infected, and 19 children were born with congenital syphilis.

COVID's effect on 30-somethings

In a similar fashion as individuals in their 20s, people in their 30s also postponed marriage, cohabitated more or lived with their parents longer.[56] In addition, birth rates were seen to decline in women aged 30-34.

With regard to employment during COVID, a study from the Netherlands in February 2022 found that increased age correlated positively with psychological well-being during the pandemic.[57] They found that older workers were more resilient to the stresses that COVID brought due to their being able to reframe the crisis and see it as an opportunity for personal growth.

Indeed, the resilience observed in older workers during COVID is not an isolated phenomenon. Linkov et al. found that the older population in general were better at coping with stressful life changes than their younger counterparts.[58] Moreover, a study from 2013 by Jeste et al. suggested that resilience in older age was as important as physical health in self-rated successful ageing.[59] This finding correlates with the changing slope of the U-shaped curve of happiness as we get older. Age provides more resilience perhaps due to a combination of decreasing regret and diminished expectations. We will explore this relationship more in the next chapter.

Despite being more resilient, workers aged 30-45 showed disproportionately higher rates of quitting during the pandemic. As a result, the employment atmosphere heavily favored hiring for a period of time. However, as fears of a global recession increased, many of the tech companies that went on a hiring binge early on were the same companies who purged themselves as the pandemic officially came to an end. All totaled, tech layoffs by early 2023 amounted to nearly 70,000 hoodies and skinny jeans no longer strolling in at 10:30 am.[60]

The larger degree of quitting may have been due to deeper reassessments of life choices coupled with greater financial security in this time of adulthood compared to adults in their 20s. In spite of the uncertainty of the job market, people in their 30s often continued to choose quality of life over gainful employment.[61] This was their means of transforming crisis into well-being.

＊

My 30s were a decade of age-appropriate productivity, self-evaluation and need for validation. For my 35th birthday, I rented out 111 Minna, a hip art gallery and lounge that would turn into a dance club and was located in the trendy South of Market area of San Francisco. An open bar was provided, and I invited everyone I knew and their significant and insignificant others and rocked out to the likes of "Poker Face" and a young Pitbull. That evening checked all the boxes and included but was not limited to crowd surfing, friends vomiting outside a club and friends challenging friends to how fast they could eat a Johnny Rockets burger at 2am after said surfing and vomiting. It was wonderful. The point of all this was of course to feel liked, seen and successful.

For many of us, the 30s are a time where hopefully our health, resources, time and appreciation converge and share equal potency. It is possibly the first time in our adult lives when we can do almost anything we want. Unfortunately, it's also a period marked by simmering panic, when we find ourselves firmly strapped to our hedonic treadmill, seemingly locked into a set quantity of happiness with no easy way off. The day of reckoning is coming, when your dreams, age and reality will meet full force, but that must wait. For now, you have no choice but to forge ahead, into your 40s.

7

Your 40s: Wait For It…

Life really does begin at forty. Up until then, you are just doing research.
—Carl G. Jung

At the age of twenty, we don't care what the world thinks of us; at thirty, we worry about what it is thinking of us; at forty, we discover that it wasn't thinking of us at all.
—Anonymous

Well you have arrived at this most pivotal of decade in your life. There is perhaps more made of turning 40 than any other age, and for good reason. This is when that U-shaped curve of happiness often finds its nadir, as a confluence of biologic and social factors conspire to summon our undivided attention. We are often oblivious to our own ageing, and though our health may not be outright declining, the advancing age of our contemporaries, parents and children are all undeniably apparent. While in our 30s we may have taken some moments to gauge our relative progress, it is in our 40s that we truly assess what we have accomplished in our lives, and this assessment invariably falls short of the vision we had for ourselves in our younger years. The combination of disappointment of our past achievements and uncertainty about our future possibilities makes for a vicious one-two punch.

Though we are aware and thankful for the gifts we have been granted—health, resources, relationships and time—the fear of losing those very things puts us ill at ease. We may also be at the age when the relationships and careers we were re-evaluating in our 30s take their last breath. Put all of this upheaval in the context of the happiness curve bottoming, and not even the most resilient of us can pass unscathed through this decade. It is truly a rite of passage in our hero's quest, and there is no going around it.

During this decade, our career accomplishments and future outlook are brought sharply to the forefront of our attention. And regardless of where you are at, you might ask yourself again, *Is this it?* Pulitzer Prize winning American author, historian, actor, and broadcaster Studs Terkel—now *that's* a name—wrote in his book, *Working*,[62] "Perhaps it is this specter that most haunts working men and women: the planned obsolescence of people that is of a piece with the planned obsolescence of the things they make." He found this was true for the more than one hundred people across all professions that he interviewed. Though written in 1974, it still rings true today. We work our asses off for years, most times too busy to stop and question what lies at the end of the path. We have committed too much of our lives and resources, made too many personal sacrifices to allow ourselves even a sliver of doubt. Nevertheless, little by little, we recognize that our sharpness and skills are slipping, hopefully imperceptible to anyone else.

Sheehy refers to the time in our mid-30s to our mid-40s as the

"Deadline Decade."[63] She writes, "Somewhere between 35-45 if we let ourselves, most of us will have a full-out authenticity crisis." In order to grow from this crisis, we must bring awareness to it, and for this pivotal topic I have devoted an entire chapter. Awareness, however, is only the beginning. Action is also necessary. All this, and more, is coming up right after the break.

Alcohol and Suicide During the Pandemic

Across all age groups, excessive drinking increased 32% for men and 54% for women during the pandemic.[64,65] During the first year, the number and rate of alcohol-related deaths increased about 25%. Prior to the pandemic, there was a 2.2% mean annual percentage increase between 1999 and 2017.[66] Drinking is not considered a good means of transforming crisis into well-being.

The rate of suicide counterintuitively dropped during the pandemic, despite traditionally following an upward trend with age, achieving an initial peak between 45-64. One theory for this drop is that people were freed from the stress of their work environment. Another suggestion is that suicides were "artificially depressed because people [couldn't] get out of their homes." [67] Ultimately, following the absolute number of suicides may be an oversimplification of the complexity of this situation in the context of the pandemic.

The Makings of a Crisis

At this point, we have been shown data about humanity's intrinsic optimism bias. In addition, we have good reason to believe that humans have a hedonic setpoint. So, what happens when our optimism bias keeps running into the wall that is our hedonic setpoint as we age?

Economist Hannes Schwandt has an answer for this. He authored a study titled, "Unmet Aspirations as an Explanation for the Age U-Shape in Wellbeing"[68] (2016), and in it, he provides a compelling reason for the U-shaped happiness curve. Using data from the German Socio-Economic Panel, he matched 132,609 life satisfaction expectations to subsequent realizations. He found that people consistently mispredicted they would be happier earlier in life and less happy later in life, when it was in fact the opposite. Early in life, he found participants had relatively high expectations, which continue to be unmet. At the same time, current life satisfaction is declining. When participants reached their 50s, their expectations leveled out, and simultaneously their current life satisfaction starts to increase. And toward the later part of that decade, their current life satisfaction *exceeds* their expectations. This continues to increase for the next two decades, and then they eventually die. Ultimately, Schwandt concludes, "the U-shape is caused by unmet expectations that are felt painfully in midlife but beneficially abandoned and experienced with less regret during old age."

Additional data from Schwandt's study shows that optimism decreases linearly over participants' lifetimes while regret forms a hump-shaped curve, peaking around age –you guessed it—45-50. Not surprisingly, this data is consistent with Graham and Pozuelo's data reviewed earlier showing a similar hump-shaped curve tracking stress levels over a lifetime.[69]

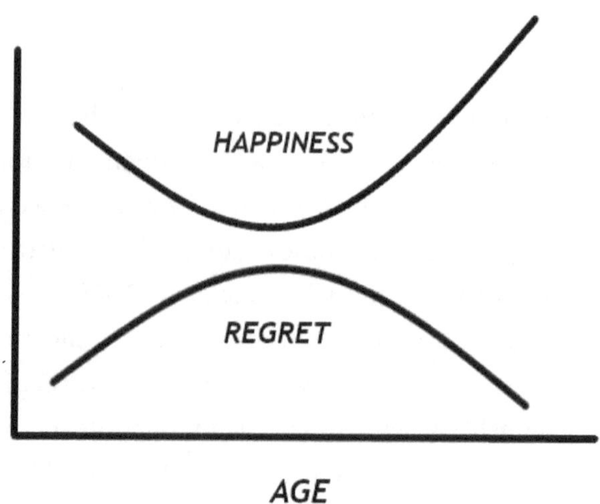

Source: Schwandt, Hannes (2016). "Unmet aspirations as an explanation for the age U-shape in wellbeing." Journal of Economic Behavior & Organization 122: 75-87.

The cumulative result of these reported data is that a negative feedback cycle exists in that regret about unmet expectations further decreases the already diminished life satisfaction. Schwandt suggests that rather than trying to quell high expectations in younger adults that instead we try to limit regret in older adults by providing reinforcement about the normality of their situation and suggesting means of optimizing their social, spiritual and physical lives. This is my book in a nutshell.

Why are our expectations so out of proportion to our reality? Part of the explanation may come from Sharot's work on optimism bias.[70] From her research, we are hard-wired to be optimistic, the purpose of which may be for the greater good of the species. This tendency though sets us up to be disappointed for the first half of our lives. Then why does this correct itself at midlife? Though there is likely no single explanation, the possible contributors are natural biologic changes to our brain as we age as well as the accumulated experiences that slowly alter our expectations and our priorities – in other words, our wisdom. In the following chapters, we will explore the fascinating neurobiology underlying our inaccurate expectations and possible mechanisms to circumvent this.

In conclusion, Sharot's and Schwandt's work may reveal a biologic explanation for the U-shaped curve of happiness and the low we experience at midlife. That being said, knowing why midlife crisis occurs does not equate with knowing the best route going forward. We need to translate this recognition into actions that improve our well-being. In so doing, we can transform crisis into emotional growth and healthier bodies. This will be the focus of the remainder of the book, where I have attempted to curate a path that provides relevant data and actionable goals. All of the COVID and midlife crisis discussion we have had thus far has been a lead-up to the discussion to follow. The best way to make sense out of life's hardship is to let it be a motivation for change, and there can be no better change than improving emotional well-being and longevity.

My Midlife Crisis

It was evening, December 16, and I had just come home from the local bank parking lot selling Christmas trees. I purchased two of them – one large, one small. The large tree I brought into my house and set up on its stand. The smaller one I placed sideways into the backseat of my sedan, which I had already packed. I went back into my home, hugged and kissed my three-year-old daughter and said goodbye to my wife of twelve years. I drove twenty minutes to a one-bedroom apartment I had arranged to sublet, and in two trips to the parking structure, brought in all my things and the tree.

I set up the tree, sat down on the sofa and exhaled. I was 42, and I had hit rock bottom. This was not how I saw my life unfolding, and I had no idea how to get through this.

In those first few dark months, my little girl was my savior. Whether it was building sofa cushion forts or eating cereal for dinner at 11pm, she reminded me that there was something special to live for. On the days I did not have her, it was a struggle. I am generally a positive person, and there is no history of mental illness in my family. So I was surprised and frightened when self-harmful thoughts flitted into me. I had bought a case of Lagunita's India pale ale, none of which I drank those first few months. Instead, I would curl up on the couch, crack open a library copy of *Wuthering Heights*, and read.

During our initial separation and to this day, my ex and I stayed amicable, doing what we needed to prioritize our little girl's well-being. At the same time, we wrapped up our marriage in the shortest interval legally possible with the assistance of a mediator. And despite that, it was still really, really hard.

I remember walking around the old neighborhood where my apartment was, full of older single-family homes. The lots were small, but the streets had mature trees that filtered the evening sunlight perfectly. I remember seeing a porch with two rocking chairs on it, side by side, with a small table between them. And that made me long for the life I had imagined and that now seemed out of reach.

My rock bottom did not last long, and for that I am grateful. That said, my funk did linger for some time, my emotions scraping bottom for a while until I could get my bearings again. I developed new relationships during that time, and at another period in my life, a couple of them could have been great. But I wasn't exactly working on all of my emotional thrusters, and I knew that. Timing is everything.

During this time, I remained true to my friendships, my daughter and my purpose to help others, and these pursuits sustained me. It took a few years, but when I emerged from my midlife malaise, what caught my attention was an emotional wave of relief that I didn't even know I needed. It was such a revelation that I felt compelled to explore it, and here we are.

* * *

As we progress through our 40s, many of us will reach an existential crossroads. We will re-evaluate the work we have put into our careers and into our relationships. Many of us will push harder in our profession to maintain the same production despite decreased cognitive computing power. Apprentices will no longer be an honor to teach; they will become a threat. And at home, some of us will witness the maturation of our offspring or simply the ageing of ourselves and our furnishings. We are left with the option of revitalizing appearances or rethinking our aspirations. The fork in the road for the breadwinner and the homemaker is dead ahead, and there are only difficult choices to be made. Sheehy reminds us, "If physical strength and pleasures of the senses are held to be life's greatest values, then we deny ourselves anything beyond youth but a dull ebb of all experience…Yet the delights of self-discovery are always available."[71]

In the next part of the book, we will move on from crisis to find paths for growth and self-discovery.

II

ADAPT

We don't see things as they are. We see things as we are.
— Anaïs Nin

8

Emotional Well-Being: The Lay of the Land

Forty is the old age of youth and fifty the youth of old age.
—*Victor Hugo*

There is no normal life that is free of pain. It's the very wrestling with our problems that can be the impetus for our growth.
—*Fred Rogers*

In high school AP biology lab, we learned that there are indeed many ways to skin a cat. In the same way, there are multiple paths for growth and adaptation following midlife or other crises, and the more tools we have at our disposal, the better. In the pages ahead, I will discuss specific and attainable objectives like developing awareness and managing expectations, practicing kindness and nurturing your relationships, breaking out of your comfort zone, repurposing yourself, and just having fun. Ultimately, the greater end to all these pursuits is living a full and present life. Sometimes, well-being is the result, and many other times, it is not. We may instead experience frustration, hardship and emotional tumult. *Many a tear has to fall, but it's all in the game.*

Different authors talk about transitions in this latter part of life. Arthur Brooks discusses finding "deep purpose."[72] James Hollis talks about finding "meaning."[73] Gail Sheehy refers to a "renewal" that can occur at this point in life, stating, "…people who have seen, felt, and incorporate their private truths during midlife passage no longer expect the impossible dream."[74]

The caveat here is that adaptation does not happen overnight or without intentionality. *The Great One* said, "I skate to where the puck is going to be, not where it has been." In the same way, challenges must be anticipated and appropriately acted on. Fortunately, there are many intelligent minds past and present who have given us insight and advice on the path ahead.

There are many ways to adapt to crisis and transform it into well-being, but you could divide it into internal and external work. There are pivotal shifts in our mindset that are necessary, and these must be translated into tangible actions. Most often, the internal changes occur first, and they are followed with external actions. *Part II: Adapt* will focus on the psychological preparatory work necessary, and *Part III: Evolve* will discuss the physical execution of the plan.

Whether you have arrived at midlife or are just experiencing your personal crisis, I have attempted to make the following chapters a helpful survival guide by including a copious volume of research and expert opinion. Simultaneously, I have strived to make it an entertaining read, with minimal fluff and maximal actionable goals.

* * *

John Welwood, an American clinical psychologist known for integrating psychological and spiritual concepts, states, "The basic human wound, which is prevalent in the modern world, forms around not feeling loved or intrinsically lovable as we are."[75] Our ability to feel loved is intimately related to our self-esteem and self-worth.

Many psychologists make a distinction between self-esteem and self-worth.[76] Self-esteem is a factor that is more affected by external influences such as personal achievement and appearance and is often dependent on others' perceptions, making it a volatile state of mind. Self-worth, on the other hand, has been defined as a trait that is less easily affected by external forces and that plays a more consistent role in the overall psychological health of an individual. Self-worth describes a person's belief that they are deserving of love and acceptance regardless of whatever their perceived flaws are and represents a much more stable state of mind.

In similar fashion to how Lykken drew a genetic connection to our happiness set point, a Swedish study from 2016 that looked at data from 14,875 twins concluded that 52% of a person's self-worth is genetically based.[77] This would suggest that almost half of a person's self-worth is influenceable by their environment and is therefore within their control.

One could see a relationship between the U-shaped happiness curve, the theorized influence of expectations and the traits of self-esteem and self-worth. As we have already discussed, with age our expected satisfaction decreases at the same time our actual satisfaction increases. When the two values cross in our 40s to 50s, that marks the upturn of the U-curve. In a similar fashion, perhaps the upturn can also be attributed to a recalibrating of our self-esteem and self-worth that occurs around the same age. Less and less dependent on external forces, our self-esteem heads north, and whatever intrinsic self-worth we are born with determines the pace of our happiness acceleration.

Psychologist Guy Winch talks about practicing *emotional hygiene*, which is taking care of our emotions and our minds with the same diligence we use to take care of our bodies.[78] Research has consistently shown that in the context of low self-esteem, that a person is more vulnerable to stress, anxiety and depression. Yet, as Winch reminds us, in cases when our self-esteem has just taken an injury, many people will paradoxically pile on to themselves and generate reasons they were just rejected or why they just failed. Why would we do this? Winch states it is a failure of prioritizing our psychological health. He says, "Failure is so common a human experience that what distinguishes us from one another is not that we fail but rather how we respond when we do."

In the end, only when we have learned to take care of our sense of self-worth can we set ourselves up for emotional well-being. In the next chapter, we will start to see that there is no direct route to getting to our happy place. Instead, it will be like riding the bus when you don't have a bus pass. You buy one ticket, then you need to get it punched so you can use it as a transfer to get on another bus that kind of goes in the right direction, and if you game it right, you can keep getting transfers to get closer to the mall, and by the time you finally walk the last mile you'll have only paid one bus fare. You high five your mate while playing video games but then get so carried away that you have to walk home because you spent all your quarters. The point is the route to happiness is circuitous and is often best enjoyed together. All aboard.

9

Do Not Pursue Happiness

Happiness is not achieved by the conscious pursuit of happiness; it is generally the by-product of other activities.
—Aldous Huxley

Happiness never lays its finger on its pulse.
—Adam Smith

When you try hard is when you die hard.
—Kanye West

Albert Einstein is famous for thinking, doing and saying many things. What he is not famous for is the proper use of hair product. One widely misunderstood thing that he said was, "God does not play dice with the universe." This has been misinterpreted in a couple ways. First, Einstein did not believe in God, as evidenced when he said, "I do not believe in…God." The other misinterpretation of the quote is that he was stating a belief in destiny. He was not. Where am I going with this? Stay with me.

What he is decrying in the quote is the lack of precision that other notable scientists of his era purported exists in nature. Specifically, in the field of quantum physics, one of the central tenets is that one cannot know precisely what the position and speed of a subatomic particle is. Measuring one of those variables affects our ability to measure the other precisely. The other variable can only be calculated in mathematical *probabilities*. This was described mathematically in the Heisenberg Uncertainty Principle and metaphorically in the thought experiment whose main tragic actor is Schrödinger's cat.*

> *Erwin Schrödinger was an Austrian Nobel laureate. In a well-known thought experiment to demonstrate the concept of quantum uncertainty on a macro level, a hypothetical cat, Schrödinger's cat, may be considered simultaneously both alive and dead, while it is unobserved in a closed box, as a result of its fate being linked to a random subatomic event that may or may not occur. Only after the box is opened and the cat actually observed can its poor fate be determined. Until that observation is made, it theoretically exists in a no-man's-land, so-called quantum superposition, both alive and dead.*

Einstein lost his quantum mind hearing this. He believed that everything in the physical universe could be measured precisely and was not having any of it. This is the context in which he uttered his phrase about God not playing dice. Sadly, he was so fixated on rejecting the Uncertainty Principle that he refused to account for it in his search for a Unified Theory of physics,* isolated himself from his scientific brethren, and ultimately failed to formulate a working theory before his death. The point of this Einsteinian detour is to say that we can't know everything with certainty and trying to measure it can change it. This applies to the subatomic world, and as I will describe shortly, also to the world of happiness. I know, it's a stretch.

> *A Unified Field Theory is a phrase coined by Einstein who tried to combine his General Theory of Relativity that relates to gravity with the concepts and mathematics of electromagnetism, which relates to subatomic particles. It's also been referred to as the Theory of Everything and the Grand Unified Theory. Essentially, physicists want to be able to have a set of rules that govern everything from stars to subatomic particles. They have yet to discover this.*

The physicists of the early 1900s went on to wax even more philosophical. Heisenberg said, "{We} have to remember that what we observe is not nature in itself but nature exposed to our method of questioning."[79] In other words, our observation of a state of being is just that, an observation. It is not actually that state of being. Although these physicists were speaking of subatomic particles, one can see how this applies to life on the larger scale. What method of questioning do we use to evaluate our own happiness? And what are the consequences of that process? As will be described later, when we attempt to access and assess our own emotions, it creates a ripple effect within our brains that changes our experience of that emotion.

In the rest of this chapter, we will explore the psychological research that revolves around the pursuit of happiness. We'll first look at the behavior called *affective forecasting*, which refers to the human attempt to predict the emotional effects of what we do in the present on our future selves. As it turns out, we are often wrong in our predictions. In the second half of the chapter, we will look at how our attempts to pursue and predict happiness in our lives also results in unintended consequences.

Just as physicists realize their observations of nature are scientifically created constructs, when we speak of emotions and use words like anger or fear or regret or happiness, it's important to remember that these words are representations of the emotions, not the emotions themselves. The actual emotions are the result of complex neuro-chemistry. For example, though an oversimplification, dopamine regulates joy, norepinephrine fear and anger, and serotonins disgust and sadness.[80] And beyond just these neurotransmitters, there are countless and as yet immeasurable interactions that happen in our brains to produce the feeling we have in any particular moment. Our experience of emotions is far more complex than any single word could ever describe, and yet, we still need to communicate them. Like physicists, we are just trying to understand and produce a set of rules for the world we live in, external and internal.

And so what happens when people try to create a set of rules for the achievement of happiness? If happiness is the goal, that evaluation must include a means of measuring if we have achieved it. Unfortunately, this is where things can backfire. David Wootton states that we have built "a whole culture around a futile, self-defeating enterprise: the pursuit of happiness."[81] Indeed, though Jefferson deemed it an *unalienable right*, he did not have the benefit of peer-reviewed research studies. Now we realize that this pursuit that has possibly defined much of American culture and history is perhaps a fool's errand. Let's delve into it.

* * *

Iris Mauss, a professor of Psychology at the University of California at Berkeley, is known for her research specifically looking at the negative effects of valuing happiness.[82] In her study from *Emotion* (2011),[83] she and researchers state, "Paradoxically, therefore, valuing happiness may lead people to be less happy just when happiness is within reach." The proposed mechanism by which this paradox occurs is the following. When we value something, we seek to achieve it and then subsequently evaluate our achievement against that value.[84] They use an example where someone who values academic achievement and therefore judges themselves on their grade. That in and of itself is fine, as getting a low grade does not preclude them from trying harder and being a motivator for getting a better grade. However, when one applies this reasoning to pursuing happiness, that is when the paradox may occur. If your *goal* is happiness, and you do not achieve it, you have set yourself up to be unhappy, because "the outcome of one's evaluation (i.e., disappointment and discontent) is incompatible with one's goal (i.e., happiness)." And therein lies the trap. Your brain be saying, "Does not compute. Does not compute."

Happiness is not a concrete thing, like an A grade, which you either have or you don't. The more you value happiness, Mauss proposes, the higher the standard you will create for it and the less likely it is achievable. And as Mauss and others subsequently have shown, it is your disappointment in not being happy (or happy enough) that leads to your sense of failure. Have you ever been that person who was not happy at your own birthday party? You expected to have a certain degree of happiness, and if you failed to achieve that predetermined level of it, that made you unhappy. This is how having a *happiness or bust* attitude can backfire.

In a study by McGuirk et.al (2018),[85] researchers asked, "...could the overpromotion of happiness have a downside?" In their experimental design, they looked at the effect emphasizing the importance of happiness as well the avoidance of negative emotions. In both cases, they found that both of these behavior patterns resulted in increased rumination to failure, which ultimately had "downstream consequences for well-being."

Psychologist Mike Rucker, author of, *The Fun Habit: How The Disciplined Pursuit of Joy And Wonder Can Change Your Life* (2023),[86] expresses a parallel viewpoint. He writes, "Happiness is really an evaluation…You are constantly asking yourself what is going right and what is going wrong. It can become a trap… Happiness begins to slip away as soon as we grab it."

An interesting study was done by Kim and Maglio in 2018. Titled, "Vanishing time in the pursuit of happiness," they found that pursuing happiness reduces our perception of the availability of time, which reduces our happiness.[87] Only when happiness seems like it has been achieved or will be quickly achieved are the negative effects of less time availability on happiness reduced.

The neurotransmitter dopamine is known to play a role in many brain functions ranging from pleasure, reward, and motivation to attention and cognition.[88] The link between dopamine and the brain's judgment of time is well-established, though not completely understood.[89,90] It has been observed that activation of dopamine neurons slows down our estimation and time, and inhibition of them speeds it up. When we are bored out of our gourd, time seems to slow to a crawl, because we are acutely aware of it. But when our estimation of time is slowed down from dopamine release (i.e., pleasurable or rewarding experiences), our internal clocks are slowed down, and we have a sense that time is sped up. (I know, this is perhaps a bit nonintuitive). This neural phenomenon explains why time seems to fly when we are having fun. In Kim and Maglio's study, the pursuit of happiness may stimulate dopamine release in the anticipation of pleasure, thereby speeding up the perception of time for that individual. If the reward is not achieved, however, there is disappointment. Not surprisingly, the role of dopamine will also be shown to play an important role in expectations and happiness, as will be described in the next chapter.

One important consideration when looking at happiness research is to note that much of the research has been based in Western countries such as the U.S. and therefore may not be applicable globally. To this end, psychologists Eid and Diener did work on cultural differences in how we experience emotion.[91] In their study, "Norms for experiencing emotions in different cultures: inter- and intranational differences" (2001), they looked at nations they classified as individualistic (United States, Australia) vs collectivistic (China, Taiwan). Not surprisingly, they found that there was significant international variability in the extent to which people experience happiness in each of these types of nations. They "unexpectedly" found that individualistic nations were actually the most uniform in norms for pleasant emotions. Individualistic and collectivistic nations differed most noticeably in norms for self-reflective emotions (e.g., pride and guilt).

An intriguing follow-up to this research showed that indeed, the pursuit of happiness may not be all bad, as long as you are not American. An article by Ford et al. entitled, "Culture shapes whether the pursuit of happiness predicts higher or lower well-being" (2015)[92] suggested that in some cultures, the pursuit of happiness is not self-defeating. They found that pursuing happiness predicted lower well-being in the United States, did not predict well-being in Germany, and predicted higher well-being in Russia and in East Asia. Their explanation was that in collectivistic (vs. individualistic) cultures, pursuing happiness may be more successful because happiness is viewed—and thus pursued—in relatively socially engaged ways. Social engagement, in turn, leads to greater happiness. This will be detailed further in the chapter, "It's Your Relationships, Stupid."

There are many other published articles as well as online commentary that now reinforce the belief that the ardent pursuit of happiness is self-defeating to the very well-being we are trying to achieve, many of which were written during the pandemic years. This makes sense as perhaps many people perhaps realized that their relentless pursuit of happiness via career achievement at the cost of all else in their lives is ultimately a self-sabotaging goal.

Affective Forecasting

So why is the pursuit of happiness so seemingly fraught with paradoxical disappointment? All we are trying to do is anticipate what actions and behaviors will lead to happiness, which is clearly a favorable state in which to exist. It turns out that predicting what will provide lasting happiness (as well as sadness and every emotion in-between), referred to as *affective forecasting*, is not a human strong suit. We are actually consistently bad at it. In their seminal work on this topic entitled, you guessed it, "Affective forecasting," psychologists Wilson and Gilbert found that although people are good at predicting both whether an event will lead to a positive or negative emotion (referred to as "valence" in their study) and the specific emotion they will have from an event, they are much less accurate about forecasting the intensity and duration of that reaction.[93] This applies to both positive and negative events.

In all the important decisions we make in our lives –be it in relationships, career choice, having children, manual or automatic transmission, etc., we naturally try to predict their effects on our long-term emotional state. And we are often wrong. Regardless of the nature of the decision, we often miss the mark in our forecast of how much happier we will be and how long we will stay happy. Moreover, the same tendency occurs when negative life events occur. We overestimate how intensely and how long they will weigh on us.[94] This inaccuracy of prediction applies to not just anticipated events, but also experienced events, again both negative and positive ones.

If this sounds a lot like the section earlier in the book where I wrote about the hedonic treadmill and a happiness set point ("Your 30s"), that's because it is. Though we may anticipate greater happiness or greater unhappiness from a life event, it is our set point that eventually brings us back to our baseline emotional state. Accepting both of these principles as valid is a bit emotionally deflating, given we can neither predict our happiness nor is it sustained even when good things happen. Do not despair though. There is a path forward, so read on!

In their article, "Pursuing happiness: The architecture of sustainable change" (2005), Lyubomirsky et al. discuss three factors that govern a person's level of happiness.[95] These are (1) the *happiness set-point* which is genetically predetermined and most difficult (though not impossible) to change and two other factors that are unfixed, (2) *circumstantial factors* and (3) *activities and practices*.

They define circumstantial factors as events that happen to people such as trauma and life status variables such as personal health, relationship and occupational status. Examples of activities and practices that positively influence happiness include exercising regularly or being kind to others. Her research puts a strong emphasis on the potential for the last factor –activities and practices—to play a large role in determining individual happiness in that they are actionable. We will explore this further in the chapter, "Kindness, Gratefulness and Awe."

Ultimately, Lyubomirsky and researchers suggested that genetics accounts for approximately 50% of the happiness variation, circumstances for approximately 10% and intentional activity for the remaining 40%. Compared to the original estimate of 80% heritability of happiness suggested by Lykken and Tellegen in 1996, this is an almost two-fold reduction of the degree of purported genetic predisposition to happiness. If true, this would translate to our having more agency in facilitating our well-being and subsequently being less subject to our happiness set points and hedonic treadmills.

Other authors have suggested throwing out the treadmill altogether. In the article, "Beyond the hedonic treadmill: revising the adaptation theory of well-being" by Diener et.al. (2006),[96] they suggested several revisions to the original fixed hedonic setpoint theory set forth by Lykken and Tellegen. They are:

1. Individuals' setpoints are not hedonically neutral (the mean human subjective well-being is well above neutral).
2. People have different set points, which are partly dependent on their temperaments.

3. A single person may have multiple happiness set points: Different components of well-being such as pleasant emotions, unpleasant emotions, and life satisfaction can move it in different directions.

4. Well-being set points can change under some conditions. Individuals differ in their adaptation to events, with some individuals changing their set point and others not changing in reaction to some external event.

Professor Lykken responded in kind to Diener's study (2007),[97] and while he acknowledged validity in revisions 1 and 2, he took some umbrage for revisions 3 and 4. In a scathing commentary, he states he "…is not persuaded" by Diener and researchers' revisions to the setpoint theory and that their conclusions "…seem unreasonable." Oh snap! He concludes by writing, "…the set point to which SWB (subjective well-being) in the normal brain returns after each drop or bounce seems to be stable." Mic drop.

So, we went from an 80% influence of genetics for our happiness set point to a 50% impact to well, maybe it's all fluid, and there is wiggle room. Whatever the reality of our happiness set point is, by understanding our individual emotional underpinnings more, we will be better able to adapt and respond to them, rather than being surprised by and victim to them.

Researchers have looked more deeply into why our affective forecasting tends to be inaccurate. Wilson and Gilbert give three main and related reasons: Impact bias, focalism and immune neglect.[98] Impact bias is the most common error and refers to overestimating the overall power of an event, both in terms of intensity and length. Whether it is landing your dream job or getting dumped by your dreamboat, the emotional impact does not last as long as we hope or fear. Impact bias often results from focalism, which is seeing events in isolation and not as part of the bigger picture of your life with elements that can offset the effect of that event, for better or for worse. The elation we feel meeting our future wife, then the other feeling we get meeting her parents. Alternatively, focalism also refers to how we forget about the benefits our social supports bring us during hard times, and how disruptive they might be in comparatively good times. Finally, immune neglect is failing to realize we have a psychological immune system that is in place to protect us when bad things happen, making us more likely to overestimate the emotional impact of negative events. Elements of this emotional safety belt system include our optimism bias and other emotional hygiene products we all carry around with us, such as humor, intellectualization, compartmentalization and sublimation.

The work of psychologists is often utilized in the science of economics, namely the study of affective forecasting. Economists want to know how people are going to spend their money. It is presumed that consumers are rational and will make decisions that serve them best. As a case in point, Daniel Kahneman, an Israeli-born psychologist, is known for his incorporation of psychological research about decision-making into economic science. Much of his work examined human judgment and decision making under uncertainty, specifically at loss aversion. Loss aversion is a cognitive bias whereby people are much more negatively affected by loss than they are positively affected by an equivalent gain.[99] Kahneman's work suggested that a potential gain needed to be about twice as much as the potential loss to cause people to choose that option.[100] Looked at differently, it is often easier to spur decisions based on pointing out what might be lost as opposed to just what might be gained. Work he did with Amos Tversky resulted in Prospect Theory[101] and won them the Nobel Prize for Economics in 2002.

In their work, Kahneman and other scholars discuss the utility of making decisions.[102,103,104] They subcategorized utility into decision utility and experienced utility. Decision utility is our prediction of utility before we experience it. Experienced utility is the actual outcome from that action. So, even though we may be inaccurate in our assessment of experienced utility, there is still value in making a choice that provides optimal decision utility. If economists can understand both of these aspects of utility, they can more accurately model how consumers and larger populations may behave.

Kahneman and scholars cite four main causes that negatively affect our experienced utility forecasting, which are similar in many ways to Wilson and Gilbert's causes for affective forecasting errors:

- Where the emotional or motivational state of the decision-maker is very different at the time of the decision versus time of consumption
- Where the nature of the decision focuses attention on aspects of the outcome that will not be relevant when it is actually experienced
- When choices are made on the basis of flawed evaluations of past experiences
- When people inaccurately forecast their future ability to adjust to new life circumstances.

Empathic Forecasting

Our poor ability to affectively forecast our own emotional lives impacts us on more than just a personal level. It plays a role in situations where we inaccurately assess the impact of a negative event on another person, referred to *empathic forecasting*. Typically, we *overestimate* the impact a negative emotional event has on someone else. For instance, in a study of 104 partnered couples by Green et al. entitled, "Victims versus perpetrators: Affective and empathic forecasting regarding transgressions in romantic relationships," (2013)[105] researchers asked the couples to predict the degree to which they (affective forecast) and their partner (empathic forecast) would feel wronged after 20 (twenty!) types of relationship transgressions, in both victim and perpetrator roles. What the study showed was a consistent affective and empathic overestimation of emotional harm caused by relationship transgressions. In both the victim and perpetrator role, participants believed they would feel worse than they actually did, and they also believed their partner would feel worse than they actually did. Participants accurately forecasted they would be more unhappy in the perpetrator role than the victim role, but inaccurately predicted that their partner would be more unhappy in the victim than the perpetrator role.

In the legal system, inaccurate empathic forecasting is also in play. When victims are remunerated for harm they have suffered, overestimation of damages can lead to overcompensation. This is recognized on enough of a level that the majority of states in the U.S. have tort reform laws that cap the maximal amount of malpractice damages.[106]

Our overestimation of other people's suffering has also been demonstrated in studies showing that spinal cord injury patients are happier than we would expect.[107] In an article by Duggan et al. (2016), they found that the majority of spinal cord injury victims identified themselves as happy. They ascribed their resilience to their good social support, a spiritual connection, and their own personality. These factors are all in line with both Kahneman's and Wilson and Gilbert's causes for our poor affective forecasting. In this case, we the outsiders fail to consider these aspects of the victim's emotional recovery team and therefore predict a higher degree of unhappiness for the them than they actually experience.

On the other end of the spectrum, the high frequency of victim blaming in cases of sexual harassment is thought to occur partly because we wrongly empathically forecast that we know what we would do and feel in the victim's circumstances.[108]

And finally, in the medical field, poor affective forecasting can lead to under- and over-treatment of ailments based on both the provider's and the patient's prediction of how quality of life will be affected. In the one study, researchers found that both patients and providers make similar affective and empathic forecasting errors.[109] Both parties often poorly predict the patient's ability to adapt to adversity. This can lead to both overtreatment and undertreatment in medical decision making.

For instance, if a patient believes they will not be able to endure the discomfort, pain and life inconvenience after a procedure, they may opt not to pursue it, despite it likely providing long term benefit. Moreover, if the provider empathically forecasts their patient will have significant emotional hardship from a procedure, they may not recommend it, even if it might help them. In contrast, the provider and the patient may both have unrealistically high expectations, leading to unnecessary or unsuccessful treatments.

* * *

In summary, we have seen that attempting to pursue or even just gauge our happiness often takes us further away from it. In addition, despite considering ourselves highly evolved and empathic beings, we often fail both in predicting another person's level of happiness as well as their level of unhappiness from life events. In the following chapters, I will describe alternatives to happiness fixation that *are* achievable and that form a sustainable psychological foundation from which it can sprout. But first, the pursuit of happiness has to get even more infuriating.

When I was in high school, I would routinely keep a hand-written, folded-up list of my top three, nay, my top five romantic prospects at any particular time. This list was a spreadsheet that detailed pros and cons to each lucky candidate. From time to time, the list would need to get updated and those on the waitlist could get moved up if, say, candidate number three told me to go climb a tree. Not that that ever happened. Suffice it to say, the end goal of creating this list was not to secure a life partner. I wasn't even allowed to date, truth be known, because I would of course induce spontaneous pregnancy, fail all my classes and in all other manner of ways ruin my life. What the lists did do for me was give me something to look forward to. Well-knowing nothing would likely ever come of the list did not prevent me from feeling anticipation and joy. Joy in making it, joy in parsing it out with friends, joy in simply knowing I had amorous aspirations. Though I had no idea neural science has an explanation for my unrequited source of happiness, I knew it made me feel good.

In the next chapter, we will explore the mechanisms by which we can hack our happiness via our expectations, sometimes to our gain and other times not so much.

10

Winning the Expectations Game

Expectation is the root of all heartache.
—Shakespeare

The key to happiness is low expectations. Lower. Nope, even lower. There you go.
—Anonymous

If your coffee order is more than four words, you are part of the problem.
—Anonymous

Let's resume our path toward happiness. I believe I have presented compelling data that forces us to acknowledge that a direct bum rush approach to it is doomed to disappoint, especially if you are American. This is thought to be due to our innate inaccuracy in predicting what will make us happy. However, if we know ahead of time that our damn happiness set point will eventually throw us right back onto our old hedonic treadmill, perhaps we can figure out a workaround.

Recall economist Schwandt's study from the chapter on "Your 40s" that accounted for the shape of the U-curve of happiness and ascribed it to unmet expectations.[110] If our failure to achieve happiness is in large part due to our inaccurate estimations, it stands to reason that changing our expectations may be helpful in staving off the low in our happiness curve. Excessively lowering them, however, may just result in net lower well-being and may not be beneficial for humanity at large. Perhaps there is a middle-ground though where we can minimize expectations as well as the emotions that come up as a result of unmet expectations. In this chapter, we will explore the neural biology underlying expectations and then analyze the real-world impact of that biology.

On the subject of expectations, a friend has shared a couple of gems. The first is "Five twos make a ten." And the second, "Lower the standard. Increase the average." More than a math lesson, my friend's attitude reflects an approach to let's say life that has resulted in their being generally even tempered over the many years I have known them.

Before I understood the wisdom of keeping my expectations low, I met my favorite future ex-wife at a loft party in the trendy South End neighborhood of Boston. My friend's friend knew someone who had a friend who was possibly invited. After first telling me I had no shot, my friends then physically shoved me in her direction, and I proceeded to say the first thing that came to my mind: "Excuse me. What's your favorite color?" And the rest is history. Going into that exchange, I had not just low expectations; I had no expectations. I believe Churchill once said, "The most dangerous bloke at the shindig is the bloke with no expectations."

Keeping your expectations low in the psychological world is referred to as *defensive pessimism.* To Tali Sharot, the prominent optimism bias researcher, them's fightin' words. Although there are some researchers who believe that unmitigated pessimism is ultimately an unhealthy path toward happiness, there is also literature showing that high expectations are equally detrimental. Let's look at the data regarding each strategy.

Expectations and Neural Biology

One of the first studies drawing a specific neural connection between expectations and happiness was entitled, "A computational and neural model of momentary subjective well-being" (2014).[111] In this article, Rutledge and researchers used functional MRI to track cortical responses to tested outcomes, correlating neural activity with how happy subjects reported being at that time. They employed a gambling game in which a small amount of real money was gained or lost, and twenty-six participants were asked, "How happy are you at this moment?" at multiple timepoints after each gambling game. In a second part of the study, they expanded their participant pool using a smartphone-based game modeling the one used in the lab. This included an additional 18,420 unpaid participants, and the results correlated with those found in the lab.

By tracking self-reported levels of moment-to-moment happiness and correlating them with neural activity, the researchers were able to corroborate the presence of a hedonic setpoint. They demonstrated that beyond a finite timepoint, previous rewards had no influence on current happiness as measured by fMRI brain cortical responses. In other words, the study participants' brains showed normalized neural signals after a certain point in time from receiving a reward, and the neurotransmitter dopamine was found to play a central role in this response (or lack thereof).* In effect, more than forty years after Brickman and Campbell proposed the hedonic setpoint idea from a theoretical standpoint, Rutledge and his team were able to confirm this at the neural level. Their key finding, they state, was that "conscious emotional states can be precisely manipulated and characterized using computational models in a similar manner to studies of conscious perception." In other words, they figured out how to mess with people's state of happiness and quantitatively study it.

> *In Rutledge's study, they studied the right anterior insula and tracked its level of activity. This area is known to be a target for ascending dopamine projections. Recall that dopamine is thought to play a role in feeling pleasure, satisfaction and motivation in the brain (and perception of time!).*

In addition to validating the presence of a hedonic setpoint, the more surprising finding they made was "the important role for expectations in determining happiness." The manner in which they looked at the effect of expectations was quite ingenious. In one set of experiments the researchers designed, the gambling outcomes were not revealed consistently, enabling the researchers to differentiate the effect of expectation of the outcome and of the actual outcome on the participants reported level of happiness. What they found is expectations affect happiness even before outcomes are revealed. For instance, even if the prize is $0, if the alternative prize was losing $2, the participants reported being happier. However, if the alternative was winning $2, they were less happy. These findings held true even if the outcome is never revealed. As long as the participant believed they had made a favorable choice, they reported being happier. The researchers compared this to real-life decisions by stating, "rewards associated with life decisions are often not realized for a long time (e.g., jobs, marriage) and our results suggest that expectations related to those decisions, both good and bad, do have an impact on happiness."

Ultimately, they concluded that "momentary happiness is a state that reflects not how well things are going but instead whether things are going better than expected. This includes positive and negative expectations, even in the absence of outcomes. Our results are in accord with well-being studies suggesting that the ongoing state of happiness varies around a hedonic set point." Positive expectations reduced the overall impact of trials with positive outcomes, and conversely, negative expectations reduced the emotional impact of trials with negative outcomes.

Rutledge and workers concluded that "the overall effect of expectations on happiness is negative." So, does this mean we should have low expectations? Not quite. In the end, Rutledge and colleague voiced an equivocal conclusion about the advantages and disadvantages of keeping expectations low. On the one hand, lower expectations create a higher probability of a positively perceived outcome. On the other hand, having lower expectations potentially decreases well-being before the outcome arrives, potentially offsetting any benefit to it. Being told a plane will arrive 6 hours late which then comes only 3 hours late is nice, but for those first 3 hours you are really pissed.

Defensive Pessimism

So from Rutledge's study, we are given data that suggests that on a neural level, lower expectations are of some benefit to our level of moment-to-moment happiness. Having low expectations comes in two psychological flavors: defensive pessimism and self-handicapping. Let's first look more closely at the former.

Defensive pessimism is defined as the cognitive strategy of setting low expectations and visualizing worst-case-scenarios prior to an achievement pursuit, despite past successes.[112] The idea is that it "can help people manage their anxiety so that it does not interfere with—and may even facilitate—their efforts to reach their goals."[113] The approach of the defensive pessimist is in contrast to those of *strategic optimists,* who set high expectations and avoid thinking about what might happen, whether good or ill. Julie Norem from Wellesley College has done a lot of work on defensive pessimism. In her contrarian book, *The Power of Negative Thinking* (2002), [114] she outlines the benefits of defensive pessimism and brings attention to the possible ineffectiveness of positive thinking.

Though having low expectations can be conducive to happiness, there are downsides to defensive pessimism. Those who employ this strategy are more pessimistic about things that have not happened even when they have performed as well as strategic optimists in the past. Strategic optimists also tend to have higher rated self-esteem than defensive optimists. [115]

On the surface, it would seem that strategic optimism is a better cognitive coping strategy than defensive pessimism. It turns out that it is not that clear cut. In one study by Brower and Ketterhagen from the *Journal of Social Issues* (2004),[116] they found that African American college students at predominantly white institutions were more likely to employ defensive pessimism strategies than those students at historically black colleges. In so doing, these students were found to have college retention rates comparable to those of white students. In contrast, black students who did not use defensive pessimism had significantly lower retention rates. The researchers argued that by employing this defensive strategy, the students identified the sources of their anxiety and acted accordingly in order to prevent negative outcomes. Basically, they studied harder.

An important point to make is that defensive pessimists do not ruminate; that is, they do not have recurrent negative thoughts about the past, as this is a counterproductive behavioral pattern. They focus on the future, and in so doing, can more specifically direct their efforts toward avoiding all the possible negative outcomes they can imagine. Norem refers to this as "positive negativity."

Defensive pessimists lean toward engaging in *prefactual thinking*, while strategic optimists prefer *counterfactual thinking*.[117] We introduced the concept of counterfactual thinking in Part I of the book. The difference is in the timing. *Before* an event, prefactual thinkers imagine possible outcomes (negative ones in the case of pessimists) and take steps to limit negative outcomes. In contrast, counterfactual thinking is imagining other possible outcomes *after* an event has occurred. In the case of optimists, they often engage in what is referred to as downward counterfactual thinking, which is imagining outcomes that are more negative than what happened. In so doing, they are reframing what may be a disappointing result into something less so. This is a type of *mood-repair* strategy that is part of our psychological immune system I described in the previous chapter. This type of thinking is a component of gratefulness, which will be explored more later.

Studies of counterfactual thinking have typically looked at the tendency to think about how bad things could have been worse, aka, counting your blessings. *But did you die?* is the meme that comes to mind to exemplify the idea of downward counterfactual thinking after hearing about someone else's misfortune (source: Ken Jeong, *The Hangover Part II*). In contrast, there has not been as much study or recognition of the possible benefits of downward counterfactual thinking after a *positive* event. It's just not intuitive to count your blessings after something good happens to you.

In a study by Koo et al. entitled, "It's a Wonderful Life: Mentally Subtracting Positive Events Improves People's Affective States, Contrary to Their Affective Forecasts" (2008),[118] researchers were the first to demonstrate the "George Bailey" effect. They found that when participants wrote about positive events never happening (downward counterfactual thinking after a good thing), they were happier than participants who simply wrote about good things that did happen. The study suggested that taking time to "mentally subtract" something good from our lives might improve our well-being more so than just being grateful for it being present (more on gratefulness in a later chapter). For instance, imagining you never met your significant other may improve your relationship well-being more than simply recounting how you did.

In the end, there does not appear to be a straightforward answer as to which cognitive strategy is better. As it turns out, trying to make a defensive pessimist act and think more like a strategic optimist leads to poorer performance.[119] The reason is thought to be that pessimists use their negative predictions as a motivator to work harder, thereby improving their performance. Norem states, "there are considerable costs of strategic optimism for those who are anxious." In a similar fashion, trying to get an optimist to think more pessimistically also creates a poorer outcome. They utilize their optimism in a manner to not focus on any negative outcome which in turn allows them to perform better, and when asked to think more like a pessimist, they too perform worse. As Norem states, "Strategies are unlikely to be universally maladaptive or effective; rather, their costs and benefits are likely to depend on who is using them under what circumstances."[120]

So I have described the neural mechanism whereby expectations influence a person's moment-to-moment happiness. Then we talked about two opposing cognitive strategies to manage expectations and pursue achievement. In the end, there is no clear-cut winning approach. There is, however, one other strategy I'll touch on that is definitively not advantageous for subjective well-being.

Self-handicapping

A behavioral strategy that shares commonality with defensive pessimism is self-handicapping.[121],[122] Psychologists Elliot and Church define it as "a strategy with the primary aim of protecting one's self-esteem in the event of failure."[123] Though both approaches share a similar motivation–that is, the avoidance of disappointment—where they differ is in the execution of that plan and in the final outcome.

Whereas defensive pessimists use their strategy to identify their anxieties and prefactually act on them, self-handicappers artificially create barriers to success, such as effort withdrawal. This way, if and when they fail, they can ascribe it to something other than their own lack of merit. Self-handicappers place more importance on the avoidance of negative emotions than the attainment of their goals. In fact, they seem to show a lack of concern about achievement altogether, possibly due to their inability to feel pride even with success. So, in the end, not being successful is hardly a sacrifice.

Ultimately, self-handicapping behavior undermines performance and personal success, and not surprisingly, self-handicappers have low subjective well-being.[124] Bottom line, this is not a cognitive strategy you want to adopt.

The problem is of course that self-handicappers' behavior puts them more at risk for failure and the concomitant negative emotions that stem from that. How does their psyche reconcile this paradox? Elliot and Church explain this behavioral paradox by distinguishing between two types of failure: "specific failure on a task in a given situation and global failure as an intellect or person." The self-handicapper has no problem failing on a specific task as long as they can ascribe it to the obstacles (they have placed) and not to their own self. This so-called "attributional ambiguity" eliminates the risk that they will see themselves as global failures, which is their primary goal. In this way, self-handicappers' behavior is goal-reinforcing, in contrast to happiness pursuers' behavior, where the emotional result of failure is unhappiness, which is irreconcilable with the original goal of happiness.

Conclusions and the Path Forward

Ever the optimist, Sharot states, "Our belief that happiness is just around the corner is, ironically enough, what keeps our spirits high in the present. Imagining a better future...maintains our well-being." This glass-half-full attitude seemingly stands in stark contrast to the research just presented demonstrating the disadvantages of high expectations. In the end, perhaps it is our expectations that get us out of bed, our defensive pessimism that helps us navigate inevitable disappointment and our strategic optimism that stops us from climbing right back in.

In the real world, falling into a high expectations trap is akin to stubbornly pursuing and evaluating our happiness. Both approaches are often a setup for disappointment. On the other hand, being persistently pessimistic without having a plan of action is counterproductive as well. And on top of all that, if we're not supposed to pursue happiness, what's the point of it all? Given these two psychological dead-ends, what is the path forward?

It might be that as individuals we simply need to recognize where we are on the happiness and expectations spectrum. What is our individual hedonic setpoint? Do we lean more toward strategic optimism, defensive pessimism or self-handicapping? In so knowing, we should be more able to anticipate and emotionally respond to whatever crisis life presents us and less likely to try to fit into a mold that does not suit us. So, if our outward expeditions toward happiness are marked by psychological booby traps galore, perhaps then we need to go *inward* to figure it out. And to go inward, we need to become more self-aware. Let's go!

11

Awareness and Self-Care

There is nothing either good or bad, but thinking makes it so.
—Hamlet

You yourself, as much as anybody in the entire universe, deserve your love
and affection.
—Buddha

There is a power in naming something. On the most elemental level, people name things to communicate about them, and on the most intimate level, our own names are what embody us. Whether it is something, someone, or some feeling, we just can't go around saying, "You know, that person did that thing, and then I felt something." On a different level, people name things to feel some sense of control in a world that may otherwise seem chaotic. Bulgarian writer Elias Canetti wrote, "You have but to know an object by its proper name for it to lose its dangerous magic." From physics to psychology to cocktail parties, giving something or someone a name allows us to quickly categorize it, cast our judgments on that categorization, and then act in a way that we deem appropriate, for better and for worse.

To name something, we need to be *aware* of it. So here we go, the touchy-feely part. You knew this was coming. You might even say you forecasted it. There is a vast history and science describing awareness practices and their central role in psychological well-being, and I cannot possibly expect to do justice summarizing them in one section of one chapter. But I'll give it a shot.

Let's first go East and start with Buddhism. The four central tenets of Buddhism, called the *Four Noble Truths*,[125] are:

1. Suffering exists.
2. There is a cause to suffering.
3. Suffering can end.
4. There are ways to make suffering end.

William Goldman paraphrased Buddhism's take on suffering thus: "Life is pain, Highness. Anyone who tells you differently is selling something." But there is a workaround. Suffering can only occur if there is an *I*, if there is a self. So, if there is no self, there can be no suffering. So how do we get to the state Buddhists call *no self*, the *unwavering band of light* that Vonnegut wrote of?

Buddhism teaches us that nothing exists outside of our awareness.[126] This can be interpreted literally. Until we place our awareness on something, it does not exist for us. This can be an object, a person, an emotion, a thought. We can call any of these things *form*, and Buddhism teaches that form does not exist outside of awareness. Another key and related Buddhist concept is that of *emptiness*, and it is often a source of confusion. It does not refer to a void or nothingness but rather points to the lack of individual relevance—an emptiness—of anything outside of its relationship to everything else. Emptiness means "empty of a separate self."[127] Whether it is an emotion, an experience or a subatomic particle, each is individually "empty of self-essence" when taken in isolation.[128] Emptiness then refers to the "interdependence of all phenomena, both mental and physical,"[129] and indeed being empty of a separate self then means being full of everything. Vietnamese (woot-woot!) Buddhist monk superstar Thích Nhất Hạnh (1926-2022) refers to this as *the fullness of emptiness* and declares, "Long Live Emptiness."[130] Taken together, one can make the philosophical leap that form and emptiness are one and the same. They are both impermanent and interdependent, and when we truly grasp this, suffering ends. If your suffering has ended, you can stop reading here. Otherwise, please continue.

Embracing the idea of emptiness or no self in Buddhism has led to the unfortunate and popular Western misinterpretation that Buddhism advocates for *egolessness*.[131] The pursuit of egolessness was thought to be necessary because it is our ego—our sense of self—that causes us to act in unhealthy ways to both ourselves and to others. And by extension, it is the clinging to that notion of self that is the source of all suffering. To that end, many Buddhist teachers in the West relentlessly condemned the ego, made it into a four-letter word and their life goal to see it burned to the ground.

From this rejection of the ego arose the Western fad of self-hatred. The story goes that when the Dalai Lama was posed with a question about self-hatred by Western Buddhist teachers, it took ten minutes of conferring with his interpreter to try to understand the question.[132] His response in the end was, "Whatchu be talkin' about Willis?" followed by, "But that's a mistake…Every being is precious."

Unfortunately, many people from the West have internalized the idea of egolessness and transformed it into self-hatred, putting the Buddha's "stamp of approval"[133] on it. Though Western thinkers have suggested this represents a flaw in Buddhist teachings, more recent opinion is that it is more a misinterpretation of the original texts. Basically, some balding Americans with ponytails misread thousand-year-old Buddhist texts, disseminated harmful misinformation, then claimed Buddha didn't know what he was talking about. Right.

Moving on to Austria, Freudian psychoanalytic theory posits that the *ego* serves as an important intermediary between the primal desires and impulses of the *id* and the moralistic, idealistic boundaries of the *superego*.[134] Modern Buddhist teaching has also recognized the importance of the ego.[135] Thanissaro Bhikkhu, an American Theravada Buddhist monk, states, "A person devoid of ego functions would be self-destructive: either a beast with uncontrolled impulses, or a neurotic, repressed automaton with no mind of their own, or an infantile monster thrashing erratically between these two extremes."[136] Sounds like a Friday night on-call in the O.R.

Regardless of whether you adopt the Freudian or the Buddhist idea of the ego, a common goal exists: finding a healthy balance of influence to give it. Too much ego, and our personal investment in everything blows us and others out of the water. Too little ego, and we are rudderless in an ocean of emotional and situational turmoil. States psychiatrist Mark Epstein, "…when we let the ego have free rein, we suffer. But when it learns to let go, we are free."[137]

So how do we manage our sense of self, use it to navigate the world and make sense of our emotional state of being *and* at the same time not let it hijack our lives and continually skew us toward a *me versus the world* perspective? Awareness.

Awareness and Mindfulness

In recent times, these words and the purported practice of them have become common in popular culture, and as a result, somewhat bemoaned.[138],[139] Reactions range from eye-rolling to downright irritation. How does a lotus pose and *om*-ing help you recover from a breakup or getting fired? The feelings are still there.

These concepts are more about creating a separation between you and the emotional experience you are having than pretending that you are just a meditating wave of energy. In so doing, you have allowed yourself some space to step back and witness the bigger picture of your life and to hopefully see that this is just one moment.

So what's the difference between awareness and mindfulness? These concepts are intertwined, and some modern Buddhist teachers consider them complementary practices. Mindfulness can be thought of as the overarching manner in which we experience the world while awareness is more the response we bring to specific experiences, emotional and physical.

Though in the most basic sense, awareness represents our perception of self and our surroundings, a well-developed capability for awareness allows us to filter all the incoming stimuli and decide what deserves our attention and what is just another manifestation of our so-called *monkey mind.** The monkey mind can be thought of as our permanently installed self-critic. It's that voice that has got something to say about every thought, action or inaction we experience. It is the unhealthy component of our ego, always critical and as a result counterproductive to our growth.[140] One of the main purposes of developing our awareness is to get this monkey to STFU.

> ** The "monkey mind" concept has origins back 2,000 years to Buddhist teachings. The phrase is translated to mean, "unsettled, restless, capricious, uncontrollable." One story goes that a man received a magical monkey that would do anything he asked. At first, this was great, as he asked for all the things he wanted. After each task was completed, the monkey would return, asking for another directive. It is when the man ran out of tasks that the constant beckoning of the monkey got to him. He could not get rid of it and its incessant need for attention. What the Buddhists were making an analogy to is how our own minds, though serving us in many ways, often do not give us any peace, constantly screeching and chattering and generally causing havoc while bouncing between one annoying thought to the next, incessantly demanding our attention.*

Awareness allows you to be grounded. In mindfulness parlance, to ground means to come back from wherever our attention has wandered to. When you come back, you are present. So why is it so important to be present? When we are present, we are not plagued by our monkey mind. We can devote our full energy to what is in front of us or within us, whether it be a task, a meal, natural beauty, another human being or an emotion. Being present connects you with what is happening in that moment, and by doing this, you can maximize your experience in any given pursuit and minimize any given emotion's ability to derail your mental health.

We can't talk about awareness without talking about Ram Dass (a pretty badass name, meaning "servant of God"). Dass was an American psychologist and writer who helped popularize Eastern spirituality in the West and is widely thought of as one of the most influential modern spiritual teachers.[141] Born Richard Alpert into a wealthy family in Boston, he writes that he derived from "a Jewish anxiety-ridden high-achieving tradition." Lecturing at Berkeley, Stanford and Harvard, he lived the storied life of the privileged and successful American who found enlightenment at the "traditional headwater of mystical rivers, India."[142]

In the 1960s, he hung out with the likes of Timothy— "turn on, tune in and drop out"—Leary and did all sorts of far-out shit. For instance, in 1962, with fellow Harvard Professor Leary and graduate student Walter Pahnke, he co-devised the first controlled, double-blind study of drugs and the mystical experience, called the "Good Friday Experiment."[143] In this study, Pahnke showed that psilocybin, the active ingredient in "magic mushrooms," was effective in inducing a profound spiritual experience similar or identical to that described by the "mystics of all ages, cultures, and religions." A follow up study twenty-five years later found persisting positive and virtually no negative changes in attitude and behavior.[144] All but one of the subjects in the experiment described their experience as having "a genuine mystical nature and characterized it as one of the high points of their spiritual life." This study and other spirituality-seeking shenanigans Dass and Leary pursued made them personae non gratae and eventually got them booted from Harvard in 1963.

Sorry, where were again? Oh right, awareness. In his seminal book, *Be Here Now* (1971), Dass writes, "Be here now."[145] With regard to awareness, he states, "Everything changes once we identify with being the witness to the story instead of the actor in it." In other words, when we separate our ego—our sense of self—from the experience we are having, that is when we can grow and learn instead of just react. Not to take himself too seriously, he also writes, "Just because you are seeing divine light, experiencing waves of bliss, or conversing with Gods and Goddesses is no reason to not know your zip code."

In our lives we all need to have mediators of awareness. Someone who will challenge us and make us feel uncomfortable because they love us. For me at midlife, it is my daughter. With her accusing eyes and youthful sneers, she calls me out on my lapses in attention and deficiencies in kindness. With her advancing age, I cannot fail to recognize my own. With her burgeoning sense of self, I am compelled to reassess my own identity. For all of these things, I am immeasurably grateful to her.

Meditation

In wrapping up with this section on awareness, I will briefly touch on the tiny topic that is meditation. If mindfulness is our destination, meditation is one path that can lead us there. Dubbed the "Father of Mindfulness," Thích Nhất Hạnh has prolifically shared his insights on this practice, with his top five mindfulness techniques being:[146]

1. Mindful Breathing: "The greatest of all miracles is to be alive, and when you breathe in, you touch that miracle. Therefore, your breathing can be a celebration of life."
2. Concentration: "Breathing out, I follow my out-breath all the way through. From the beginning of my out-breath to the end of my out-breath, my mind is always with it. Therefore, mindfulness becomes uninterrupted, and the quality of your

concentration is improved."

3. Awareness of Body: "Breathing in, I am aware of my body. Breathing out, I am aware of my body."

4. Releasing Tension: "Breathing in, I'm aware of my body. Breathing out, I release the tension in my body."

5. Walking Meditation: "The real miracle is not to fly or walk on fire. The real miracle is to walk on the Earth, and you can perform that miracle at any time. Just bring your mind home to your body, become alive, and perform the miracle of walking on Earth."

As is apparent, each practice builds upon the other. All of them are dependent on the breath though, which in and of itself can constitute someone's entire awareness practice. Buddhist teacher and author Dzogchen Ponlop Rinpoche states, "The practice of meditation is basically a process of getting to know yourself by becoming familiar with your mind... {it is} intended to increase our mindfulness and awareness, strengthen our sense of inner peace, and improve our ability to deal with our emotions as well."[147]

My personal meditation practice is as follows:

1. Light a candle. Optional: set timer and cue relaxing music
2. Sit quietly and comfortably
3. Focus on my breath
4. Notice my thoughts and physical sensations—pleasant and unpleasant—and let them run rampant, but do not try to engage them, get away from them, or stop them
5. Go back to step 3

Headspace co-founder and former Buddhist monk Andy Puddicombe (not a badass name) states that being present is the "cornerstone of meditation and mindfulness ... Most people assume that meditation is all about stopping thoughts, getting rid of emotions, somehow controlling the mind. But actually it's…about stepping back, seeing the thought clearly, witnessing it coming and going."

In addition to psychological benefits, mindfulness practices can also lead to objective physiological gains. Psychologist Richard Davidson is known for his research looking at emotion and the brain as well as its downstream effects on our physiology.[148] When comparing the brains of meditators vs. non-meditators, his work has demonstrated differences in immune response, [149] brain activation, and neural responses to pain.[150] Davidson and colleagues found that compared with non-meditators, meditators had increased activation of the part of their brain associated with positive affect and intriguingly made more antibodies in response to the flu vaccine.

In Davidson's study looking at pain response, pain was inflicted with the TSA-2001 thermal stimulator, an Israeli developed device that is MRI compatible and can deliver heat up to 120 degrees Fahrenheit to the desired body part.[151] Of note, it was found that expert meditators (defined as having at least 10,000 hours of practice) reported equal pain intensity, but less unpleasantness compared to non-meditators. Moreover, using functional MRI, these mindfulness masters showed minimal anticipatory neural responses prior to the painful stimuli; in other words, they did not flinch. Researchers equated these findings as the neural represdentation of "being in the moment," one of the significant benefits of mindfulness. The meditators did not suffer ahead of time. In contrast, the non-meditators' activated the part of their brain called the amygdala—responsible for fear and threat detection—*before* the painful stimulus. In other words, they preemptively suffered. In everyday life, we are all guilty to some extent of worrying when we don't need to, grieving when there is not yet a cause. Also known as anticipatory anxiety or future-tripping, this study provides an intriguing mindfulness workaround for this annoying human tendency.

In psychiatrist Dan Siegel's, *Aware: The Science and Practice of Presence* (2020),[152] he takes an in-depth look at the science that underlies mindfulness' health benefits. A pivotal axiom that he explores is that *neurons that fire together wire together.* This phrase was first used by neuropsychologist Donald Hebb in 1949 and is the central concept behind neuroplasticity. The meaning is simple: experiences re-wire the brain and when those experiences are repeated, those connections get reinforced. This is the basis of memory and learning. More than that, when it happens, all sorts of magical things might occur in your body. To better conceptualize one's awareness practice, Siegel describes "three pillars" of mindfulness. They are focused attention, open awareness and kind intention. When we are successful in optimizing these pillars, research he reviews is associated with benefits to our cardiovascular and immune systems, improvement in our DNA repair mechanisms, and reductions in our stress and inflammatory responses. We will review some of these processes in the chapter, "What Does a Body Good? It's your DNA, Stupid."

Now before you run off and sign up for that mindfulness retreat in the hopes of hacking your brain, know that it's not going to be that easy. As a case in point, some early studies suggested that the trendy 8-week mindfulness-based stress reduction (MBSR) program[153] can induce changes in the brain similar to that seen after long term mindfulness practice.[154,155,156] MBSR was developed at the University of Massachusetts Medical Center in the 1970s by Professor Jon Kabat-

Zinn, and it uses techniques such as meditation, yoga and other touchy-feely exercises with treatment applications ranging from high blood pressure to skin disorders to even cancer.[157]

While a study from 2011 by the dynamic duo Niazi and Niazi[158] showed that there is certainly benefit of MBSR in helping patients *cope* with chronic illness, there is not yet conclusive data to say that it actually improves any of those conditions. That said, if there is one take-home point from learning about awareness, it's that how we emotionally cope with difficult life situations makes a huge difference in how we experience it.

Regarding MBSR leading to neural changes, however, that is doubtful with just an 8-week course. A high-quality study that was published May 2022 by Davidson and colleagues failed to show any structural brain changes.[159] There were no alterations in gray matter volume, gray matter density or cortical thickness. Alas, though MBSR may not give you the 6-minute gray matter six-pack you seek, there is little debate about the other multiple emotional and psychological benefits of these practices and the healthy behavioral changes they may spur.

* * *

The common message of any awareness practice, be it meditation or otherwise, is that the *real you* is the witness in your emotional and physical lives, not the source of the emotion or the action themselves. After all, how can your thoughts be coming from the real you if you are hearing them? In a way, your thoughts are the ultimate reality show, and you are the viewer. Thoughts may be entertaining, frightening or just ordinary; but they are separate from the real you. By learning to be present with an uncomfortable emotional or physical experience instead of trying to run away from it, we give ourselves the opportunity to examine it more closely. When we do this, we often realize that the situation is more granular, not black and white. Pain and suffering are just labels we place on circumstances and not absolute qualities of them. This is perhaps the most significant benefit of mindfulness habits. The more we practice awareness, the more we may realize that there is a world out there that we process through our minds and paying attention to how our minds process that world changes the world that we experience. We will come back to this practice often as we discuss the changes we can choose to make in the second half of our lives.

Spiritual Bypassing, Toxic Positivity and Tragic Optimism

Moving on, I'll just spend a moment discussing the evil twin of awareness, its archnemesis if you will. Taking a path to pursue mindfulness without the benefit of personal growth has been referred to as *spiritual bypassing*.[160],[161] Described by Buddhist teacher and psychotherapist John Welwood in 1980, it refers to the "widespread tendency to use spiritual ideas and practices to sidestep or avoid facing unresolved emotional issues, psychological wounds, and unfinished developmental tasks." The commonly described example is someone who goes on a spiritual retreat to learn to mindfully disregard the issues causing turmoil in their lives. When they return to their normal lives, they feel temporarily enlightened, only to be victim to the same issues that plagued them in the first place. Examples of spiritual bypassing include:[162]

- Not focusing on the here and now; living in a "spiritual realm" much of the time.
- Overemphasizing the positive and avoiding the negative.
- Being self-righteous about the concept of enlightenment.
- Being overly detached.
- Being overly idealistic.
- Having feelings of entitlement.
- Exhibiting frequent anger.
- Engaging in cognitive dissonance (the state of having inconsistent thoughts, beliefs, or attitudes, especially as relating to behavioral decisions and attitude change)
- Being overly compassionate.
- Pretending that everything is okay even though the situation is not okay.

Toxic positivity is a common external expression of spiritual bypassing. It is the act of disregarding or even denying a harsh reality of life and choosing only to look on the bright side. It might be regarded as an unhealthy extreme of gratitude. The origin of the phrase *toxic positivity* is not clear, but its use seems to have increased around the early 2020s, i.e., during the COVID-19 pandemic. During this period, many people expected themselves and others to maintain a positive attitude despite the overwhelmingly negative circumstances. Many articles have been written about its widespread presence and the downsides to it.[163,164] Denying the tragedy of the pandemic backfired by stripping a person of the opportunity for emotional growth, as psychological research demonstrates that struggle and hardship actually increase a person's appreciation for their lives and facilitates personal growth.[165,166,167]

Admittedly, I have been a perpetrator of toxic positivity in my life.

Recognizing that I have enjoyed a fairly blessed existence, it has been easy for me to disregard out of hand any negative circumstances I encounter, and by extension, other people's adverse situations. I have frequently reminded my young daughter to be grateful and not complain about her mean teachers. I have cut off friends' gripes about their coworkers. I have disregarded my own feelings of not feeling loved or being chosen because what right do I have to feel bad? In so doing, I now realize I have denied myself and those around me the opportunity to fully have their negative experiences and grow from them.

The antidote to toxic positivity is said to be *tragic optimism,* a phrase coined by the psychologist and Holocaust survivor Viktor Frankl.[168] Tragic optimism was his method to search for meaning in the face of human suffering and tragedy. Instead of trying to regard negative events in a positive light, his approach acknowledges the reality of the suffering, but attempts to reframe them with a growth perspective. Frankl's approach to psychotherapy is called *logotherapy,* which translates to "healing through meaning." Its premise is that the primary motivational force of an individual is to find meaning in life. It contrasts with the two other contemporary schools of psychotherapy –Sigmund Freud's and Alfred Adler's—where the individual is motivated by pleasure or power, respectively.

* * *

In summary, awareness forms the foundational basis from which we experience any emotion. Practicing awareness and mindfulness are essential for successfully piloting our way through our emotional lives. Along with the management of expectations we discussed in the previous chapter, awareness underpins all our life circumstances and allows us to shed light on the psychological frictions that resist change.

Using awareness, we can uncouple our sense of self from our thoughts, and that allows us to notice the experience of emotions without being caught up in them. According to Dass, awareness is who is "minding the store." It is the "I" that exists "independent of social and physical identity." Even though this is an attractive concept when we are trying to detach from negative emotions, we must remember that it also applies when we are experiencing positive ones like happiness and thus not become too absorbed in them either. In the words of Dass, "It's all real and it's all illusory: that's Awareness!"

With a foundation of awareness, we have one key to well-being. The next step is learning to love ourselves, to put our oxygen masks on first.

Self-Care and Loving Kindness

"I ain't got time to bleed." –Jesse 'The Body' Ventura, from "Predator"

The history of self-care is thought to go way back to So-crates, with his famous injunction, carved into stone at the entrance to Apollo's temple at Delphi: "Know Thyself." Sounds a lot like "Be Aware," right? To Socrates, to know oneself is the means through which one cares for oneself and therefore justifies self-care.[169] By extension, practicing awareness could be viewed in a similar fashion as a means of self-care.

Fast forward to the twentieth century, and the promotion of self-care was initially connected to the field of medicine and the treatment of the mentally ill and the dependent elderly.[170] From there, the concept of self-love has been linked to the Beat Generation of the 1950s and to the Hippies later in the 1960s. The second wave of the feminist movement and the civil rights movement in the same era also adopted self-care as a central tenet.[171] In the 1980s, Audre Lorde, a black writer and activist, famously stated, "Caring for myself is not self-indulgence, it is self-preservation…"[172] It was during these decades that self-care became more than just an individual concept and additionally transformed into a political statement.

In more recent times, self-care has been brought back to the forefront by two key events. Google searches for self-care spiked in the months preceding and up to Trump's election win in November 2016, with approximately three times the queries compared to years earlier.[173] Indeed, some studies looking at the mental health of Americans following that election showed a measurable decline, with one study by Yan et al. demonstrating that there were 54.6 million more days of poor mental health in December 2016 compared to October 2016 in states that voted for Hillary Clinton.[174] That equates to a *lot* of bon-bons and binge-watching. Since November 2016, self-care searches have gone on to *quadruple*.[175]

And even more recently, during this pandemic, self-care has been trending, with seventy-two million posts on Instagram as I write this. Here are a couple of good ones: "When in doubt, zen it out." And, "People who wonder if the glass is half full or half empty miss the point. The glass is refillable." Clearly, there is current and unprecedented interest in self-care and self-love, and in the remainder of this chapter, we'll unpack these ideas and their associated behaviors, both productive and unproductive.

* * *

"What do I need now?"

According to Kristin Neff and Christopher Germer, authors of *The Mindful Self-Compassion Workbook: A Proven Way to Accept Yourself, Build Inner Strength, and Thrive* (2018), asking yourself this single question can lead to self-care and self-love in the times that we most need it.[176] Let's start by defining self-care. On one level, it includes brushing your teeth, exercising, going to bed on time, managing your finances and eating well. And on another level, it is having healthy relationships, recognizing when we need emotional help and knowing how to refill our tanks.

Though some aspects of self-care seem relatively straightforward, others are decidedly more complex. Yet, we often fail in even the simpler aspects of self-care. Why? Some reasons include negativity bias, shame, misconstruing the meaning of self-care and setting our expectations too high.[177] Let's look at each of them.

Negativity bias is one reason we may not choose to make healthy decisions for ourselves. It is a psychological concept described by psychologists Rozin and Royzman in 2001 and is defined as "a general bias…in animals and humans to give greater weight to negative entities (e.g., events, objects, personal traits)…" than to positive ones.[178] Baumeister et al. put it much more succinctly in their study entitled, "Bad is Stronger than Good" (2001).[179] Negativity bias results in bad events having more impact on us than equally good or neutral ones. Be it bad emotions, bad parents or bad ceviche, these emotional experiences stick with us longer and more intensely than positive ones.

A biological explanation for negativity bias is that our brains actually give negative information more computing bandwidth than good information. From a survival standpoint, it makes sense to place more emphasis and remember the things that can kill us rather than on the things that will love us. This behavioral pattern is purported to exist in the young developing brain and as such, would not simply be the result of environmental conditioning.[180] Negativity bias and loss aversion (described in, "Do Not Seek Happiness") likely derive from the same neural fabric.

Everyday examples of the negativity bias include the fact that bad news always sells better than good news and how bad impressions and bad stereotypes form quicker and are more resistant to disconfirmation than good ones.[181]

An interesting research finding is the tendency of individuals with greater negativity bias to support conservative politics and those with less negativity bias to support more liberal politics.[182] As a result, conservative policies tend to be aimed at threat reduction and social order as opposed to liberal policies which are more accepting of diverse social groups due to their placing less weight on the potential social unrest that might occur as a result of those policies.

So when it comes to self-care, negativity bias makes it harder to perceive its benefits. If your gaze is constantly fixated on the negative events of your past, it paralyzes you to act positively in the present for yourself. As result, finding motivation to initiate self-care habits becomes more difficult.

In relationships, negativity bias leads us to expect the worse in our partners. Subsequently, when anything gets triggered, your shields go up, and you're on red alert. Throw in some confirmation bias,* and now you've got yourself an argument and fall into that deep *you're-always-like-this* hole. Paradoxically, because of negativity bias, we may be more likely to remain in unhealthy relationships because of the disproportionate weight that heartbreak and loneliness carry compared with how we remember our happy relationship moments.

> *Confirmation bias is a common cognitive bias whereby we tend to filter all information available and only look for and acknowledge as true that information which fits into our overall beliefs. I'll write more about this in the chapter about breaking out of your comfort zone.*

But you might ask, what about optimism bias? Would this not offset negativity bias? Not really. Recall that optimism bias describes the tendency for someone to believe they are less likely than someone else to experience a negative event. And as we just discussed, negativity bias is the tendency to place greater recollection weight on negative events than positive ones. So in the same person, these two biases can coexist. Optimism bias is about the future while negativity bias is about the past. You can simultaneously be optimistic about events that have not yet occurred but be very negative about those that have. Complex and confusing creatures we are.

When I was a medical student, negativity bias was always in play. One of the harder lessons was the rule that one "oops" undoes ten "good jobs!" I could be the alpha med-student, checking labs and being consistently on time for 6 am rounds for the entire rotation, but because I passed gas once during a bowel procedure, all the good work I had done previously gets overlooked.

In the end, how do we overcome negativity bias? Mindfulness, duh. In a randomized study by psychologists Kiken and Shook entitled, "Looking up: Mindfulness increases positive judgments and reduces negativity bias" (2011),[183] they found that when they introduced a mindfulness exercise to study participants, they demonstrated less negativity bias and more positive judgments. The decrease in negativity was attributable to better categorization of positive stimuli, not less categorization of negative stimuli. In the real world, the study suggests that when we are mindful, we will be less likely to succumb to the trap of negativity bias because we will proportionately weight our positive life events.

To be successful in initiating any self-care activities, we should attempt to do so with the clarity of mindfulness. Given, our brains will over-emphasize negative past events. Being aware of this, however, if we can perceive the explicit triggers of our negativity bias, we might see that it serves us better to address the specific past events that led to it in this particular context, and in so doing, work on undoing that trigger. When past events come to mind, invariably the ones with negative outcomes, we can remind ourselves that our brains are selectively curating our memories and picking out the moments when we and others were at their worst. At the same time, we can make an effort to remember all the times things worked out well. If we are successful, we might be able to resist the impulse to act instinctively in an attempt to avoid a repeat of our over-weighted past negativity. Only with consistent practice can we fully open ourselves to opportunities for self-care and growth.

* * *

Another reason we may fail in self-care is because when we acknowledge we need it, we are also admitting we have not been doing something right in the first place. And with this comes some degree of *shame*. Left unchecked, shame can spiral into self-hatred. Recall the tendency of some Western Buddhist teachings to cultivate this behavior in the interest of achieving the state of no self. Quite paradoxically, in these cases, the path to mindfulness and self-help can lead some to this dead-end path of shame, which poisons any attempt to love yourself. Only by falling back to awareness and naming the shame can we start to take some of its power away and move forward.

We may also fail in our attempts to love ourselves due to an inaccurate definition of what self-love is. Perhaps because of the same misconstrued line of reasoning some people adopt self-hatred, others will look at self-care as self-indulgence, self-coddling or just plain selfishness, and as a result, find a convenient reason not to pursue it. More than one religious teaching will tell you that succumbing to the desires of the self is the root of all evil.

And at the other extreme of misdefining self-care, some can justify being flakey or not committing to something under its guise. Instead of breaking out of their comfort zone, (described later) they take "personal days" as a means of not giving up control and preventing the unpredictable from happening in their lives. As a result, their individual growth may be stunted, and the frequency and strength of their social connections are likely diminished.

A final reason we often fail in self-care is when we set our expectations too high (sound familiar?). Often, we will make these grandiose plans when we are feeling our best from an emotional and physical standpoint. But when it comes down to action, we may be under-slept, overfed or just undermotivated. We set ourselves up to fail, and when we do, we feel shame and dig ourselves just a little deeper into that hole.

So how do we define self-care in a positive light and set reasonable objectives for ourselves? Repeat after me: Awareness. We acknowledge there are downsides to the abuse of the self-care mantra, and we stay vigilant to them, carefully examining the decisions we make to bow out of activities, previously pledged to or otherwise. We continuously take into account what our specific life situation is and commit to small and achievable targets, one step at time.

When we fail to care for ourselves properly, it becomes harder and harder to care for others. One commonly recognized consequence of failing to provide proper self-care is a phenomenon referred to as *compassion fatigue*. This phrase was used in a study from 1992 by C. Joinson who described nurses' "loss of...ability to nurture." [184] It has been defined as "the deep physical, emotional, and spiritual exhaustion that can result from working day to day in an intense caregiving environment."[185] Health care providers continue to be significantly affected by it, more so in the aftermath of the pandemic.[186,187] However, anyone in a caring profession can be affected –from therapists to first responders to veterinarians.[188] It's not hard to imagine how compassion fatigue can lead to compromise in patient care while on the job and outside of work, worsening of relationships and even more significant psychological conditions.

One means of limiting compassion fatigue in healthcare is learning how to compartmentalize our emotional reactions while taking care of people. Whatever comes up, we push it down, put it in that box, and plan to deal with it later. To compartmentalize successfully, however, we have to take emotion out of the equation altogether—throwing out the baby of compassion with the bathwater of anxiety, sadness and stress.

To be sure, to stay sane, working in health care requires us to be able to compartmentalize. While we cannot always succeed in stopping a disease or injury process from harming our patient, we must still move on with the next step in their treatment and attend to the others who are in need our help. At the same time we must learn from experience (and complications), we cannot let that occupy our mind so much as to negatively affect our next patient. Sometimes we have the luxury of reflection and analysis when things do not go as planned, and other times, as with an intra-operative mishap, we must immediately move forward, resort to our plan B, finish the procedure, close up our patient and get them off the table.

In his brilliant first book, *Complications*,[189] Atul Gawande reminds us of the common criticism of surgeons, "Sometimes wrong; never in doubt." He reminds us that despite the uncertainty that is a pervasive, "ground state" in the practice of medicine, we must carry on for the sake of our patients. Thus, though temporarily practical in specific critical situations, compartmentalizing only takes you so far. At some point, you have to deal with that stuff that came up.

So whether it is in medicine or just life in general, we are all in some degree charged with the care of more than just ourselves. In the long term, it serves us well to practice awareness and occasionally take inventory of our self-care tank. *Metta* is the word for loving-kindness in Sanskrit, and in Buddhism, it is one of the qualities of an enlightened mind. In her book, *Loving-Kindness For Dummies*, just kidding, it's *called Lovingkindness: The Revolutionary Art of Happiness* (2002),[190] Sharon Salzberg states, "The foundation of metta practice is to know how to be our own friend." Buddhist teaching tells us that there is no one other than our own selves who is more deserving of our love and affection. Unfortunately, in our daily lives, we often spread ourselves so thin, there is little left to give ourselves.

My Introduction to Self-Care

I did not learn how to cook in my childhood. I did not learn how to cook in my adolescence or young adulthood. I had a meal plan throughout my college years in Berkeley (and I loved it). For my first two years that I was in medical school in Boston, my mom would regularly overnight a box of three dozen or so home-cooked meals, lovingly prepared with items from all the food groups. I was the envy of my med-school dorm friends, and I made sure to point out between each savory bite that my mother clearly loved me more than theirs.

The first meals I started making for myself were in my 30s. They were mostly simple meals (and still are), with only natural ingredients like salmon, chicken and sriracha. Garlic would always be involved. Two necessary steps of the preparatory ritual were putting on music –often the likes of Billie Holiday or Thievery Corporation, then cracking open a beer or opening a bottle of wine (red, of course, more on this later!). What were the results? Did I find that I missed my calling as a

Michelin star chef? Haha. There were more than a few meals where my only comfort was in knowing that I and I alone had to eat it. Yes, *had* to eat, because I made it, and you don't waste food, Bobby. In the end, most were fairly edible. None were amazing.

What I realized in this process of cooking for myself was that even though the quality of end product was always in question, I just felt good doing it, for me. I was not cooking for anyone else most of the time, thank god. The time and energy I spent were all for me. The effort and care I devoted to the process were all for me. Cooking became a way for me to show love to myself for perhaps the first time in my life. Even as I write this now, I feel a little odd in my body. As if I'm professing something simultaneously obvious and at the same time a little criminal. Of course I should cook for myself. And how dare I take care of just—myself?

Fast forward to the present day. I often leave work late after finishing cases. It's dark. I'm starving. There is an In-N-Out on the way home from the hospital, at the intersection I turn at to get home. Do I go there? OK, sometimes. But when I don't, it's because I have my meal waiting to be made at home. My go-to comfort meal is what I like to call the specialty of the house: Spaghetti Bolognese a la Nguyen which consists of a full box of thick spaghetti, a pound of 85% lean ground beef, a bottle of spicy marinara sauce, a few cloves of garlic, a whole shallot, and my secret ingredient, a heaping spoonful of brown sugar. I cue the music, crack the beer and feel the love for myself.

It was not laziness that stopped me from cooking for myself all those years but rather my lack of awareness in how to take care of myself. Or for that matter, that I even needed to take care of myself. I never asked, "What do I need now?" Other people needed taking care of, not me. Though I can't tease out what part of this thinking comes from my Vietnamese upbringing, from being raised in the United States, or from being in the medical profession, I do think there is a pervasive modern mentality that expects that you simultaneously provide maximal care for others and minimal care for yourself.

As a result of the conflicting messages we receive about considering our own needs, our self-care muscles have traditionally been underdeveloped. Fortunately, in recent times, there seems to be more attention getting paid to wailing on our self-care pecs, as it were. Ultimately, we have to remember that an empty tank will take us nowhere. Only by coming from a place of internal abundance and a ripped self-care physique can we be fully available to others.

In the following chapter, moving from our base of awareness and metta, we will explore other mindfulness practices that can enrich our collective human experience and that can lead to well-being as their byproduct. We will investigate what I consider the *Greatest Hits* of these practices: Kindness, Gratefulness and Awe. In each instance, awareness and mindfulness are prerequisites to initiate the behavior, maximize the benefits of those actions, and maintain a lifestyle that facilitates those changes.

12

Kindness, Gratefulness and Awe

Be kind, for everyone you meet is fighting a hard battle.
—Ian MacLaren

We should certainly count our blessings, but we should also make our
blessings count.
—Neal A. Maxwell

There are two ways to live: you can live as if nothing is a miracle; you can live as if everything is a miracle. The most beautiful thing we can experience is the mysterious. It is the source of all true art and all science. He to whom this emotion is a stranger, who can no longer pause to wonder and stand rapt in awe, is as good as dead: his eyes are closed. –Albert Einstein

In the Beginning...

When my parents fled the only home they knew, they did so literally*
with only the clothes on their backs and us, who were also sometimes

on their backs. Us meaning four kids – my oldest sister aged 8, my big brother aged 7, my other sister aged 3, and me, aged 18 months. Because of unforeseen circumstances, my dad left first, which left my mom saddled with all of us. Remember that none of this could be openly or extensively planned out, but my parents realized that the fall of Saigon and the end of the Vietnam war were imminent. The date we escaped with my mom was April 29, 1975. Saigon fell April 30, 1975.

> *As an aside, are there any other linguists out there deeply perturbed by the rampant misuse of the word literally? People are literally using it when their statement is in fact not literal. "OMG, I like literally died..." In an article Elizabeth East,[191] she explains how literally has literally been misused as far back as 1789 and goes on to give other examples of these so-called Janus words. Frequently described as words that are their own opposites, Janus words are also known as contranyms, antagonyms, or auto-antonyms. For instance, oversight originally meant watchful care, but then grew to also mean errors of omission. Which begs the question, what exactly is Congressional oversight? Similarly, sanctioning something can either mean disallowing it or approving of it. The point is, literally is not the only word used in English that can mean its opposite. Alas, in the end, persnickety people will literally just have to bite their tongue. But I digress.*

I like to think of myself as being able to travel light and at a moment's notice, packing only carry-on even for international trips. But if I forget my toiletry bag, iPhone charger, trashy sci-fi novel, eye mask, ear plugs, cozy slippers, favorite hoodie and other unmentionables, I'm a hot mess. I'm pretty sure my mom did not pack any of these.

What's more, we've all seen the inevitable chaos during air travel with one toddler and two parents. Now add another toddler and two older kids, with my oldest sister having Down syndrome, put it in the context of oh, say, life and death, multiply all this by a gazillion, and that might approximate a fraction of the kind of day my mom was having.

So when we finally got to Salinas, California and reunited with my dad, life was very good. Except, we had no money and no worldly possessions. Enter Pastor "O" of the neighborhood church, who upon seeing us at the shelter during one of his visits, gifted us a small home to live in and a Chevrolet to get around in. Though my recollection of him at that time is nonexistent, I met him several times after I had grown up, the last time just after I had gotten married and two years before he passed away.

To me, he and his wife seemed like Californian versions of Mr. and Mrs. Claus. Warm and abundantly fleshed, his temperament was unflappable, and her cookies were irresistible. They lived in Forest Ranch, a town just north of Chico. To my father, Pastor O represented the dad he had not seen since leaving home at age 18. His and his wife's kindness in my family's time of greatest need can rightly be described as divine.

* * *

In this chapter, we will explore three happiness hacks: kindness, gratefulness and awe. All of these behaviors most times require little of the participant and yet can yield enormous emotional benefit. None of these behaviors require enlightenment or even any planning. What they all involve though is awareness.

Sonja Lyubomirsky is a professor of psychology at the University of California, and she is considered a top researcher in the field of human happiness. We had previously looked into her work in the chapter on {not pursuing} happiness.[192] There she discussed the three main factors she thinks are most influential in determining a person's level of happiness. To recap, they are the individual's happiness set point, circumstantial factors in that individual's life and that person's chosen activities and practices. In this same article, she and researchers described "happiness interventions." These included committing acts of kindness, practicing grateful thinking and bringing intentionality and variability to everyday acts. Let's unpack each of these.

Being Kind

Lyubomirsky's work has looked at the strategy of committing acts of kindness as a means of increasing happiness.[193] She and workers proposed several mechanisms by which this may occur. Kind acts may foster one's sense of community and belonging and create opportunities for cooperation and interdependence. In addition, kind acts may remind that person of their own good fortune. People who demonstrate acts of kindness also may perceive themselves as altruistic and feel more confident, effective and in control. Furthermore, people who act kindly are often liked more by others, are more attractive mates, and can benefit from reciprocally kind acts.[194,195] Finally, kindness may "satisfy a basic human need for relatedness."[196]

An interesting nuance was observed when they analyzed the positive effect of acts of kindness on well-being. Timing was critical. In their study, participants were asked to perform five acts of kindness per week over a 6-week period. They could choose to carry out all five acts in a single day or spread them out over the whole week. It turns out that only when the kind acts were carried out in a single day was the participant's well-being significantly increased.

It is possible that a similar neural mechanism that determines the hedonic setpoint discussed in Rutledge's fMRI studies[197] is at play here. Just as he demonstrated that past a finite point in time, previous rewards had no effect on current happiness in study participants, perhaps spreading out the time in which acts of kindness are carried out leads to diminution of their benefits to well-being. Given too much time between kind acts, our *kind-act-setpoint* (yes, I just made that up) resets, and we do not psychologically benefit from that act. Recall the role that dopamine plays in the perception of time[198],[199] and its role in Rutledge's expectation-related happiness study, and it should not be surprising that close timing of kind events should have a more dramatic effect than temporally spaced-out acts of kindness.

The takeaway here may be that in order for kindness to lead to well-being, the acts need to be consistent and not just one-off.

Feeling Gratefulness

Let's talk about the second happiness intervention Lyubomirsky describes: gratitude. Emmons and McCullough (2003) found that practicing grateful thinking on a regular basis can enhance concurrent well-being.[200] "Gratitude promotes the savoring of positive life experiences and situations so that maximum satisfaction and enjoyment are distilled from one's circumstances." This is not rocket science. Remind yourself of how good you have it on the regular, and your mood is typically improved. What is interesting to note is the mechanism by which this may work. Gratitude can be thought of as directly counteracting the effects of the hedonic treadmill. Instead of our level of happiness drifting back down to its setpoint after a positive event, practicing gratitude theoretically bolsters it and reminds us that indeed, we do have something to be happy about. In addition, we can employ the same emotional muscles we use to practice gratitude to reframe difficult and stressful life events. Finally, gratitude may help us be and stay happy simply because it is hard to feel envious, angry or greedy when we are feeling grateful.

In Lyubomirsky's study, participants were asked to have grateful thoughts either once a week or three times a week. In an interesting twist, the frequency of grateful thoughts proved to be *inversely* related to the participants' increase in well-being. That is to say, there were diminishing returns, and only the people who had grateful thoughts once a week were shown to have a significant increase in well-being. Those who did it three times a week paradoxically did *not* show similar improvement. Perhaps there is an inverse hedonic relationship to feeling grateful and its positive effect on well-being. Do too much of it, and your brain figures out you are trying to hack it, and the jig is up. One might call this the *reverse-hedonic-gratitude-treadmill.*

The devil's advocate might call gratitude a "tool for narcissistic self-improvement."[201] The indictment being that people might often just be grateful for what *they* have and what has happened to *them*, failing to acknowledge that the world as a whole has provided them with the reasons to feel grateful.

To counteract this tendency, instead of just feeling gratitude (about our own life circumstances), we also express gratitude to others. In addition, experts have suggested that instead of adopting gratitude, which is seen as a fleeting and situational emotion based on a specific present circumstance, that instead we embrace gratefulness. This is definable as an "overall orientation" that is "not contingent on something happening to us, but rather a way that we arrive to life."[202] In the same light, Jans-Baker and Wong make a distinction between "existential gratitude" and "dispositional gratitude."[203] The former is a pervasive emotional state and is associated with increased well-being while the latter is a situational feeling that is not.

* * *

On the whole, we can intuitively accept Lyubomirsky's and other's research findings as being true in the real world. Being kind and expressing gratitude to others makes both us and the recipient happier. It's a win-win situation, so why is it that we don't do this more often? One theory as to why not is called the *prosocial paradox*. Psychologist Nancy Eisenberg defines prosocial behavior as "voluntary behavior intended to benefit another,"[204] with examples including offering social support, giving compliments and expressing gratitude toward someone.

What's more, prosocial behavior begets more prosocial behavior. In their study, "A little thanks goes a long way: Explaining why gratitude expressions motivate prosocial behavior (2010),"[205] researchers Grant and Gino demonstrate that gratitude expressions motivated helpers to provide even more assistance to the original receiver of help and moreover to others whom they had not yet helped. This effect was mediated by gratitude expressions enabling individuals to feel more socially valued.

Researchers Epley et al. examined the prosocial paradox in their study entitled, "A Prosociality Paradox: How Miscalibrated Social Cognition Creates a Misplaced Barrier to Prosocial Action" (2023).[206] They found that people consistently underestimate the value their kind actions will have on recipients. As a result, they are less likely to do those prosocial things. They found that the underestimation was due to an overemphasis on competency on the part of the giver when in fact what the receiver valued most was the kindness that the act represented and the "warmth" with which it was provided. As a result of this inaction, a person may look selfish when in fact they are not. Because of this paradox, both giver and recipient have lost an opportunity to improve their well-being via an action that typically requires minimal time, effort or money.

The prosocial paradox is reminiscent of our poor abilities in empathic forecasting I talked about in the "Do Not Seek Happiness" chapter. With empathic forecasting, we typically *overestimate* the emotional impact a negative event has on someone. In the case of the prosocial paradox, it seems, we typically *underestimate* the emotional benefit our actions can have on others. It seems we just can't get it right.

Intentionality and Variability

Intentionality and variability are modifiers to the happiness interventions that Lyubomirsky describes, and when they are applied to everyday events, we may derive happiness from otherwise mundane or routine experiences. Intentionality is definable as the quality of being done on purpose and with resolve, bringing focused *awareness* to our chosen wellness-inducing activity. In other words, being present and noticing what we are doing are necessary for the happiness intervention to be successful. With regard to variability, she and researchers suggest that varying focus and timing in how the activity is implemented will avoid habituation and loss of psychologic benefit— thereby avoiding the hedonic treadmill effect. One of their pithy conclusions is that "variety is the spice of happiness."[207] Ultimately, they state, "…if one can remember to appreciate or actively engage with the object or circumstance (i.e., pause to savor the new Mercedes or take advantage of the California weather), then stable objects and circumstances may not be stable after all.." and "…only life changes involving intentional activity can be expected to lead to sustainable changes in well-being."

Lyubomirsky's findings that associate variability and intentionality to increases in well-being could be looked at as related to Jachimowicz's study (in the "Your 30s" chapter) describing the benefits of active leisure versus passive leisure in terms of happiness frequency.[208] In both instances, I would argue that the common element leading to greater well-being is none other than awareness. When we bring our full attention to an activity, we have much more to gain from it.

In follow up research, Lyubomirsky, Sheldon and colleagues went on to further delineate other variables by which happiness interventions work best.[209,210] First, you have to *want* to be happy. Meaning, even if Mr. or Mrs. Grumpy MacGrumpster performed an act of kindness or displayed gratitude, that would not automatically make them happy. That is to say, "if people do not want to become happier, do not believe it is possible, or are not willing to invest the energy," they are unlikely to improve their well-being, regardless of the intervention. The other important aspect that is important is the actual *content* of the activity. For it to enhance well-being, the activity needs to "provide an opportunity for positive experiences and personal growth." Examples of experimentally supported growth activities include: "contemplating best possible selves, cultivating gratitude, being kind, replaying happy life events, savoring daily experiences, and employing one's strengths."

Following Lyubomirsky's research that associated variability with happiness, variety has been further examined and reinforced as a moderator of happiness in a subsequent study by marketing experts Etkin and Mogilner.[211] In their 2016 article, "Does Variety Among Activities Increase Happiness?" they found that the perception of time was an important mitigating factor in variety's effect on happiness. When more activities were spread out over longer periods like a day, variety does increase happiness. However, over shorter periods like an hour, too much variety decreases happiness. They reason this difference in effect of variety had to do with a person's sense that life can feel either more stimulating or less productive depending on whether variety is experienced over a greater or shorter time interval, respectively.

Interestingly, they found the effects to be consistent over actual and perceived variety and actual and perceived time duration and also across multiple types of activities. In other words, it is the person's *sense* of variety and time interval that influences happiness, not the actual time, variety or even the activity itself, whether it be work or leisure, self-selected or imposed, social or solo. For example, in the final set of experiments they conducted, they had participants complete a variety of tasks over a 15-minute duration. When they "encouraged participants to perceive 15 minutes as longer,"* they found variety did *not* result in a decrease in happiness, offsetting the usual negative effect variety has during short time frames. Nor, however, did it result in an increase in happiness, suggesting that you can't make 15 minutes seem all that long. One wonders if that cute little neurotransmitter dopamine is playing a role here.

** How, you might ask, did the researchers change the participants' perception of time? According to Mogilner, they used a "simple manipulation," where they asked some participants to write a paragraph about how fifteen minutes is a long period of time and other participants to write about how it is a short period of time.*

Etkin and Mogilner suggest that there are clear and practical implications of their research. Regardless of whether we are at work, at home or out and about, we all want to feel that we are making the most of our time. There are caveats though, and context is key. For instance, in the workplace, task variety can decrease boredom, increase engagement and increase productivity. However, the introduction of too much variety in tasks can lead to frustration, errors and decreased productivity. Alternatively, instead of adding excessive variety to the work itself, employers might do well to encourage employees to increase variety in different ways. For instance, instead of remaining at their workspaces at lunch, workers might be incentivized to take their lunch elsewhere, with employers possibly building in extra time for walking or travel time. Feeling refreshed at midday may lead to a happier, more productive worker, offsetting the lost work time.

Variety is not always feasible either in the arena of our personal relationships—where the benefits of variety to spice things up are constantly exhorted. Realistically, there is often a gamut of domestic daily must-do items that interfere with this. However, by understanding the nuances of how variety can be a force for happiness or frustration depending on the time frame, we can adjust our domestic schedules accordingly. Mogilner states that the best practical takeaway from her research is to optimize the way that we schedule our calendars. Depending on whether we have an hour, a day or a week, we can accordingly decide what level of activity variety we plan in order to maximize our sense of well-being and limit our feelings of being unproductive. She adds, for people who may not have much control of their schedule, they can titrate their sense of variety or similarity to suit their individual circumstances. This takes advantage of the powerful role that the perception of variety and time plays. In so doing, according to Mogilner, one could "pull out the optimal or ideal level of happiness."[212]

Awe

The final happiness hack we will briefly explore is awe. Psychologist Paul Pearsall, author of, *AWE: The Delights and Dangers of Our Eleventh Emotion* (2007)[213], defines awe as an "overwhelming and bewildering sense of connection with a startling universe that is usually far beyond the narrow band of our consciousness." And Dacher Kelter, author of *Awe: The New Science of Everyday Wonder and How It Can Transform Your Life* (2023),[214] writes that "Awe is the feeling of being in the presence of something vast that transcends your understanding of the world."

As far as emotions go, awe represents a field of study still in its infancy. From what has been learned though, experiencing awe grounds people in the present moment. In a study by Rudd et al. called, "Awe expands people's perception of time, alters decision making, and enhances well-being" (2012)[215], it was found that participants who felt awe perceived that they had more time available, were accordingly less impatient, were willing to be more prosocial with their time, were more strongly gravitated toward experiential living as opposed to materialistic goals, and ultimately experienced greater life satisfaction. Sign me up! In another study, the experience of awe was found to be associated with reduced daily stress levels. The researchers suggest that awe can put daily stressors into a healthier, re-framed perspective, and in so doing, increase well-being.[216]

The other significant effect of awe is that it quiets the ego and brings us closer to that sense of no self that is the holy grail of Buddhism. (I know, Siddhartha might cringe at my mixed religion metaphor). Keltner states that awe transforms us "by quieting the nagging, self-critical, overbearing, status-conscious voice of our self, or ego, and empowering us to collaborate, to open our minds to wonders, and to see the deep patterns of life."[217]

This is all great, so how do we experience awe? Common paths to awe include taking in a natural wonder, witnessing a perfect act of musical or sports performance or experiencing a spiritual revelation. These are not always available during lunch time though. A simpler, more available means of experiencing awe is to be childlike. For many people, that may not pose much of a problem. However, what being childlike in the context of experiencing awe means looking at things as if it were the first time you saw them. Or looking at things you have seen tons of times but in a different way. Just yesterday, my daughter marveled at "this really big fluffy dog in the bagel shop."

Manifesting awe means that you don't just stop and smell the roses. You really look at them, at their brilliance and variety of colors, touch the petals and notice the geometrical perfection of their arrangement. No roses around? Try this: next time you're walking around outside, instead of reflexively reaching for that phone, just look up. Look at the sky – gray, blue, cloudy, it doesn't matter. And if there are trees that's even better. Make sure you don't walk right into traffic or any rigid objects. If you can do this for even just a couple of seconds, you might notice you can break that trance of neurotic fixation that most of us are all afflicted with for much of our days. And when this stupor is broken, if only temporarily, the momentary reset may allow you to rethink and reassess some situation that has been plaguing you and by so doing, move past it, lightening your daily psychological load, crushing one pebble at a time. I learned this practice while on a trail walk, feeling annoyed about an argument I just had that morning with my 11-year-old daughter about something trivial. It wasn't necessarily awe that I felt at that moment. It was just a feeling of stepping outside of my mind and my body, witnessing the emotional turmoil that was happening and no longer being attached to the event that led to it.

John O'Leary is author of the book, *In Awe: Rediscover Your Childlike Wonder to Unleash Inspiration, Meaning, and Joy,*[218] When he was nine and playing with matches and gasoline in the garage, an explosion occurred that threw him against the wall, causing burns to 100% of his body and made his risk of death 99%. He survived and went on to become a college graduate, husband, father, best-selling author and an internationally sought-after inspirational speaker. If that's not awesome, I don't know what is. He says, "Expect amazing. Expect beauty. Expect awesome. Expect joy. It will dramatically influence what you see. And what happens."

* * *

One sunny afternoon I was in the Lake Merritt area of Oakland, late to meet a person of interest. On the side of the road I was walking there was a mom and her 2 kids standing next to a car with a flat tire. As I briskly moved by them, I noticed the looks of their faces, their large, unmoving eyes. I looked away and kept walking. After a few more steps, I turned around, came back, and offered my assistance. I jacked up the car, removed the lug nuts and wrenched and tugged on the wheel but failed in getting it off, as the bolts had seized and were locked onto the hub. Sweating profusely, hands stained with dirt and grease, I sat on the curb and waited with them until they were able to call a tow truck. They smiled, thanked me, and I wished them the best.

Social inertia is real, and most of us are in some kind of self-inflicted urgency mode during our days. However, slowing down to express gratitude, experience a little awe, or just to be kind often takes minimal effort, has the ability to simultaneously improve ours and others' well-being, and is something we never regret. So next time something nice pops into your head to say to that coworker, say it. Next time a service provider is polite and efficient, tell them how much you appreciate it.* And next time you see something that was otherwise ordinary and common, try to see the awe-someness in it.

** For great ideas of random acts of kindness, check out this website: https://www.randomactsofkindness.org/*

* * *

In the following section, we will make the transition from our internal processes to their outward manifestations. We have seen that trying to take a beeline to happiness is not going to work. We were also read the riot act on managing our expectations appropriately, not going too high and not staying too low. We then learned that the pillars of awareness and self-love are necessary supports for practicing kindness, feeling gratefulness and experiencing awe. This has all been psychological foreplay, if you will, but like the real kind, it sets us up for the tasty events to follow.

However, in order to enjoy said tasty events, we must first clear the table for the next course. And by table, I mean, us. And by course, I mean the big components of our lives that we give our time to— our purpose. Whether it is our career horizon or our offspring's moving truck that is coming into view, the purpose each served in our lives will dramatically change, and we must change with it. We must repurpose. Like old skis turned into a bench, repurposing is using something in a way for which it was not originally intended but that remains valuable in a different manner. Though at one time we were used to carve down the mountain, now we will get sat on, and that's OK. Repurposing is the first step to evolving after crisis, and we will start there in the Part III.

Awe: Boston, The Prudential Tower, photo by the author (2003)

III

EVOLVE

It is not the strongest of the species that survives, nor the most intelligent, but the one most responsive to change.
—Charles Darwin

13

Before You Wreck Yourself, Repurpose Yourself.

Life is never made unbearable by circumstances, but only by lack of meaning and purpose.
—Viktor Frankl, concentration camp survivor, Austrian psychiatrist, author of Man's Search for Meaning

The afternoon of life is just as full of meaning as the morning; only, its meaning and purpose are different....
—Carl Jung

Adapting, though important, is not enough. It is only the first step in responding to crisis. Adaptation stops you from dying, but it does not move you forward. Growth requires more than this. To turn disadvantage into advantage and make ourselves more resistant to future havoc involves more than just a recalibration of our psychology. It demands an evolution in the way we view ourselves and interact with the world.

This section takes us beyond our internal fixes and translates them into external overhauls. Each of us is likely aware of some of the specific changes we would benefit from, and in Part III, I review what I believe constitutes a significant swath of them. From finding new purpose to inviting discomfort to having fun to fostering our relationships, this is where the rubber hits the road, where we evolve from who we were into who we will become.

* * *

So you've spent most of your adult life in the pursuit of a few critical things: social relationships, personal health and financial stability. Wherever you are at, and with whomever you share your days, your purpose has taken you here. When you were young, purpose was a four-letter word that got thrown around at you by older people. Now, *you* are those older people. Purpose is a weighty word, and as such, it's somewhat off-putting and even daunting. As a result, some people try to make it more psychologically digestible by saying don't talk about purpose, just think of it as what's important or meaningful. Not me. Important is taking the trash out on Thursday night. Meaningful is the ending of *Shawshank Redemption*. And with all due respect to Mr.'s Freeman and Robbins, purpose goes beyond those descriptors and should not be diluted.

And now, a side rant. My daughter just finished 5th grade and elementary school and has now proceeded on to middle school. Now around these parts and nowadays, this transition is not called "Graduation" anymore. Why? Because doing so would give these 11-year-olds the idea that this is the end of their academic road, obviously.

In order to prevent them from becoming dropouts, the ceremony is instead called "Promotion," which will of course motivate them to continue their education, listen to their parents and eat their broccoli. The ideas of promotion and participation trophies spring from the same mentality that tells us we need to manage our kids' emotions, when in fact most of them are probably more resilient than we adults with our fragile egos. The point of my diatribe is this. Let the little people have their moment. Don't dumb it down. Make it the little big deal that it is, as life only gets more complicated from here on out. If I didn't respect my daughter's wish for me to not be *that* parent, I would cut and paste this paragraph and send it to the superintendent.

Now back to purpose. In the same way, I shall not oversimplify talking about purpose. It is a big deal, and like it or not, it's time to put on your big-non-binary pants. At its simplest level, purpose is about survival; at its most privileged level, purpose is about discovering what unique qualities you have to contribute to humanity and then applying that skillset. At any level, however, purpose carries the benefit of diminishing the effects of personal suffering, muting our monkey minds and allowing us to see ourselves as part of something bigger. Research has shown that purpose can also enhance our self-worth, give us hope and allow us to experience flow states.* People with purpose adopt healthier lifestyles, exercising more and engaging in more preventative health services.[219] Moreover, individuals with a sense of life purpose are also less likely to have heart attacks, strokes, and dementia.[220] Finally, greater purpose in life is associated with a reduced risk of Alzheimer's disease and all-cause mortality among community-dwelling older persons, starting from age 50.[221,222] This is what is at stake and therefore warrants placing purpose on a psychological pedestal.

> *Coined by psychologist Mihály Csíkszentmihályi in 1970, flow or flow state refers to being "in the zone," a mental state in which we are fully immersed in an activity, where our perception of time is altered, and despite the activity being physically and/or psychologically complex, it is also seemingly effortless. More on this topic in the chapter, "Laugh and Have Fun. But Don't Die."*

Without purpose, we languish, ruminate and have no answer to the question of what's the point of it all? We seek out activities, people and purchases that might give us that dopamine hit, but in the end, we run out of people to call and things to buy and often resort to self-destructive activities. All this being said, I think the case for having purpose is quite clear.

Our purpose changes throughout life. When we move beyond survival, we can find external causes to drive us, and alternatively, we may discover our purpose is in simply knowing our own selves better. Purpose does not have to be grand; but it needs to be true to what each of us finds meaningful. And what is meaningful is bound to change as we do ourselves.

Even the Queen of tidiness herself, Marie Kondo, has rethought her purpose. Three kids and two Netflix series later, she admits, "My home is messy…the way I am spending my time is the right way for me at this time at this stage of my life…I have kind of given up on that in a good way for me. Now I realize what is important to me is enjoying spending time with my children at home."[223]

One of the most inspirational modern examples of repurposing is perhaps J.K. Rowling's story. Described as a "penniless divorcee hitting the jackpot" following the success of her first two *Harry Potter* novels,[224] just 4 years prior, she was thrown out by her abusive Portuguese husband and needed police to regain custody of their 4-month-old daughter. With a draft of her first *Potter* novel in her suitcase, she moved to Scotland and needed government assistance to pay for her self-described rodent-ridden flat. Working as a secretary while simultaneously getting her teaching credentials, she suffered depression as a single parent and contemplated suicide. In the end, Rowling found new purpose in writing, and her feelings about "love, loss, separation, death ... are reflected in the first book."[225] *Forbes* declared her the "first billion-dollar author,"[226] but due to her charitable contributions and high UK taxes, she did not remain so.

Though Rowling was not at midlife during these difficult years in her life, she clearly needed to find new purpose to take care of herself and her infant daughter. Once you do arrive at midlife, however, your purpose often gets a full makeover. Everything that got you here might need to get thrown out the window. Well, maybe not thrown out yet, but you need to start looking for a window and making sure it will open. That window represents your exit plan, and like it or not, we all need one.

For many of us in our 50s, we are at the top of our career ladder. According to Statista.com, the average age of CEOs in 2018 in the U.S. was 54 years old, compared to 46 years old in 2005.[227] In healthcare, the average age of a practicing physician in 2021 was 53 years old.[228] One of the ironies of retiring is that we do it exactly when we have had the most experience in our professions.

Average retirement age in the U.S. has increased compared to three decades ago. In 1990, it ranged between 57-59, and in 2022, it was between 61-65.[229] Reasons for this trend include the ability to stay effective and productive later into life due to better lifestyles coupled with less physically demanding occupations, changing pension and social security incentives, new anti-discrimination laws, evolving social norms, and health insurance coverage.

Two other factors affecting retirement age are recessionary influences and the impact of COVID. Recessions in general increase the retirement age as people try to recoup losses in their 401k's, home values and other investments. However, the COVID-induced recession thus far has had the opposite effect, causing people to retire *earlier* –due to layoffs and the previously discussed *f*ck it* effect.[230]

With all this being said, why the hell should we be thinking about repurposing ourselves at this point when we are in the prime earning and experience phases of our careers? To be sure, in addition to income, working longer carries with it other advantages. Mental and physical stimulation, continued social engagement and simply a reason to get up in the morning are a few of them.[231] However, the path we take after 50 cannot just be a continuation of the one we took to get there. As Arthur Brooks bluntly points out in his book, *From Strength to Strength: Finding Success, Happiness and Deep Purpose in the Second Half of Life (2022)*,[232] "Decline is unavoidable." Though experience and wisdom increase with time in a career, effectiveness will diminish. Regardless of profession, according to Brooks, cognitive decline is a given starting as early as your mid-30s and as late as your early-50s. As we discussed at the end of the chapter on your 40s, it is in this period of our midlives that you can, with awareness, look within yourself and ahead far enough, and start to reinvent your purpose.

Benjamin Franklin said, "By failing to prepare, you are preparing to fail." In the business world, failing to prepare and repurpose has notoriously led to the downfall of once-megacompanies like Polaroid, Blockbuster and Blackberry. Good old Abe Lincoln pronounced, "Give me six hours to chop down a tree and I will spend the first four sharpening the axe." The tree that eventually has to come down is our careers. And for the first 20-30 years of it, we have been sharpening our skills, hacking our way through the workplace jungle. But starting at the back our minds, the thought and reality of our successor creeps forward and looms larger little by little each year. In any relationship that must eventually end, you can choose to either go out on your own terms or somebody else's.

So, on one end of the repurposing spectrum, we are simply planning our exit strategy, our career offramp as it were. What do we do once we have retired from our current profession? And on the other end of repurposing, we are calling into question the job itself. Is this it? Is it too late to start a different path altogether? Though different questions, a lot of the calculations necessary to make an informed decision are the same for each scenario. We'll address this below.

Motivation

Before we talk about to what ends we are repurposing ourselves, we need to explore the driving force for any change –motivation. Motivation can be thought of as a situational variable, as the reason we initiate, continue or terminate a behavior. Motivation pushes us toward accomplishing our goals, which in turn align with our purpose. Psychologists divide motivation into two types, extrinsic and intrinsic.[233],[234], [235] Extrinsically motivated activities rely on end results, rewards and outside validation to provide value. In contrast, intrinsically motivated activities are those that we genuinely derive pleasure from, those where we enjoy the process itself and where there is no obvious external reward.

Psychologists Deci and Ryan were developers of Self-Determination Theory (SDT), one of the most influential theories of human motivation.[236,237,238] In stark contrast to the historically prevailing idea that getting humans to perform tasks is best done with rewards, SDT states human motivation is the result of the satisfaction of three basic psychological needs: autonomy, competence and relatedness.

In an early study looking at extrinsic and intrinsic motivation in 1971 titled, "Effects of externally mediated rewards on intrinsic motivation,"[239] when undergraduate subjects were given money as a reward for completing a task, intrinsic motivation decreased. Deci proposes that money led to a "cognitive reevaluation" of the activity because subjects sensed that money is a control mechanism. However, when verbal reinforcement and positive feedback were provided, intrinsic motivation to perform the activity increased.

In a later study by Lepper and Greene from Stanford titled, "Turning play into work: Effects of adult surveillance and extrinsic rewards on children's intrinsic motivation" (1975), they found that preschoolers who were offered the extrinsic reward of playing with "highly attractive toys" by engaging in a specific activity lost some of their intrinsic interest in that activity subsequently.[240] In addition, the kids who were told their activity would be monitored by a television camera also showed less subsequent interest in the prescribed activity. These last two studies demonstrate that extrinsic incentives can undermine intrinsic interest in both preschoolers and undergraduates, some of whom act like preschoolers.

Other research has shown that high school and college athletes with scholarships in a variety of sports enjoyed playing their sports less than those without scholarships. In one study, Division I athletes who had scholarships demonstrated less interest in the that sport even decades later.[241],[242] Vallerand (2012) summarized this phenomenon by stating, "unfortunately, scholarship recipients may come to feel that they play more to justify the scholarship they have received than for the pleasure of the game."[243]

Applications of Deci and Ryan's SDT principles of autonomy, competence and relatedness range from the classroom and the homestead to the stadium and the workplace. When we support children's autonomy, parenting and learning are benefited.[244],[245] When driven athletes feel capable, they perform at elite levels.[246] When employees are incentivized to work together in a cause they truly believe in, the results are more long lasting and consistent.[247] In contrast, when an individual's perception of their competence is decreased, their intrinsic motivation also decreases.[248]

Repurposing

So what type of motivation will we employ to repurpose ourselves in midlife? Though extrinsic and intrinsic motivation are distinguishable by certain criteria in SDT, they are not mutually exclusive in the pursuit of a particular goal. They exist on a continuum, and both contribute to self-determination. In any phase of our lives, we are best served by choosing a path that draws energy from a strong internal drive but that also benefits from external rewards. For instance, students may have intrinsic interest in a subject and at the same time may want to make their parents and teachers proud of their achievements. And in early adult life, someone can pursue and find a profession that they love and that also benefits them from an extrinsic perspective. It is in this first act of our lives that we build up the external resources –both monetary and social—that we will rely upon for the next act. Plays and life often fall into a three-act structure: the Setup, the Confrontation, and the Resolution.[249] Hopefully, by the end of your first act, you have set yourself up properly for the next.

In the second act of our lives, one of the essential conflicts is between choosing to try to keep the status quo and remain on the same path you have forged up to that point or flipping the script and reevaluating your purpose. Not uncommonly, after a 20-30 year career, the balance of influence that keeps us on the same path is weighted heavily in the extrinsic motivation column. For those who decide to change course, the drive is often to derive purpose by finding more intrinsically motivated activities. However, the freedom to pursue these types of activities is dependent on the aforementioned financial solvency and social resources that hopefully exist for you in your 50s, which free you from a dependence on extrinsic motivation. Midlife repurposing is not without sacrifice, and indeed, in order to make a successful run at redefining our purpose, the concept of opportunity cost must be considered and understood.

Opportunity Cost and the Sunk Cost Fallacy

From an economic standpoint, opportunity cost is the value of what is not chosen in favor of a mutually exclusive alternative. For instance, if you have $50, you can only spend it on one thing; the thing you have not spent it on represents the opportunity cost. In non-economic terms, it is what is missed out on as a result of a particular decision. Jeff Bezos understood this concept very well when he first walked away from a job as vice president at Banker's Trust, then walked away again as a V.P. at the hedge fund D.E. Shaw in 1994. Successful and 30 years-old, Bezos still realized that staying in those respectable positions would not allow him to do what he truly believed in. There was an opportunity cost to keeping those jobs, and he realized he "might sincerely regret" not pursuing his idea of starting an internet-based bookseller.[250] Perhaps you've heard of it.

There are opportunity costs to every decision we make in life. Seinfeld's "morning guy" and "night guy" bit is an example of opportunity cost at work. Opportunity costs can be further divided into explicit and implicit costs. Without getting into economic minutiae, explicit costs are readily identifiable and quantifiable whereas implicit costs are less tangible and less definable. For example, governmental spending during the pandemic resulted in explicit costs –for vaccine distribution, medical bills and economic stimulus checks. On the other hand, the implicit costs of the pandemic included weakened social connections, lost productivity and slower economic growth.

Perhaps the most significant implicit cost of any decision is time itself. As my mom says, "There are only 24 hours in a day." And this is where we segway into repurposing ourselves. Whatever we chose to spend our first 50 years doing, the opportunity cost was everything else we were not doing. Beyond the physical, energetic and resource expenditures we put into those pursuits, the inescapable implicit cost was time. Invariably, it dawns on us all that this time is not coming back to us no matter how hard we work. Thus, at this midlife point, we need to take opportunity cost into account as we ponder the path we will choose for the latter half of our lives.

Not surprisingly, a mid-career crisis more often than not goes hand in hand with your midlife crisis years –when the happiness curve reaches its low, typically between 45-55. As if right on cue, feelings of stagnation, burnout, futility and regret seem to commonly exist for many at this point in their careers, even in what is seemingly a successful one. Counterfactual thinking reaches a deafening level, and the nagging questions persist: Do I need to work this hard? Is this really all I have to look forward to until I retire and die?

Mind you, not everyone who has these thoughts should immediately be telling their bosses to take this job and shove it. How, then, do you deal with them? Awareness. With awareness, we can step back from the emotions that are coming up, create separation, and look at our lives in their entirety, instead of just focusing in on the possible dissatisfaction we are having in that moment with our careers. If we did not take the path we did, we would not have the relationships we have, and we would not have turned into the person we are now. Ultimately, we made the best decision we could with the available information at that time. And even if choosing a different path seems like it would have been better, that is at best an educated guess and at worst, an illusion.

What is not an illusion are the feelings of love and companionship we have toward the people in our lives in this moment. Love is real, and that is the gift that awareness gives us any time we go back to it. Kieran Setiya, professor in the Department of Linguistics and Philosophy at MIT (who knew MIT had these departments?), elegantly writes, "Love is a counterweight to regret."[251] There is no such thing as a life without second thoughts or without regret. And for that we should be grateful, because a life without regret is a life without choices.

Your conclusion after all these considerations may be that when it's all said and done, the career path you have chosen, though not the only one available, is still the best one for you in this moment. If, however, after due reflection, you decide that a drastic directional change is necessary, additional planning is then required. You not only have to have your offramp planned, but you have to change the interstate you are on.

Jill Schlesinger is an Emmy and Gracie Award winning business analyst for CBS News, and she has advice for people wanting to change career interstates – to follow their passion in a different career, to move somewhere else, or to quit altogether. In her podcast, "Can I afford to quit my job?,"[252] she outlines the steps below. In order to make an informed decision, she states, these calculations have to be made.

1. Look at your assets –e.g., income, home equity, 401k, pension, subsidized health insurance
2. Look at your liabilities –long-term debt, monthly expenses, unanticipated financial obligations
3. Ask yourself what you are looking to reset and how does mortgage/rent play into this?
4. Look at your expenses and ask yourself if you can really spend less, and secondarily if your dependents/partners are willing and able to spend less
5. Consider obligations you have to others –siblings/parental care
6. Figure out endpoints: worst case, middle case, best case scenarios and ask yourself if you could live with them.

Regardless of the conviction of our decision –either to transition from our career to retirement, to another occupation, or to no occupation, change will not be easy. If the need for some adjustment is so clear, however, why would we have such a hard time rethinking our direction at midlife and then acting on it? A common trap we fall into that prevents us from cutting our losses is referred to as the *sunk cost fallacy.* In economic terms, this refers to the erroneous logic that leads us to believe that since we have invested so many resources –time, money, energy—into something, we should stick with that {bad} investment in order to not waste what we have already contributed.[253], [254,255] The reality and fallacy is we are never getting any of those investments back no matter how long we stick it out.

For instance, in the creation of a new product, the resources used for research and development, building, marketing, etc., are sunk costs and will never be recouped. The fallacy occurs when we believe we need to continue investing in that failing product even though those investments are already lost. Other expressions describing the idea of a sunk cost are "water under the bridge," "crying over spilt milk" and "throwing good money after bad." You would think that with so many ways to describe the same thing, we might be less likely to succumb to this fallacy. But alas, we are human; we contain multitudes.

Psychologists Arkes and Ayton gently ribbed adult humans in their article, "The Sunk Cost and Concorde* Effects: Are Humans Less Rational Than Lower Animals?"(1999).[256] In their article, they pointed out that children and "phylogenetically humble organisms" do not commit the same cognitive error. Sunk cost fallacy plays a major role not just in bad business decisions, but also in why people may continue unhealthy committed relationships.[257] And back to the topic at hand, this fallacy is likewise a reason people may stick with a job that is not serving them well in the present moment, and it can also be the reason that makes them unable to separate from that job when the time comes to plan for retirement.

> *In January 1976, the supersonic Concorde jet took its first commercial flight—at a cost of $2.8 billion from the British and French governments. But even when it was clear that the plane wasn't profitable, investors continued to pour money into the failing project for another 27 years.*

And herein—during the most vulnerable portion of our U-curves—is where opportunity cost and sunk cost come crashing together. When we allow ourselves to realize that being in this job and in this life came at the cost of not following a different path *and* we simultaneously give ourselves permission to move on from these sunk costs, we have our midlife moment. Existential crisis hath no fury like sunk cost scorned. Stated a different way, when, at midlife, we find the reasons and courage to say *f*ck it!* to our greatest sunk costs—time and energy—and drastically alter our life trajectory, it is unequivocally frightening.

A slightly different take on the question of purpose comes from a trio of Yale professors who teach the most popular course at the university. In their book version of the class, *Life Worth Living: A Guide to What Matters Most (2023),*[258] Volf, Croasmun and McAnnally-Linz encourage us to abandon the question, "What do I want?" in favor of asking instead, "What is *worth* wanting?" By asking this question, the professors argue that we "de-center the self," and in so doing, break away from overvaluing our individual desires, which they call "slippery, fickle things" that "billion-dollar corporations" manipulate. Oh, snap! By asking what is worth wanting, we are by necessity taking other people's values—and by extension, humanity's values—into consideration and are not resting the full weight of our lives on our "arbitrary" desires.

In the end, the concepts of worth, meaning and purpose are all songs on the same playlist. Asking what is worth wanting is not very different from asking what gives life meaning or what purpose you should pursue. Nevertheless, the reality behind the answers to any of these questions is that they are moving targets. Few things last the test of time, and even well-thought-out paths that are absolutely true for us at one age may be the furthest from true for us at another. I believe for all of us who are fortunate enough to reach midlife and to have the luxury of re-contemplating our purpose, we have the ability to look at our lives, see what got us here and realize that there are many new paths of exploration and growth that we are blessed to choose from.

The catch is, you don't have all the time in the world, and you can't select all of them. Choosing one path means not choosing another one, and that's life. To start something, sometimes you have to quit something. Quitting, however, is anathema to the American way. If you grew up in this country, it is almost impossible to not be indoctrinated into this line of thinking. We are collectively infatuated with the success stories of those who persisted despite adversity. Rarely, however, do we make heroes out of people who abandon their hard-earned success to seek a different calling. Vince Lombardi said, "Winners never quit, and quitters never win." He didn't read my book though. Because if he did, he might have said, "Winners sometimes repurpose."

At the end of the day, if you allow it, awareness may facilitate your decision to drastically deviate from your life heading should you choose. But then you will find yourself at the bottom of a deep existential hole. In the following chapters, we will explore some directions that can lead you to find new purpose. We will start with learning how to break out of your comfort zone to find an optimal state of anxiety in your life. Then we will find out about the benefits having fun. Following that, we'll come back to what makes it all worth it—our relationships. Enhancing your life skills in just these three areas in turn opens doors to redefining your purpose in midlife, or at any point in life for that matter.

*** *** ***

Tom Brady was the 199th pick of the 2000 NFL draft, and he carried that chip on his shoulder pads to 7 super bowl victories and retired at the age of 45. In many ways, I'm like Tom Brady. From the time I was jilted in 5th grade, I harnessed and repurposed that heartache to become the scrappy guy who never quit, took pleasure in defying expectations and refused to be ignored. That approach to life served me quite well, until it didn't. Despite taking a great job in a highly competitive specialty in the San Francisco Bay Area, I still felt an unending need to prove myself. This was my life's purpose.

Unfortunately, my inability to turn it off doubtlessly made relationships with me untenable for many people, and it was only after I became a parent that my perspective on what's important changed. My need to show them how it's done was replaced by my overriding purpose to be the best dad I can be. Don't get me wrong, I still need other motives to get off the couch—like writing this book or reducing a shoulder fracture-dislocation. Fatherhood has just taken the edge off of me, for the better.

14

Break Out of Your Comfort Zone: Finding Optimal Anxiety

One can choose to go back toward safety or forward toward growth. Growth must be chosen again and again; fear must be overcome again and again.
—Abraham Maslow

Life is either a daring adventure or nothing...To keep our faces toward change and behave like free spirits in the presence of fate is strength undefeatable.
—Helen Keller

When I was 8, I owned a poop-brown Huffy bike with a banana seat and handlebar tassels. As per usual, it had a kickstand bolted to the left chain stay, and my typical dismounting procedure would be leaning the bike to the left, getting off, then extending the kickstand. One evening while visiting my next-door neighbor, who was one year older, freckled and kind of cute but really more my sister's friend, I was in a real hurry because mom was making Stove Top stuffing. So

I rode one house over to her driveway and since her front door was on the right, I decided I could shave some time by getting off the bike on the right side. Not having the muscle memory to do this, I lost my balance and my bike tipped over. I fell on my forearm, breaking it and my comfort zone at the same time.

Breaking out of your comfort zone has been a mantra preached for reasons ranging from spurring creativity and personal growth, to building confidence and resilience in the face of difficulty, to meeting new people and appreciating different ways of life. That said, it does not escape me that having the luxury to break out of your comfort zone presumes you had a comfort zone to begin with, where "uncertainty, scarcity and vulnerability are minimized" and where love and food are not in short supply.[259]

Judith Bardwick, author of, *Danger In The Comfort Zone: From boardroom to mailroom- How to break the entitlement habit that's killing American Business* (1991)[260], used this phrase in the context of getting millennials I mean employees to work harder. Though work gets done when someone operates within their comfort zone, there is minimal growth and innovation. She states, "The comfort zone is a behavioral state within which a person operates in an anxiety-neutral condition, using a limited set of behaviors to deliver a steady level of performance, usually without a sense of risk." Apparently, the boardroom may not be all that different than some bedrooms.

And if we go way back to 1908, the idea of the comfort zone was studied on a literal, not metaphoric basis by the chaps Yerkes and Dodson, who electrically shocked mice in progressive levels and found that they completed mazes with more gusto, but only up to a certain intensity level, after which they began to hide.[261] Shocking, truly. And thus was humanely born the idea of *optimal anxiety*, where stress improves performance or growth up to a point, beyond which both deteriorate. Melinda Beck from the *Wall Street Journal* states, "Somewhere between checked out and freaked out lies an anxiety sweet spot."[262] I'm not sure the mice would agree the spot is quite that sweet.

The Yerkes-Dodson curve

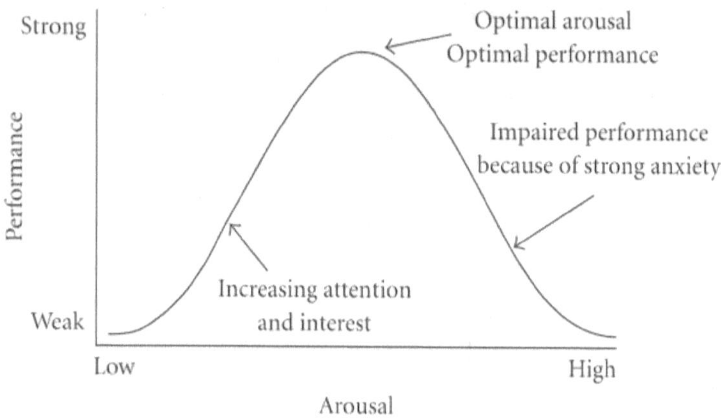

Source: Wikimedia

Optimal anxiety is defined as the apprehension level where mental productivity and performance reach their peak. In this state, you realize your aspirations, set novel goals, and maybe even find new purpose. From a neurologic standpoint, it is where there is an optimal zone of arousal, also referred to as our "window of tolerance." This concept was described by psychiatrist Dan Siegel (referenced in the Awareness chapter) in 1999 and describes an ideal state of emotional stimulation or stress that motivates us to grow and allows us to function well but does not overwhelm us.[263] According to Siegel, your window of tolerance is not fixed (unlike how some psychologists believe your hedonic setpoint is) and is influenced by variables such as individual temperament, history of trauma, social context, and how long it's been since you ate.

While under-stimulation leads to boredom, inaction, and awkward conversations, overwhelming our emotional stress response is also counterproductive. According to Siegel, excessive anxiety "leads neurologically to the inhibition of higher perceptions and thoughts; more basic somatic and sensory input is favored. In this situation, people don't think; they feel something intensely and act impulsively." Our brains basically go into low power mode and advanced decision-making functions are offline. The goal is to find the balancing point between these two extremes, our state of optimal anxiety. In this state, with our awareness and potential for growth maximized, we can find new paths that lead to well-being. Though there are multiple manners in which we can achieve this objective of being socially uncomfortable, I've chosen three to focus on: ditching your friends, being contrarian and changing your location. So without further ado, let's launch into these ways to put some ants in your pants.

Ditch your Friends (temporarily)

Recall the phenomenon I described of losing your friends that commonly occurs in your 30s.[264] Though this was often not an active decision but rather a consequence of major career and relationship choices that are made at this time in life, the result was a disruption of your comfort zone. Indeed, at midlife as well, finding new friends or simply taking time off from your regular companions may be the single most powerful way to break out of your comfort zone and create optimal anxiety. This is because your friends represent a source of social friction when it comes to breaking out of your comfort zone. They may not want you to change, because that might make them feel uncomfortable, forcing them out of their own comfort zones. With friends, we often fall into a practiced manner of behavior, with well-rehearsed quips and retorts and familiar but stale types of and locales for interacting.

Remaining in our social comfort zone fits into the sociologic phenomenon referred to as homophily, the tendency to for people to gravitate to other people with similar characteristics like gender, age, background, social class, beliefs and values. Birds of feather, as the saying goes. There are obvious advantages to homophily—such as increased efficiency of action and combination of like resources which in turn can lead to success for that particular group. Homophily also leads to assortative mating, whereby people (and other species) mate with others who are like them from physical and genetic standpoints. In humans, this type of mating is thought to perpetuate socioeconomic inequalities.[265]

Persistence of homophily can lead to problems from literal and metaphoric inbreeding. Stagnation of ideas, lack of inclusion of minorities, 12 fingers and mullets are but a few of them. Perhaps nowhere else are the limitations and potential harm of homophily seen as with modern social media outlets.[266,267] In these forums, opinions, misinformation and confirmation bias can flourish unchecked. Terms like "echo chambers" and "filter bubbles" have been used to describe these online environments. Research by Ciampaglia and Menczer in 2018 demonstrate that "individuals, institutions and even entire societies can be manipulated on social media" and demonstrate "complex vulnerabilities" due to different biases. [268] Sean Parker, the founding ex-president of Facebook, candidly professed that Facebook had no qualms "exploiting {this} vulnerability in human psychology."[269]

In her TED talk, "Why we need more friction on social media,"[270] Yaël Eisenstat states that the mantra of our times and especially the mantra of social media platforms is to be "first, fast, free and frictionless." She states that Facebook profits from being frictionless, and as a result, misinformation is more easily spread. Despite recognizing this and having tools to build in friction, Facebook and Twitter (now X) choose not to, and understandably so. Force-feeding content is the foundation upon which they make their money, and any process to slow it down is antithetical to this model. She states, the "world [is] optimized for frictionless virality."

Enter the opposite type of interaction, heterophily, or intermingling of people who are from a different physical, genetic or socioeconomic background. Sociologist Everett Rogers first termed this idea in his book, *Diffusion of Innovations* (1962).[271] He believed that while homophily was a better means of *communicating* information, heterophily had advantages in *diffusing* information and sparking innovation. Though Rogers' book was mainly about the way people adopt new products and ideas, the same concepts might be applied to interpersonal relationships.

When we ditch our friends and seek out interactions with people who are not like us, we put ourselves in a place to find optimal anxiety. Though it requires us to overcome social inertia, once we do, more possibilities for growth exist. It could be as simple as going to a different café to work from home or joining a new meetup group or as committed as doing an overseas humanitarian mission (more on this in the next section on travel).

Mind you, I am not suggesting that you permanently ditch your lifelong friends. At this latter point in your existence, in fact, friends are a key component to maintaining physical well-being, and we will explore this in detail in the chapter ahead about relationships. However, flipping the friend script can lead to your starting a whole new act in midlife, with scene changes and plot twists galore.

There is a potential downside to heterophily. In a study by Kim and Kim (last names, not sure if they are related), they found that with "upward status heterophily" –i.e., interacting with groups who are disproportionately more socioeconomically advantaged, subjective well-being and physical health were negatively affected in the less privileged group.[272] These findings could be extrapolated to suggest that attempting to befriend or socialize with a group that is very far outside of your comfort range may be counterproductive. Just as in the state of flow (discussed more in the next chapter), where there is an optimal state of difficulty for an activity—not too easy, and not too difficult—it may also be reasonable to believe that there is an optimal state of heterophily to seek out in order to facilitate psychological growth. In other words, Ubering from a jazz bar to an EDM club may prove not to be slay; perhaps trying Applebee's instead of TGI Fridays may be more palatable.

In summary, it's clear that finding out how other people choose to live their lives—and not just the people you have seen every workday for the past twenty years—may give you a few new ideas for your own repurposing at midlife. Overall, heterophily can be thought of as increasing social friction, with its concomitant chafing and irritation. I do believe that in the right context, the stimulation justifies the inconvenience. In the end, if we have the luxury of time and come from a place of psychological openness and abundance, intermittently abandoning your friends might just be what the doctor ordered.

* * *

The first job I took after completing my east coast residency was in Tuba City, Arizona. Situated one hour northeast of the Grand Canyon, it is the most populous community within the Navajo Nation, with a population of about 8,600. Newly wed, I worked at the Tuba City Regional Health Care Corporation, which services an area of 6000 square miles (Connecticut is 4800 square miles) and is the largest employer for an 80-mile radius.[273] I did not know the word heterophily at that time, but I did know I wanted a different kind of life experience. And on that land, on their land, I cut my orthopedic teeth, learned to ride a horse while taking ER calls about rodeo injuries and caught a glimpse into the lives of this country's original caretakers.

In the next section, I will briefly touch on the idea of rejecting popular opinion as a means of breaking out of your comfort zone. Ironically, it's been trending as of late.

Be Contrarian.

We all know that person who feigns enlightenment by contradicting even the most basic of statements. To be sure, there are irritating ways to be contrarian. However, contrarianism is also a means of questioning our comfort status quo. It accomplishes this by mitigating our confirmation bias, which is the tendency to seek out, recall, interpret or favor information that already conforms with our pre-existing beliefs.[274,275] Stated simply, this cognitive bias represents our inability to recognize our own blind spots (while at the same time we find it quite simple to identify others'), despite believing we are rational creatures. George Carlin had a bit where he asked, "Have you ever noticed that anybody driving slower than you is an idiot, and anyone going faster than you is a maniac?"

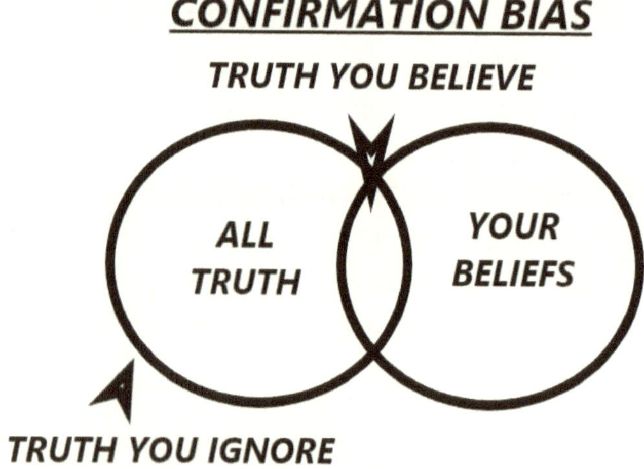

Confirmation bias may be the most common type of human cognitive bias and as such, has effects on a wide range of political, financial, social media and scientific contexts. No field is unaffected by it, and nobody is immune to it.

Back in the day, the perpetuation of bloodletting for all varieties of ailments was the result of confirmation bias in the medical community. Practitioners believed bloodletting helped cure disease. When people got better after bloodletting treatment, they concluded it was the bloodletting. And by contrast, if they did not get better, they concluded it was some other cause, not that bloodletting treatment was ineffective. In more modern times, confirmation bias leads practitioners to continue a course of management for a patient based on their initial diagnostic assumptions rather than on potentially contradictory new data.[276],[277]

On an interpersonal level, confirmation bias undoubtedly hurts relationships. If you believe your partner to be: messy, thoughtless, lazy, detached, fill-in-the-blank negative quality, you will always be able to find examples of those behaviors. And equally so, you will neglect to notice when they are not those things. And finally, your recall will be selectively skewed toward what you perceive as their faults and away from remembering all the wonderful things they have also done in the relationship.

In many ways, exhibiting confirmation bias is about living within your comfort zone, where you don't have to question yourself. It's only natural to want to exist there, all warm and cuddly and stuff. When confirmation bias is not in effect, we feel emotionally conflicted, often leading to a condition called *cognitive dissonance*.[278] As discussed before, in this state, we believe in things or behave in ways that seem incompatible with our pre-existing values. In order to not experience this emotional indigestion, we reject, rationalize and avoid information that conflicts with our beliefs. To that point, American science fiction author and aeronautical engineer Robert Heilein said, "Man is not a rational animal; he is a rationalizing animal."

Recognizing the pitfalls of this confirmation bias, how can we limit it? One method is to pick a personal belief and search out ways in which you might be wrong about it, instead of just ways you are right about it. Be contrarian. Test that belief against the opposite idea. Ask yourself, if this belief is true, then what must not be true? If that confirmation fails, then you must be willing to give up that belief.

Bohr's statement I started this book with is an affirmation of the value of adopting contrarian thinking. A great truth is recognized by the fact that its opposite is also a great truth. Being contrarian is not simply about being contradictory; it's really about fostering curiosity about the world we live in. Whether it is people, social mores or scientific principles, the bigger the issue, the more important it becomes for us to be curious because the more likely it is that a contrarian truth exists. From our careers to our relationships to our cellular processes (to be discussed in Part IV), it is often the case that the ideas that we are most attached to and the truths that seem most concrete are equally valid when turned on their heads. It is when we are most convinced that we should be most vigilant of alternative truths.

Another means of avoiding the comforts of confirmation bias is to be aware of something called *repetition bias*, also known as the *illusory truth effect*.[279] In this scenario, you begin to think something is true simply because you have heard it more than once.[280] In some studies, hearing something only 2-3 times is enough to make it believable, in the absence of any other evidence. The neurologic mechanism thought to account for this is called *processing fluency*, whereby the more often we hear something, the more familiar it becomes and the less time it takes for our brains to process it. Our brain in turn interprets and equates familiarity and ease of processing—i.e., fluency—with truth. It does this as a means of energetic efficiency, true or not. This neurologic backdoor, as it were, has obvious and often sinister applications in advertising, politics and the propagation of misinformation, i.e., "fake news."

While we can certainly try to challenge our own beliefs, this is easier said than done because it requires us to challenge our own logic, our sense of right and wrong. Instead, having friends who contest you is a great way to accomplish this. Friends who follow the same marching orders may not do this consistently though. When we seek out friends from different walks of life, it makes it more likely they will have different confirmation biases than yours and therefore will be able to call you out on your B.S., and you on theirs. It's a win-win! So now, with the 1-2 punch of ditching your friends and becoming contrarian, you are well on your way to finding that optimal anxiety sweet spot. If you are successful in recognizing and circumventing the triggers to your confirmation bias, this is what it may look like:

NEW AND IMPROVED CONFIRMATION BIAS

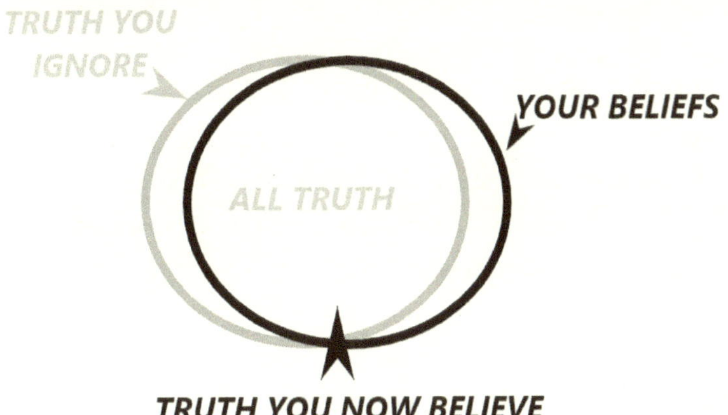

Changing Your Location

The final and perhaps the potentially most fun way to create optimal anxiety is to vary your geography. Changing where you are not only takes you out of your comfort zone, but it remarkably has also been shown to influence how your DNA is expressed. More on this in, "What Does a Body Good? It's Your DNA, Stupid."

At the time of this writing, I have been divorced for seven years. In that span, I have witnessed the evolution of the dating app, eagerly waiting for that unicorn to fall into my lap (horn up hopefully). In this magical dating app universe, there is an ever-evolving algorithm to curating your perfect online persona. For men, there is but one hard stop: the shirtless bathroom selfie (though interestingly not for women). Red flags for any gender include pseudo-self-deprecating statements like, *More issues than Esquire magazine* or *Fluent in sarcasm.* Other notable descriptors are the toxically positive *Good vibes only,* the criminally overused *Looking for my partner in crime,* the newly chic, *Oxford comma enthusiast,* and the cheeky, *Will mess up your lipstick, not your mascara.**

> *Here's a fun fact: Christian Rudder, co-founder of the dating website/app OkCupid, reports that their data shows that 75% of people who match and stay together are likely to answer the same way to the questions: Do you like scary movies, and have you ever travelled overseas alone?*

And in the positive column on your dating profile, for both the male and female gender, a person who travels is thought to be worthy of interest, as it represents many things simultaneously in a potential mate: means, adventurousness, a worldly perspective. More recently, though, showing that you are well-travelled is turning into a contrarian quality, as many profiles will read, "I don't care how many countries you've been to." With all this being said, travel and other means of changing your location will be the last item I investigate as a means of breaking out of your comfort zone.

In many ways, changing your location may be the easiest optimal anxiety hack to execute. For instance, by default when you travel, you are ditching most of your friends and by extension, leaving a lot of your confirmation biases at home too. This is because much of your individual beliefs and assumptions are location-specific and therefore based on experiences you have at and around home, so that when you leave this location, you also leave those conditioned beliefs. Confirmation bias doesn't fit in the overhead compartment, and who pays for checked baggage nowadays anyway?

Consequently, when you arrive somewhere new, you might come as an almost blank canvas, and by definition you are out of your comfort zone. Preconceptions are minimized, and because you now have everyday logistics to deal with that normally are a given at home— transport, food, shelter—you are fully in the moment. You left your monkey at home, and your mind is free-balling it. This feels great, until it doesn't.

The issue that often comes up when we are on vacation or out of our comfort zone anywhere is that all the stuff that normally gets pushed down when we are fulfilling our everyday checklist of obligations now finally has a chance to get noticed when you finish that third Mai Tai. This is the reason that relationships get tested while on vacation. When you are forced to break out of your auto-pilot mode, stuff gets stirred up. Like, do I really enjoy my time with this person? Who am

I when I am not defined by my relationships, my job and my other daily life responsibilities? And although it may be unknown territory, the answers to these questions may light the way to finding your new purpose.

After completing my orthopedic residency, I went on to do a trauma fellowship in Zurich, Switzerland and a sports fellowship in Sydney, Australia. In combination with my time on the Native American reservation, these travel experiences took me out of my comfort zone, allowing time and space for reflection and growth.

I will point out that travelling does not have to be far or exotic. You don't need to pack your passport to have these reflections. It might range from trying a different walk or hike or doing a weekend road trip to some place you randomly pick on Google maps. I would submit that even those of us who have the most hectic lifestyles and self-imposed obligations can spare a weekend day at least once a month. And that in and of itself may be all that is needed to partially refill your well-being tank. Equally important, breaking out of your weekend routine in this small way may stir up some emotional sediment clogging up your psychological drain. And even though what gets brought to the surface can lead to quite a bit of discomfort, it is better out than in and better sooner rather than later.

On the contrarian front, travel might be utilized by some people not as a method of self-discovery but rather as a means of escape. For instance, finding themselves unhappy and unable to form connections, they might move to a different city, state or country, each time assigning blame on the location and the community there when things don't work out. Rather than performing an awareness check, some people will attempt to silence their personal demons by altering their location. So if you happen upon a dating profile with a self-described *Globetrotter* or *Citizen of the World*, swipe right with caution. Ultimately, whether it's carry-on or checked, your baggage goes with you, and as they say, wherever you go, there you are.

* * *

My 10th grade AP Biology teacher used to say, there are only two things you have to do: go to the bathroom and die (remember, even if you die first, you will still go the bathroom). Everything else is a choice. Choosing to explore our comfort zones is a choice, and to really define its boundaries, sometimes things will become more uncomfortable than we were prepared to deal with. Stepping back, remember you are making a decision to be uncomfortable, that anxiety is an intended consequence and that you are trying to find your optimal amount of it, in the name of awareness and growth. So step back in, check in with yourself, rinse and repeat.

In Nassim Nicholas Taleb's book, *Antifragile: Things that gain from disorder* (2012),[281] he talks about how things from bones to political and economic systems to life decisions not only improve from volatility and chaos but also feed off of them in order to survive and flourish; these things are what he calls *antifragile*. Taleb states, "Antifragility is beyond resilience or robustness. The resilient resists shocks and stays the same; the antifragile gets better." As such, if we are willing to believe our minds and perhaps even our lives in general are antifragile, we might be more willing to put ourselves out there, testing our limits and trusting that some things do get better when they are disturbed. For many of us, crisis can show us that indeed we are antifragile and can thrive from hardship.

And with the conclusion of this chapter, the heavy psychological lifting portion of the book is now done. The next two chapters are relatively easy sledding, then we get our DNA science on in Part IV. For now, we have now earned the right to have fun. So come and get some!

15

Laugh and Have Fun. But Don't Die.

We cannot really love anyone with whom we never laugh.
—Agnes Repplier

Life is too short to not have fun; we are only here for a short time
compared to the sun and the moon and all that.
—Coolio

The experience of fun has been said to occupy a "place of dominant centrality" in the lives and economics of people living in the U.S.[282] In their article, "The Fun God: Sports, Recreation, Leisure, and Amusement in the United States" (2005), Bryant and Forsyth state that as a society, Americans have become "almost pathologically obsessed with fun" and that they try to integrate it into every aspect of their daily lives—at home, at work, at school, even at rest and at sleep. Furthermore, Megan Garber of *The Atlantic* notes in her article, "Are We Having Too Much Fun?" (2017), that Americans even get their "news filtered through late night comedy."[283]

Despite fun being a historically pervasive and pursued experience in this country, adults having fun has traditionally been stigmatized and carries with it connotations of frivolity, childishness and even narcissism. However, as of late, having fun has become an *en vogue* means of self-care, emerging as possibly a backlash to the antisocial habits we were all compelled to adopt during the pandemic.[284] The social acceptability of adults having fun and the opportunities to experience it seem to be enjoying a resurgence, and we will explore them in this chapter.

Fun and Laughing are Bad

What if we start in contrarian fashion and instead of assuming having fun is a good thing, let's see if we can prove it to be horrible instead? Let's go straight to death. Apparently, dying from laughter is actually a thing, typically precipitated physiologically by heart failure or asphyxiation leading to heart failure.[285] The reason intense laughter can lead to asphyxiation is that it is characterized by successive exhalation-only sequences without an inhalation phase, which has the effect of completely emptying the air from our lungs. In contrast, nonhuman primates like monkeys and apes laugh with exhalation-inhalation sequences, making death less likely.[286]

In one of the more decorated examples of death by laughter, Chrysippus, a 3rd-century B.C. Greek stoic philosopher, died laughing after he got his donkey hammered eating fermented figs, then washing it down with undiluted wine. I guess he wasn't so stoic. Other documented episodes of dying by laughter involve a woman seeing an actor in drag in good ole 18th century England, a Burmese king finding out that Venice is a free state without a king, and an Englishman watching one of the final scenes in *A Fish Called Wanda* where Otto sticks fries up K-K-Ken's nose right before eating Wanda.

So having fun can cause laughing, and laughing can make you die. Check. Moving on, let's look for evidence that having fun might be bad for your well-being without actually causing death. It turns out there is some downside to having fun, as it relates to the timing of said fun. If one's tendency is to stay up late to have fun, that can be a problem. For instance, night owls, AKA *late chronotypes,* will more likely have high blood pressure, be overweight and be at higher risk for diabetes. They get overall less sleep, leading to higher levels of the stress hormone cortisol with all of its concomitant health risks.[287] To be sure, stuff we do late at night typically doesn't fall into the healthy-for-me column. No one is eating organic kale, washing it down with a chia seed smoothie, then hitting the 24-hour fitness at 2am. In addition, many of the increased health risks of being up late may simply be associated with the disruption of circadian rhythms.[288] Effects range from cardiovascular and metabolic detriment to impaired glucose tolerance and elevated inflammatory markers. All in all, if having fun results in consistently staying up late, this is no bueno.

With regard to the integration of amusement and fun into our culture, American critic and educator Neil Postman (1931-2005) had some strong words about this. In his book, *Amusing Ourselves to Death: Public Discourse in the Age of Show Business* (1985),[289] he invectively argues that as a result of television, "…politics, religion, news, athletics, education and commerce have been transformed into congenial adjuncts of show business." He goes on further to say, "…The problem is not that television presents us with entertaining subject matter but that all subject matter is presented as entertaining." Even though at the time he wrote his book, the best modem you could purchase ran at speeds of 300 bits per second (compared to 1 gigabit per second nowadays), he was still able to recognize and fear that, "Americans no longer talk to each other, they entertain each other. They do not exchange ideas, they exchange images. They do not argue with propositions; they argue with good looks, celebrities and commercials." Oh, if Postman had only lived to the age of the internet, he would have died laughing.

Postman's argument was that we should not fear George Orwell's *1984* dystopia of oppression; rather, it is Aldous Huxley's *Brave New World* that should give us mortal pause, as we distract, entertain and laugh ourselves into oblivion, taking meaning away from life issues that deserve gravity. Nevertheless, Megan Garber astutely points out that while Postman was correct in seeing and foretelling the downsides of the universality of entertainment and humor in American society and politics, she counters by reminding us that "entertainment, engaging people as it does, can be extremely democratic."[290] Humor and fun have the power to include marginalized portions of society in political and social discourse as well as draw in others who may otherwise be ambivalent. Moreover, what Postman may have forgotten in his prescient pontifications is that more often than not, it is our failure to administer the fun and levitous antidote to the suffering that is life that is our shortcoming, not the opposite. Indeed, Viktor Frankl suggests that it was his and other prisoners' "grim sense of humor" that was one of "the soul's weapons in the fight for self-preservation."[291] Mic drop, again.

So, in the bad column for having fun: death, bad health and just a generally too-laid-back-approach to issues that should be taken seriously in life. Before moving on to the upsides of fun, let's take a moment to acknowledge that having fun is a luxury, enjoyable when other needs for survival are met, as per Maslow's hierarchy (1943).[292] Like repurposing and finding optimal anxiety, having fun presumes you are already doing pretty well. At the risk of self-loathing—which Buddha would not approve of—we who have the gall to consider how adding fun to our already full lives might do well to take a second to recognize this the next time we shriek when our Wi-Fi speed gets throttled back, or our navigation takes us to the wrong organic craft beer garden or God forbid, someone omits an Oxford comma. Now, off my soapbox.

Fun and Laughing are Good

We've covered some of the downsides of fun; let's now dive into why having fun is purported be healthy. Given there is a known strong association between socioeconomic status and health,[293] and that financial resources are important to enjoy certain types of leisure activities,[294,295] it is reasonable to infer that leisure—and by extension, fun—may be a mechanism by which socioeconomic status influences health. Granted, leisure is not the same as fun. Leisure describes an activity, and fun is an emotional experience. Though we do not have to be doing something leisurely to have fun, fun is often associated with leisure.

In one of the first studies looking at health implications of engaging in enjoyable activities, Pressman (2009) et al. demonstrated improved physiologic and psychological well-being improvement in participants after leisure activities.[296] The defined leisure activities in their study were: spending quiet time alone; spending time unwinding; visiting others; eating with others; doing fun things with others; club, fellowship, and religious group participation; vacationing;

communing with nature; sports; and hobbies. Higher self-reported enjoyment scores were associated with lower blood pressure, total cortisol, waist circumference and body mass index. In addition, perceptions of better physical function, higher levels of psychosocial states and lower levels of depression and negative affect were noted in those participants.

In a study by Berk et al. called, "Neuroendocrine and stress hormone changes during mirthful laughter" (1989),[297] laughter was associated with decreased blood levels of cortisol, epinephrine, growth hormone and dopac (derived from dopamine breakdown). Taken together, this amounts to a reversal of the body's stress response, with resultant decreases in blood pressure and blood sugar.

And this just in, laughing more makes you die less (unless you die from laughing).[298] In a study by Sakurada et al. people who laughed <1/month were almost 2 times more likely to die as those who laughed >1/week. This risk was independent of age, gender, high blood pressure, smoking, alcohol and Doritos consumption. Now that's no laughing matter.

In another study, social laughter was found to be associated with an elevated pain threshold. [299] Laughing was induced by watching a comedy video or live theatrical performances, while pain tolerance was assessed in manners that included using a frozen vacuum wine cooler sleeve, a maximally inflated blood pressure cuff, and finally, by having subjects lean against a wall with their legs at right angles until it becomes too painful and they collapse onto the ground. The researchers explain their results as due the release of endorphins—our body's natural opioids—brought on by laughter. In other words, laughing literally brings on a natural high, and it's no wonder we can feel intoxicated by it.

When looking at the reason primates laugh, the common belief is that it facilitates social bonds by inducing good vibes in listeners and reducing threat, leading to increased interaction and thereby benefiting the survival of that group.[300,301] Laughter in group settings is highly contagious and we are up to 30 times more likely to laugh at the improv than sitting on our toilet watching the same act (assuming one is alone).[302] British anthropologist and evolutionary psychologist Robin Dunbar estimates that human-like laughter first appeared 2.5 million years ago in *Homo Categoricus*.[303] He comes to this estimation by surmising that laughing is a "plausible candidate to fill the gap between primate social grooming and other evolutionarily more recent social bonding behaviours such as singing, dancing, feasting and storytelling." Try working that fun fact into your next happy-hour banter.

Overall, laughing is a contagious, addictive, endorphin-releasing experience that increases social connection between those who laugh together. Given the data presented above, laughing and having fun would appear to be win-win scenarios for both the individual and the group. Postman be damned (sorry bro), I'm ordering that "Live, Laugh, Love" key holder.

What is Fun?

Now that we have made a case for laughter and fun being good for our health, we just need to define it. Unlike conditions like happiness or well-being, fun is not as easily measurable because it is an experience. Like awe, fun has not been rigorously studied in psychological literature. One of the early articles to try to define fun came out in 2010. Authored by British psychologists McManus and Furnham and entitled, "Fun, fun, fun: Types of fun, attitudes to fun, and their relation to personality and biographical factors,"[304] they explored this "psychologically neglected concept" and found that fun is a complex experience that means different things to different people. For instance, they state, "an agreeable, conscientious, female, middle-aged introvert may have a very different conception of fun from a young, neurotic, poorly educated, sensation-seeking male." Brilliant, as Brits would say.

The different types of fun McManus and Furnham describe include: *Sociability, Contentment, Achievement, Sensual* and *Ecstatic*. And the five attitudinal factors they identify were: *Fun involving risk-taking; Fun dependent on fun people; Fun causing happiness; Money needed to have fun;* and *Spontaneity as fun*.

In subsequent research, Reis et al. declared that "Fun Is More Fun When Others Are Involved." (2017).[305] The researchers differentiate "high arousal" and "low arousal" fun as well as explore the difference between having solitary fun versus social fun.

Dacher Keltner states, "Fun, like awe, is one of several self-transcendent states, a space of emotions that transport us out of our self-focused, threat-oriented, and status quo mindset to a realm where we connect to something larger than the self." [306]

True Fun

In an attempt to unify the disparate definitions of fun and provide a blueprint for accessing fun in our lives, award-winning science journalist Catherine Price described the concept of "True Fun" in her book, *The Power of Fun: How to Feel Alive Again* (2021).[307] Price defines True Fun as the "confluence of playfulness, connection, and flow." Let's look at each of those elements.

First and foremost, true fun involves playfulness. My daughter has the endearing quality of being able to make any situation, however mundane, playful. We might be at a gas station, and she'll make a up a jingle about fueling up and filling up. We'll walk by a dentist office on the weekend and crack ourselves up staring at the people getting their teeth cleaned. And when I ask her to finish dinner quickly so we can get to her gymnastics class on time, she will chew in slow motion, mouth open and with sound effects. My daughter models what Price reminds us of when she says that it is a playful state of mind that is most important in making any activity fun and not necessarily the activity itself.

Situated in the idyllic backdrop of Carmel Valley, California, is the National Institute for Play. Psychiatrist Stuart Brown founded it, and he believes that we are "built to play and built by play."[308] He looks at play as a state of being rather than any single activity and sees it as something that everyone can access in their daily lives. He hopes to have play viewed as important a public health activity as good sleep, a balanced diet and watching "The Bachelor."*

The last item in this list may be an over-extrapolation of Dr. Brown's message about play, but I'm just messing around.

In his book, *Play: How it Shapes the Brain, Opens the Imagination, and Invigorates the Soul* (2010),[309] Brown describes play as "self-motivating…absorbing [and] apparently purposeless." Like Price, he describes play as any activity that involves a "suspension of self-consciousness and sense of time." Going all in, Brown states, "When we stop playing, we start dying." That's perhaps a bit strong. Taking it down a notch, it is still very reasonable to state that play and playfulness are well-being inducing and can be integrated into many aspects of our daily lives.

In her description of connection, Price references French sociologist Émile Durkheim's concept of "collective effervescence."[310] This refers to the feeling of harmonious energy and pleasure experienced when people are engaged in a shared and unifying ritualistic activity. Writes Durkheim, "…{collective effervescence} generates a kind of electricity that quickly transports {people} to an extraordinary degree of exaltation." Though Durkheim developed this concept to support his theory of religion in 1912, collective effervescence is believed to play a role in other social rituals as grand as sporting and performance events and as everyday as happy hour. Indeed, research has found that frequently experiencing collective effervescence is associated with well-being, and it "turns the everyday profane into the meaningful and sacred."[311] Cheers to that.

In a fascinating study about this shared fizziness entitled, "Quantifying collective effervescence: Heart-rate dynamics at a fire-walking ritual,"[312] Danish and Kiwi researchers tried to science the crap out of this phenomenon. At the peak of an annual ceremony taking place in the Spanish village of San Pedro Manrique, dozens of locals carry a beloved one on their backs across a bed of glowing coals. By measuring the heart rates of the performers and selected spectators during the ceremony, the researchers showed that there was "synchronous arousal"—seen in the elevation of heart rate—

in performers and spectators who were relatives or friends of the firewalkers. Moreover, spectators related to one firewalker were found to show similar patterns of arousal even when witnessing a firewalker they were not related to. In contrast, in spectators who were unrelated to any firewalker, there were no similar increases in heart rate seen. The researchers concluded that collective ritual effects are physiologically quantifiable and synchronous but are more complex than the qualitative notion of a general collective effervescence. Therefore, they suggest, not everyone involved in a ritual or ceremony is going to experience the same degree of connection.

The final element of True Fun is flow. Coined and described originally by Hungarian-American psychologist Mihály Csíkszentmihályi in 1970 (pronounced muh·hay·lee chik·sent·mee·hai·ee), flow refers to a mental state in which our focus becomes extraordinary, where our perception of time is altered and complex activities become seemingly effortless.[313] During flow, "the ego falls away,"[314] and we perhaps enter a state of no self.

The Father of Flow was born in 1934, the third son of a career Hungarian diplomat. One of his brothers was killed in World War II, and the other was sent to a Siberian labor camp. At age 22, the Father (much easier than writing his name) emigrated to the U.S., worked his way through college and met his future wife. He became a positive psychology pioneer and was known by colleagues as "Mike C." He passed away at the age of 87 in his home in Claremont, California.[315]

One of the key components in achieving flow according to the Father is having the proper "challenge-skill balance," something that follows the Goldilocks Rule.[316] Too easy, we get bored; too hard, we crash and burn. Indeed, throughout life, it benefits us to find challenges that fit this rule. Whether it is at the work, in your relationships or out in nature, finding an optimal state of challenge maintains motivation and interest and creates the environment for finding flow. Thus, this component of flow might be considered the moment-to-moment physical equivalent of the larger overall psychological concept of optimal anxiety as a means of personal growth that we discussed in the last chapter.

Price writes that without flow, there is no True Fun. This makes sense, as when we are really having fun, we are present, our ego is absent, and we have no sense of time passing, all of these being key elements of the flow state.

How to Have Fun

In his book, *The Fun Habit: How The Disciplined Pursuit of Joy And Wonder Can Change Your Life* (2023),[317] Mike Rucker suggests that in order to have more fun, we need to prioritize *time affluence* over financial affluence (again, a priority of the privileged). He also describes keeping a "Fun File," while Price talks about keeping a "Fun Times Journal." Both authors recognize the scarcity of time in our over-scheduled lives and therefore recommend setting aside regular blocks of it specifically for fun.

Though putting fun on your calendar may seem odd, this action is more about creating the intention and space for fun rather than formulating out the specifics of it. It's also important to remember that when it comes to fun, it's the quality, not the quantity, that matters. So even if your fun blocks come up infrequently, you can still make the most of them by choosing the best place, activity and people to experience them with. So pull out your fun-rolodex,* flip it and pick it, show up, ditch that mobile device** and see what happens.

*Rolodex, a combination of the words rolling and index, is a rolling card filing device, arranged alphabetically, that at one time was a universal desk fixture. Used originally to store business contact information, the rolodex has since been repurposed in a variety of ways—wink, wink—such as being a mini-scrapbook of sorts. Though few people still use the physical item, it is still lovingly referred to as a means of personal information storage.

**Catherine Price has written an entire book on this. Entitled, How to Break Up With Your Phone (2018, Berkeley: Ten Speed Press), she makes a strong case against our collective phone addiction, providing compelling evidence for how it damages our abilities to focus, think deeply and form new memories.

With enough forays into finding fun, you will learn what works best for you in your life. Beware though the hedonic elephant in the room. Over time, by doing the same things with the same people in the same way, you will lose that funning feeling. What's the fix for this? Recall Sonja Lyubomirsky's research that concluded that variety is the spice of happiness [318] as well as the work that Etkin and Mogilner did that demonstrated the nuanced effects that variety can have depending on the time frame involved (from the chapter on gratefulness).[319] So mix it up, but don't try to cram in too much fun over a short period of time.

Rucker expands on this variety idea and calls his spin on it "variable hedonics."[320] In addition to leading to happiness, he suggests that variety is also a factor that leads to fun. This makes a lot of sense, because much of what makes an experience fun is the unforeseen nature of it, the novelty of it. "It's fun to do the unexpected," declares Walt Disney. And 18th century German philosopher Immanuel Kant blithely states, "In everything that is to excite a lively laugh there must be something absurd." Even if it is something we have done before, variety makes it more engaging. For instance, riding a mountain bike trail for the first time has that effect on me. Without knowledge of the turns, descents and technical challenges that may come up, I am forced to be fully present, and as a result, I flow and reap the reward of fun.

In our lives, increasing the variety in which to have fun can follow the same guidelines I discussed in the previous chapter on finding optimal anxiety. These include ditching your friends, being contrarian and changing your location. Once you start to feel too much routine creeping into your fun excursions, step back, reassess and change it up a little. From time to time, ditching your go-to fun group and joining an acquaintance's might be in order. When it comes to being contrarian in your fun activities, you could test your confirmation biases against other activities that you would not think to be fun. Maybe you'll surprise yourself. Finally, maybe you keep the same fun group and do the same fun thing but find a different place to do it. This may be the easiest way to add variety and perhaps the first thing to try when it's starting to feel a little stale. To be sure, changing things up intermittently will take more work, but it is work that will be rewarded with more fun and make the world a better place, one laugh at a time.

* * *

Growing up, with few social outlets outside of school, I have always strived to make education fun. I made inappropriate noises while acing Algebra 2 exams, and I was my high school class clown. I gave my college commencement speech while wearing a superhero leotard and cape. I mouth-farted my way through a med school talent show, and one time took my pants off while PBS filmed Patch Adams and me in the lecture hall. The more serious the context, the more contrarian I behaved. Apart from this behavior being the result of not getting enough parental attention as a child, I was truly trying to share my excitement with others around me and create an experience that was both unexpected and hopefully a bit absurd.

In the next and final chapter on how to foster emotional well-being in adulthood, we will discuss arguably the most important factor: your relationships. Hopefully, when implemented, all the work that I have talked about up to this point should both strengthen your existing relationships and help cultivate new ones in your life.

16

It's Your Relationships, Stupid.

You know you're in love when you can't fall asleep because reality is finally better than your dreams.
—Dr. Seuss

Be honest, brutally honest. That is what's going to maintain relationships.
—Lauryn Hill

James Carville, a strategist for Bill Clinton's successful 1992 presidential campaign against incumbent George H.W. Bush, is given credit for famously saying, "It's the economy, stupid." Clinton's campaign successfully used the recession during Bush's term to their advantage, and this phrase became one of the major bullet points of the campaign. Since 1992, this phrase has become a snowclone,* oft repeated in American political culture. For example, "It's the deficit, stupid." Or "It's the voters, stupid." And now, here it is again. It's your relationships, stupid.

> *A snowclone is a phrasal template in which different details are added to a recognizable root phrase, such as "The mother of all [blanks]," or "[blank] is the new [blank]," or "In space, no one can hear you [blank]." The word was coined in 2004 and is a reference to the number of Innuit words for snow, incorporating a pun on the phrase snow cone. Linguist Geoffrey Pullum describes snowclones as "some-assembly-required adaptable cliché frames for lazy journalists." (source: Wikipedia)*

No one doubts the importance of relationships in contributing to our overall state of emotional well-being. What may be surprising is the influence of relationships and psychosocial factors on physical health and illness.[321] Sheldon Cohen's research focuses on the roles of stress, emotions, social support systems and personality in health and well-being.[322] For example, in one of his co-authored studies, they found that psychological stress is associated with depression, cardiovascular disease, and HIV/AIDs-related conditions.[323] In a different study, they demonstrated that people with a positive emotional style—characterized by being happy, lively, and calm—were 2.9 times less likely to get a cold than those with a negative emotional style—characterized by being anxious, hostile, and depressed.[324]

In another study, Cohen and researchers *nasally inoculated* participants with rhinovirus (a common cold virus) and found that participants with the fewest social ties (1 to 3) were *4.2 times* more likely to develop a cold than participants with the most social ties (6 or more).[325] It's rumored that the participants thought the inoculations tasted like chicken. The social ties they included were: relationships with a spouse, parents, parents-in-law, children, other close family members, close neighbors, friends, workmates, schoolmates, fellow volunteers, members of groups without religious affiliations, and members of religious groups. To have a social tie included, the participant needed to have spoken to a person at least once every two weeks. Interestingly, the data showed that it was the *variety* of social ties that mattered, not the absolute number of members in those ties. Shout out to Lyubomirsky there.[326] Variety, it seems, is not just the spice of happiness, it is also associated with the health benefits attributable to our relationships.

In addition to its role with reducing illness, relationships are tied to the mother of all health benefits, longer life. In a meta-analysis* by Holt-Lunstad et al. (2010)[327] that looked at more than 300,000 participants, they found a 50% increased probability of survival in people with stronger relationships. This was independent of age, sex, initial health status, cause of death, and follow-up period. Looked at another way, having poor social relationships is a risk factor for death that is on par with other risk factors such as smoking and alcohol consumption and is a greater risk factor for death than physical inactivity and obesity.

> *A meta-analysis refers to a type of study that combines the results of multiple other scientific studies. Coming from the Greek root meta- meaning beyond or after, meta-analyses are an attempt to pool a large amount of experimental data to confirm or deny a statistical association. In so doing, the findings of a meta-analysis may provide stronger evidence of the scientific question being asked. Nevertheless, they are still vulnerable to study bias due to criteria the researchers use to select and analyze the studies and the possible intrinsic and common biases inherent to each study selected.*

In these and other early studies, although an association between relationships and their psychosocial benefits with our physical health was consistently demonstrated, the specific biologic mechanisms by which this may occur were not elucidated. More research is being done to identify those neural pathways more clearly, and we will delve into this in the following chapter.[328],[329] In this chapter we will discuss the larger social aspects of relationships that lead to their health benefits.

* * *

One of the more well-known studies on happiness was recently reported on by Robert Waldinger and Marc Schulz. Waldinger is director of the world's longest-running scientific study of happiness, the Harvard Study of Adult Development. From the book he writes with Schulz, *The Good Life: Lessons from the World's Longest Scientific Study of Happiness (2023)*,[330] I have paraphrased the key tenets:

1. Relationships are good; loneliness is bad.
2. Relationships need to be watered, just like house plants.
3. Relationships are hard.
4. Our attention is our most precious resource.
5. Even old farts can develop and improve their relationships.

In their research, they found that "chronic loneliness increases a person's odds of death in any given year by 26 percent. The fact is that relationships serve so many functions and help us in so many ways that we are unlikely to get all we need from one person." One might interpret this last statement as the battle cry of polyamorists, but I won't go there. That said, their statement does corroborate with the association in Cohen's study just referenced demonstrating the health benefits of having a variety of relationships.[331]

I would argue, as others have, that many of Waldinger and Schulz' conclusions and recommendations are intuitive. Though, it doesn't hurt to be reminded of the critical importance of relationships to our health. Before moving on, I'll touch a bit on item 4 that has to do with attention.

Now where was I at again? Right. Much has been made of our attention span or lack thereof during this expanding age of digital distraction. Indeed, in one study, the mere presence of a smartphone makes you less smart by reducing "available cognitive capacity."[332] In her book, *How to Break Up With Your Phone: The 30-Day Plan to Take Back Your Life* (2018),[333] Catherine Price provides a cautionary tale of the impact that our electronic devices have on our ability to pay attention and its downstream effects on our social lives and relationships. Admittedly, few people would argue against these ideas in this day and age. However, like the format in her book on how to have fun, Price outlines a means of assessing your own personal level of digital dependency and then forming a plan to mitigate and moderate the effects of it on your life.

In another admonishing work, *Dopamine Nation: Finding Balance in the Age of Indulgence* (2021),[334] Stanford psychiatrist Anna Lembke calls the smartphone "the modern-day hypodermic needle, delivering digital dopamine 24/7 for a wired generation." Now that's a hook! Just as the pandemic increased the rates of alcohol abuse, Lembke argues it has also exacerbated dependence on social media and other digital addictions. Unlike substance abuse, however, where we eventually run out of the substance, the money to acquire it, or just consciousness, there is an unlimited amount of media we have access to and can consume without compromising our vital bodily functions. That said, for many people during the pandemic, their digital relationships were essential to their overall well-being and may continue to be. But now the pandemic is over, and like alcohol consumption, this COVID-induced vice could stand reassessment.

To combat our digital compulsion, Lembke recommends a "new form of asceticism" that involves unplugging and being present with whatever thoughts—however mundane or uncomfortable—pop into our awareness. In addition to compromising our attention span, she argues that reflexively resorting to the instant gratification that our devices give us reduces our ability to deal with everyday life stressors, frustration, and hardship in all its variations. She contends that to counteract the dopamine dependency we easily get from our digital sources, we need to find hard ways to get our dopamine hits, like going for a run, talking to a stranger, or reading a book on midlife crisis. This has the double benefit of resetting our brain's reward pathways and in addition bringing awareness to how our digital device use affects us and our relationships.

Lembke's suggestion for us to rediscover difficulty in our lives is reminiscent of the Buddhist path to enlightenment and its teachings about suffering: suffering exists, and there are ways to end it. To learn how to end suffering, however, we must first suffer. Thích Nhất Hạnh succinctly summarizes it thus: *No mud, No lotus.* Without the suffering that mud represents, there is no growth, no beauty. Our digital devices represent the perfect, always accessible escape to all suffering—small and big, and when we rely on them for this, we are likely setting ourselves up for greater hardship down the line.

And on the contrarian front, some researchers have called into question the significance of the neural impact that the digital age is wreaking on our cognition and ability to pay attention.[335],[336] Their studies point out that mainstream media—ironically—often overplays digital browsing's detrimental effects, and that the reality is much more complex and nuanced. However, though the specific pathways mediating this process have yet to be clarified, there is no question that time is limited, and spending it digitally is not spending it otherwise. Without a doubt, our digital devices allow us to connect to others as well as perform a variety of other daily tasks in a more efficient manner. When researchers speak of digital addiction, however, this is the not the type of use that is worrisome. Like with all things, finding moderation in pleasurable things is always the elusive goal, and when we do not achieve this with our devices, the aspects of our lives that often suffer most are our relationships.

Loneliness

Moving on, when we fail to nurture our relationships, loneliness is the result. This is in distinction to solitude, which is a choice to be alone for personal reflection and other individual pursuits. Solitude is widely supported as psychologically beneficial in that in allows you to reset your mind and body, making room for more experiences, emotional and physical.[337]   Being on your own also facilitates rediscovering yourself and finding your voice. If a task needs to be accomplished, doing it solo can improve your concentration and increase your productivity. Finally, solitude is paradoxically perhaps the best way to improve the quality of your relationships. By taking time to reflect on who you are and what you need, you will naturally make better choices for who to include in your life and be more present when in those relationships.

And now, back to loneliness. The Centers for Disease Control has called loneliness and social isolation "serious public health risks," citing data that show that more than one-third of adults over 45 feel lonely and almost one-quarter of adults over 65 are considered socially isolated.[338] Across the pond, the recognition of loneliness as a public health concern led to the establishment of a Ministry of Loneliness in 2018.[339] Pair this up with the National Institute for Play, and we have the makings of a Marvel movie. You read it here first.

In a study by Khan and Kadoya, they looked at the different features of loneliness during COVID by age group,[340] They found that loneliness was more common in younger people but more severe in older folks. The cutoff for the two groups was 65 years old. Woohoo, I'm younger! While personal finances were most associated with pandemic loneliness in the older population, gender, marital status, living status, and feelings of depression were the factors associated with loneliness in the younger group.

Regardless of age, loneliness is recognized as a serious detriment to health, leading to impaired sleep and depression in early and middle life.[341] Moreover, it is a risk factor for dementia and even death in older adults.[342,343] During the pandemic, loneliness predictably increased, with a report from Harvard in February 2021 that reported 36% of all Americans—including 61% of young adults aged 18-25 and 51% of mothers with young children—felt "serious loneliness."[344]

It's not about the size: Quality and Quantity of Relationships

In each of our lives, we have many flavors of relationships. Predominant ones are those with our partners, our family, our friends, and our co-workers. Less commonly discussed are the short-lived connections we experience for instance while traveling or during random encounters in the Whole Foods line, at the YMCA, or with our Uber driver (this paragraph was sponsored by Whole Foods, YMCA and Uber). I like to call these micro-relationships. These are brief interactions that come with no expectations or preconceived notions. As such, there is a freedom to our communication that is absent when we interact with people we know. This could be considered a momentary form of heterophily, which we discussed as a useful means of breaking out of our comfort zones. As such, micro-relationships might be a path toward finding optimal anxiety and reaping the well-being benefits thereof.

In 1973, Stanford sociology professor Mark Granovetter wrote one of the most influential sociology papers in history.[345] Entitled "The Strength of Weak Ties," the paper purports that diffusion of information and innovation, employment opportunities, and social mobility are better accomplished via acquaintance level interactions—which he defined as *weak ties*. This is due to the intrinsic diversity of the contacts and resultant increase in "local bridges." In contrast, *strong tie* relationships—between close acquaintances—are inherently handicapped in these ways due to their homogeneous composition and resultant similarity of core beliefs and social connections, often resulting in confirmation bias and stagnation of ideas.

Granovetter notes that "weak ties are indispensable to individuals' opportunities and to their integration into communities; strong ties, breeding local cohesion, lead to overall fragmentation." By pointing out this paradox, Granovetter provides the foundation upon which information dissemination theory is based, for better and for worse.

In the for better category, Steve Jobs' imagining of the Pixar building in the late 1990s called for a large central atrium where employees were forced to co-mingle, in contrast to the cubicle farms that dominated workplaces at that time. Jobs ascribed literally to Granovetter's theory and created a physical environment that "promoted encounters and unplanned collaborations."[346] And in the for worse category, weak ties have been suggested to play a significant role in how misinformation is spread,[347] because of the inherent variability of demographics in weak tie connections and the unique and expanding capability of social media to access those weak ties instantaneously.

More recent studies have expanded on the benefits of weak ties, going beyond employment opportunity and idea innovation, and have shown that weak ties are equally important to strong ties in creating and maintaining emotional well-being. Gillian Sandstrom from the University of Essex has done a lot of work in this area, consistently demonstrating the social and emotional benefits of weak ties.[348,349]

In her research, Sandstrom and colleagues discuss the barriers that prevent people from engaging in a common type of weak tie—talking to strangers—despite often being happier if they do so.[350] They describe what they call the *liking gap*, which is a systematic underestimation of how much people believe their conversation partners liked them and enjoyed their company.[351] Given the commonly unperceived benefits of reaching out to strangers, one of the goals of Sandstrom's research is to develop methods to encourage more weak tie connections—which she calls minimal social interactions.[352] In one of her studies, participants engaged in a week-long scavenger hunt that involved repeatedly seeking out strangers' assistance. Following this, those people were more confident about their conversational ability and less pessimistic about the possibility of rejection.

Sandstrom's findings tie in to two other research observations I have cited. First, Cohen and colleagues demonstrated that having a variety of relationships contributes to psychological and physiological well-being more than having homogeneous ones.[353] It stands to reason then that when we add weak ties to our relationship pool and increase its variety, we improve our health. Second, time and again—from affective forecasting[354] to empathic forecasting [355] to the *Prosociality Paradox*[356]—our ability to predict the emotional outcome of events that involve ourselves or others is often pitifully inaccurate. And now again, with the liking gap, we incorrectly underestimate the value of our minimal social interactions. In so doing, we limit our opportunities to improve both ours and someone else's psychological well-being. In the end, there is no pat rule by which we might avoid making any of these predictive errors; however, simply being aware of them is a good start.

And finally, in the intriguing and controversial category, let's talk about one last potential influence on our relationships—our micro-biome. This refers to all the non-human microscopic organisms in our bodies, including bacteria, fungi and viruses. In technical terms, the microbiome refers to the collective genomes of all of these resident microorganisms in contrast to our human genome.[357] It is estimated that our bodies are host to 2,000,000 bacterial genes compared to 20,000 human genes, a ratio of 100 to 1. Accordingly, a great deal of research is being done to examine the potential influences of those and other microbiome genes on human physiology.

Of particular interest, our gut microbes may have an effect on how we socialize. This is referred to as the microbiota-gut-brain axis, and recent and accumulating research indicates that the bacteria that naturally colonize our gastrointestinal tract (and perhaps other parts of our body as well) affect our neural pathways and social behavior.[358] (Is anyone else mildly panicked by this?) Possible pathways include immune activation, bacterial metabolites and production of various neurotransmitters.

For instance, in the study "Microbiota and the Social Brain" by Sherwin et al. (2019), certain butyric acid producing bacteria were consistently associated with higher quality of life indicators.[359,360] And in a randomized, double-blind study—sponsored in part by a probiotic company—a study showed that probiotic supplementation was associated with significantly lower depression scores in participants as well as increased accuracy at identifying facial emotions.[361] Participants who took the probiotic were also given cars and taken on lavish vacations (not really). Another study showed that *prebiotics*—typically high fiber foods that act as food for gut bacteria—significantly improved cognitive function tasks such as improving attention and problem solving. Of note, the patients studied were psychotic, and therefore the results may only apply to people in straitjackets, bosses and certain relatives.[362,363]

Medical research into therapeutic bacterial influence on emotions is called *psychobiotics*. There is a lot of buzz around it because it may provide more agency for people to manage their psychological health without traditional medications with their concomitant side effects. What's more, who wouldn't mind substituting good relationships and taking care of their emotional health for a pill full of bacteria?

As a final note, our microbiome may also play a role in chronic disease and longevity. Although the mechanism is not entirely clear, it is thought that stability and flexibility in our gut bacteria may have anti-inflammatory effects and possibly stave off the stigma of ageing.[364] As we age, the population of bacteria and other microbes changes, and this is thought to have potentially significant health effects. For example, when our microbiome is compromised with antibiotics, our cognition may be negatively affected. One study that looked at more than 14,000 middle-aged women (mean, 54 years-old) who took at least 2 months of antibiotics showed measurable declines in cognitive capacity when assessed 7 years later.[365]

We will delve more deeply in how inflammation and other factors lead to disease and ageing in the next chapter. We will also discuss how the gut microbiome may have an influence on an organism's lifespan in the immortality chapter.

As always, association does not equate with causality, and it may be that particular bacteria happen to be in happier or longer-lived people as a result of their diet (versus depressed people's altered diet). It's the chicken and the egg analogy: which came first—gut bugs or well-being and longevity? However, as researchers are wont to point out, it does make sense that our stomach bacteria would want us to be more social and live longer, as that will improve our emotional and physical well-being, making it more likely that we and our bacterial buddies will thrive and make big and microscopic offspring.

* * *

In summary, there is strong consensus that how we socialize—or do not socialize—has a strong association with our physical health. Just as research demonstrated the physiologic benefits of mindfulness practices, relationships can have analogous positive downstream effects. The frontier now being explored involves the biological mechanisms whereby that occurs, and that is one of the topics of the next section.

Closing Thoughts

Indian industrialist Ratan Tata said, "If you want to walk fast, walk alone. But if you want to walk far, walk together." Early in our lives, it was all about walking fast, getting there, competing. At midlife, we might want to slow our roll and find some hands to hold and fists to bump as the finish line comes slowly into bittersweet sight. For most of us at this point, we can expect fewer years ahead of us than behind us. However, I believe the quality of the years ahead can make up for the unequal quantity of them, and it is clear that the richness of those years is patently dependent upon the quality of our relationships, big and small, long term and short-lived.

Beyond the emotional value relationships provide, there is ample evidence associating the physiologic benefits relationships afford. However, the reality is we have only so much time and bandwidth for them. Occasionally, relationships that spurred growth and served us earlier in our lives cease to do so. Ain't nobody has time for that. Becoming aware of this, we might consider Kondo-izing those relationships to make room for others that might bring us joy, ditching those folks (lovingly or unceremoniously) and welcoming others. Because like it or not, when that cord has been pulled and you realize your stop is coming up, it's best to change plastic seats, find different chitchat companions and get different views of the world passing by.

* * *

Over the last few decades, five of the most common means studied and reported on to improve emotional well-being are practicing gratitude, mindfulness, spending time in nature, being social and exercising. I have reviewed the first four of these and their purported benefits in this and previous chapters. That being said, an article published in July 2023 by psychologists Folk and Dunn calls into question the statistical validity of the majority of the available studies purporting the benefits of these five recommended happiness strategies.[366]

After analyzing more than 500 articles, they included only 57 that they found possessed enough scientific "rigor" to have their results and conclusions be well-substantiated. While they judged that there is reasonable evidence supporting gratitude and socializing, they found weak evidence for mindfulness, exercise and spending time in nature as means to happiness. Incidentally, despite the lack of support for exercise leading to happiness, we will explore how it does have other health benefits in the chapter, "What Does Your DNA Good?"

It is important to note, says Dunn in an interview about their study results, that they are not saying all these purported happiness strategies are "snake oil."[367] They are merely pointing out that without hard evidence in the form of well-designed scientific studies with adequate statistical power,* researchers and society "need to better understand these topics because they have been so widely embraced by the public and so widely disseminated by the media."

> *Statistical power refers to the ability of a study to make a reasonable conclusion about a particular study question. Power is a direct function of the number of study participants and the rareness of the outcome. In technical terms, power is ability of a study or test to show that a difference exists between one method of doing something and another method. If there is not enough power in a study (typically because there are not enough study participants), the results of the study cannot be considered statistically significant, whether or not a difference is shown between study groups.*

Despite their findings, the researchers do voice two important caveats. First, they acknowledge that everyone is different and that people should not stop doing something if it improves their well-being. In addition, Dunn points out that patients with established psychological diagnoses who are being actively treated by a professional may still benefit from one or more of these techniques and therefore should not dismiss them as a result of their study conclusions.

Expert opinion on the study results varied, with some psychologists stating the results are "not cause for concern" as there are statistical methods to mitigate the study deficiencies pointed out. Others state that the study is a "well conducted systematic review" but point out the importance of "matching people to strategies" so that "failure doesn't hit their bank balance and their self-esteem and self-efficacy."[368]

In the end, it is important to remember that the lack of high-quality research does not disprove the validity of a particular happiness hack, just as a well-established study result does not mean its results are relevant to you. For instance, some Norwegians found that sitting in wet underwear in the cold was less comfortable than wearing dry underwear.[369] Ultimately, we all need to practice due diligence before investing our time, energy, money and expectations into purported happiness-inducing practices, and finding the right one(s) may ultimately be a process of trial and error.

IV

SURVIVE

*The really frightening thing about middle age is that you
know you'll grow out of it.*
—Doris Day

17

What Does a Body Good? It's Your DNA.

Take care of your body. It's the only place you have to live.
—*Jim Rohn*

Once we have crested our crisis peak, adapted our psychology, and evolved our social approaches, there is just one more item on the well-being to-do list: optimizing our bodies. A beautiful mind trapped inside a worn-out body is not a desirable endpoint. Some might say that talk is cheap, and it always come back to survival. To that end, in the first two chapters of this section, I will detail current research aimed at circumventing ageing, which revolves around the preservation of DNA health. No small topic, these chapters represent almost ¼ of the book and are heavily referenced. I will then move to an examination of humanity's preoccupation with achieving immortality and describe how science has incrementally moved us closer to it, with some people believing it is a possibility within a human generation. In these three chapters, we are getting down to brass tacks.* If you are lucky enough to get to midlife in one relatively preserved piece, the topics I will explore are probably at the top of your to-know-list. And finally, should we fail to find eternal life, we all need to formulate an exit strategy. I have lovingly termed this a *Death Plan* and will detail various aspects of it in the last chapter.

> **The origin of this idiom is debated, but two popular suggestions derive from the fact that brass tacks are one of the last finishing touches on leather-bound furniture and also are the last decorations put onto coffins. To get down to brass tacks then means to come the {end}point, to get to the matters of practical importance.*

* * *

What does a body good? Apparently, it might not be milk. In the 1980s, there was a barrage of very engaging commercials shot with a simple black bedsheet backdrop showing pre-pubescent kids drinking milk. They were addressing their naysayers, describing in detail all the evolutionarily glorious benefits of drinking this substance that early *Homo sapiens* likely had no means of refrigerating, all the while transforming into Amazonian beauty queens, homecoming beefsteaks or the like. The commercials all ended with the same matter of fact statement: "Milk: It does a body good." Forty years later, some people are saying milk may not be all it was chalked up to be. In a scathing 400-page diatribe entitled, *Spoiled: The Myth of Milk as a Superfood* (2023),[370] culinary historian Anne Mendelson debunks milk's inflated health status. She goes off on how cow's milk weaseled its way into "becoming a darling of the medical community," even going so far as to say we health care workers who so staunchly promoted it are uninformed at best and charlatans at worst. Oh, the humanity! Her most powerful argument about milk's overratedness is despite being undigestible by 2/3 of us, it continues to be mass-produced at great cost to cows, farmers and the environment.

Where am I going with this? First, milk is not the answer. Love is, obviously. Second, since at least the 1980s, we have concerned ourselves with how to keep our bodies healthy. In this chapter, beyond cow's milk, we will explore some newer and nuanced notions about optimizing our physiology and maintaining our physical selves. We'll focus on the building block of life itself, DNA (deoxyribonucleic acid), and look at how science has shown that health and ageing not surprisingly hinge on its integrity. We will focus on specific molecular and physiologic mechanisms that are believed to play significant roles in cellular and DNA fitness. And in the following chapter, we will look at some behaviors that are thought to have upstream influence on the pathways above. We will see that it is not simply about the double-helical sequence with which you were born. Though genetic inheritance certainly does play a role, what we will explore in this chapter is the effect that environment and behavior have on DNA and what we can do to maximize the upsides and minimize the downsides of those effects.

Please note that the molecular changes explored do not just start happening after midlife; they are relevant to simply being alive at any age. Therefore, any and all of the age-hacking interventions I will describe can be taken earlier in life. The reality is most people don't start thinking about how to slow down ageing until they feel old, which often happens around midlife. The material presented at some times will be dense, as I have strived to do justice to the relevant research and biological context underpinning the ageing process. During my investigation, rabbit holes abounded, but for readers who are connoisseurs of scientific detail, this is your section.

In the next two chapters, we will get a glimpse into the complexity and seeming paradoxes on how our cells work and our bodies age. Exciting research is being done to look at the root biological causes of ageing and develop targeted treatments to counteract them. Taken together with the psychosocial and awareness research presented earlier in the book, this information provides a more complete view of the inter-relatedness of our environment and behavior and their effects on our molecular selves. With no further ado, let's get our DNA on!

Social Genomics

In the previous chapter on Relationships, I alluded to research being done that ties relationships to physical heath.[371],[372] While it is clear from epidemiological studies that an association exists between our social environment and our physical well-being, the specific pathways dictating how this happens were not initially recognized. In the chapter on Awareness, we learned about research that identified physiologic and neural mechanisms that are benefited by mindfulness practices. Beyond this degree of understanding, there is one level deeper to investigate though—DNA.

One of the underlying biologic bases accounting for physiologic changes due to everyday life circumstances is thought to be changes in gene expression. That is to say, our socio-environmental conditions are thought to dictate what DNA gets expressed and what DNA does not expressed.* And since it is commonly believed that disease risk is associated with differential gene expression,[373] by the transitive property, our social environment may affect our disease risk. This type of correlation is the focus of *Human Social Genomics*, and it refers to the social regulation of gene expression.[374]

> *Genetics 101: The vast majority of times, a sequence of DNA codes for proteins. The process of the DNA code being turned into proteins is broken down into transcription and translation. Transcription refers to the DNA code being turned into messenger RNA. Messenger RNA then gets turned into proteins via the process of translation. Proteins are the molecular compounds that make or influence the building of other molecular compounds. When DNA gets "expressed," that means the protein it codes for gets made. If it does not get expressed, its protein does not get made. This is how each cell regulates all of its vital functions and by extension, how our body responds to its environment as a whole. Sometimes, small cellular disturbances leading to DNA expression changes can lead to significant downstream disease consequences.*

Professor Steven W. Cole from the University of California in Los Angeles has spent his career looking at social genomics.[375] In 2007, he and other researchers published the first study describing on the genomic level how social factors affect our body's stress response.[376] In this study, they identified specific genes affected by loneliness, finding that pro-inflammatory DNA was upregulated and anti-inflammatory DNA downregulated by social isolation. Thus, while in the last chapter we described how loneliness can lead to downstream conditions such as depression, dementia and even death, Cole's and others' subsequent research identified the affected DNA-expression pathways that might account for them. The hope is that this kind of work would pave the way toward genomic level therapeutics for a variety of chronic conditions.

Many of us likely think that we are what we are from a genetic standpoint, that it is written in stone, taking what parts of mom and dad nature chose to give us, and expressing it in a pre-determined manner. Not so, apparently. For example, Youssef Idaghdour and researchers found that only 5% of genomic variability in human white blood cell DNA expression was genetically determined. In contrast, environment accounted for as much as half of the gene expression variability, while geography—either urban or rural—accounted for up to 25% of it.[377],[378] Science-splaining this, although these results are about a certain type of cell in a specific group of people in a particular region of the world, the results might be extrapolated to suggest similar degrees of environmentally influenced DNA expression variability in other aspects of our physiology. This is how science works, by making small, demonstrable observations and using that data to plan other studies that may corroborate or disprove it on a larger scale.

In the kingdom of insects, there is a dramatic example of how the environment affects gene expression. This is seen in the development of bee larvae into either drones (males), workers (sterile females) or queens (fertile females). This differentiation of bees is determined by a substance called *royal jelly* [379],[380] You read that correctly. Royal jelly is a glandular honeybee proteinaceous secretion that is fed to all larvae. If the royal jelly tap is turned off after three days, you get a worker or a drone. If it is left on, you get a queen.

This phenomenon is an example of *epigenetics*, which describes the relationship of how environment and behavior influence what genes are expressed. One way to understand epigenetics is to remember that every cell in our bodies has the exact same DNA. Yet groups of cells can perform vastly different functions from organ system to organ system. The functions they perform are dictated by the genes they express. Epigenetics tries to explain this differential expression, and in so doing, provide pathways to modify aberrant or dysfunctional changes.* The allure of epigenetic factors is that once they are identified, they can be targets of intervention with significant impact on the organism, since they are only one level removed from altering the DNA itself.

> *A commonly recognized type of epigenetic phenomenon in lifeforms is represented in the stem cell. From one pluripotent stem cell, every other organ-specific cell line is derived, without changes to the DNA. There are only changes to what DNA is expressed. Depending on its molecular environment, a stem can differentiate into anything from a neuron to a liver cell to muscle. As such, uses of stem cells range from treating anemia after bone marrow transplant to therapies for Alzheimer's, Type I diabetes, heart disease and arthritis. The trick is getting the stem cell to turn into the type of cell you want it to.*

Learning about the effects of royal jelly, naturally some people decided to see what would happen if they ingested copious amounts of what basically amounts to bee saliva. While companies producing it will tout a variety of health benefits, the Food and Drug Administration poopoos those claims, so to speak.[381] However, in a study from 2012 by Morita et al.,[382] royal jelly ingested for six months improved red blood cell formation, glucose tolerance and mental health. Hot damn! The researchers hypothesized this may have been due to increased conversion of dehydroepiandrosterone sulfate (DHEA-S) to testosterone.

Back to the bees, the epigenetic mechanism by which royal jelly affects gender differentiation is via a modification of DNA known as CpG* methylation.[383] With more methylation, you get a worker or drone. With less methylation, you get a queen. Thus is the segway to investigate the ability of our environment to influence our genetic code expression.

> *DNA has four nitrogen-containing building block molecules called "bases." They are adenine (A), cytosine (C), guanine (G), and thymine (T). Because of their composition, they are able to pair up with one another and stack on top of each other, forming a continuous spiral type of structure, called a helix. Two helices then wrap around each other, and are packaged up very tightly in the nucleus of all of our cells. In mammals, DNA methylation occurs on the cytosine base. Hence, the term CpG methylation.*

DNA Methylation and Programmed Cell Death

The most studied epigenetic DNA modification associated with ageing and disease in general is DNA and histone* methylation.[384,385,386] Methylation is the addition of a molecule consisting of one carbon and three hydrogen atoms (CH3) to a segment of DNA. Most commonly, DNA methylation results in *silencing, not activation,* of the corresponding gene, often because the methyl group occupies space that would normally be taken up by gene-writing proteins.[387, 388] Differential methylation patterns are associated with diseases such as cancer, arthritis and neurodegenerative conditions like dementia.[389]

Histones are cute little round proteins that DNA binds to help form its helical structure. Their methylation can have functional effects similar to DNA methylation. For the purposes of simplicity, when discussing the effects methylation, this will refer to both DNA and histone methylation, though DNA and histones are distinct structures.

Though the causes are not completely understood, age is a significant cause of both hypo- and hypermethylation, both potentially leading to dysfunction and disease.[390] For example, in cancer, the most frequent genetic root cause is not DNA mutation, but rather *loss* of gene expression by *hyper*methylation. What kind of expression loss would lead to cancer? One kind is DNA repair gene expression loss.[391] Indeed, up to 17 types of cancer are associated with under-expressed DNA repair genes that have been hypermethylated.[392] On the other hand, *hypo*methylation can be a cause of cancer as well. This happens through *activation* of cancer-causing genes, called *oncogenes*.[393] In other words, methylation can be both detrimental and beneficial, depending on what genes are inactivated.

The natural question then becomes how we prevent or at least limit detrimental methylation patterns. In a study by Li and Tollefsbol (2010),[394] they found that green tea, soybean and plants containing isothiocyanates led to a reversal of hypermethylation-induced inactivation of key tumor suppressor genes (I know, a lot of words to follow there). This would have the effect of allowing these genes to be made into cancer-preventing proteins. Isothiocyanates are naturally occurring small molecules that are abundant in cruciferous vegetables such as broccoli, kale, watercress, Brussels sprouts, cabbage, Japanese radish, cauliflower, black and brown mustard, and root crops such as turnips and rutabagas. Over the past 20 years, research has shown isothiocyanates to be both cancer-preventative agents as well as tumor-fighting molecules.[395,396,397] In addition, folate-rich fruits, vegetables, and beans[398] as well as selenium-rich nuts, kidney and liver[399] are thought to play roles in cancer prevention.

There are several proposed pathways via which dietary substances such as isothiocyanates prevent cancer and kill tumors, and most include halting cell growth or even inducing programmed cell death. Programmed cell death is referred to as *apoptosis* (Greek for "falling of the leaves"), and it is a critical cellular failsafe pathway in any organism,[400] very similar to the U.S.S. Enterprise's auto-destruct sequence. *The effect of certain foods on apoptosis is thought to be the predominant means in which our diet may limit our risk of cancer.*[401] This effect is mediated both by their effects on methylation as well as their direct anti-tumor properties.

When aberrant methylation patterns cause apoptosis mechanisms to malfunction, cancers can arise. One gene in particular has risen to fame as the "guardian of the genome," and the product it makes is referred to as the p53 tumor suppressor protein.[402,403] This protein has two main functions: it stops the cell from replicating, allowing for the DNA repair mechanisms to do their job, and failing that, it induces apoptosis. Indeed, the p53 pathway is *inactivated* in almost all human cancers. When it goes down, we go down, and cancers can grow unchecked. Despite its big-protein-energy, p53 still humbly goes by a lower-case p.

With cancer, the fundamental cellular problem is with insufficient apoptosis, leading to uncontrolled replication of cells. The two mechanisms that allow this are an overactivation of genes that lead to cell growth—called oncogenes—or an underactivation of genes that check uncontrolled cell growth—called tumor suppressor genes. If DNA becomes damaged beyond repair, normal cells stop duplicating. In cancer, there is uninhibited reproduction of cells with damaged DNA, and once they reach a certain number and size, they are detectable as tumors. Unchecked tumor growth with their space-occupying effects and resultant organ dysfunction as well as the tumor factors they release into the bloodstream are what lead to the negative fallout seen with cancer.

Apoptosis can also go hog-wild, leading to excessive cell death and conditions including neurodegenerative diseases, ischemic damage and autoimmune disorders. For instance, in diseases including Parkinson's, Alzheimer's, Huntington's and amyotrophic lateral sclerosis, there is progressive neuron loss through unregulated apoptosis. Heart attacks—caused by loss of blood supply to a portion of it, called ischemia—also lead to apoptosis, even beyond the area of ischemia. For these types of conditions, cellular treatments are aimed at limiting unchecked apoptosis.[404]

In summary, disturbances in DNA methylation can lead to downstream aberrations in cellular function, a significant one of them being apoptosis. The scientific study of the mechanisms of apoptosis has huge implications for disease understanding and prevention. The mechanisms of these pathways are complex, with both under- and over-methylation as well as too much or too little apoptosis representing root pathways that lead to a variety of human diseases. In this section, I have presented a tiny glimpse into this world of research. The actionable takeaway is components of our diet likely play a role in mitigating the detrimental effects of aberrant methylation and its potential to allow carcinogenesis. In the next section, we'll look at the peculiar phenomenon of ageing and its relationship to the status of our DNA.

Cause of Ageing: DNA Damage and Free Radicals

One might start by first asking, why do we {need to} age in the first place? Evolutionary logic tells us that once we have passed our peak age of procreation, nature is done with us, and natural selection then becomes ambivalent to whatever genetic defects we harbor that lead to aging.[405] But what about the biologic cause of ageing? Damage to DNA is now recognized as a primary, unifying cause of ageing.[406] It turns out that DNA is highly unstable and prone to damage, and therefore a well-functioning DNA damage response (DDR) is required to maintain it. It is estimated that 100,000 incidents of DNA damage occur in *each cell per day*.[407] DDR systems cannot keep pace with this, and over time, accumulated damage leads to aging. As a striking example of this principle, when DDR systems are defective, progeria syndromes—AKA, premature aging syndromes—are the result.

The primary mechanism by which DNA damage occurs is our own metabolism—the sum of chemical reactions that occur in our body.[408] In other words, ageing is simply the byproduct of living. Go figure. Accordingly, research was initially done to look at mechanisms of not living. Seeing a dead-end to that path, scientists then focused on DNA damage and how to limit or prevent it and thereby mitigate ageing's consequences.

A major pathway whereby metabolism is believed to lead to DNA damage and ageing is via the production of free radicals and a subset of them called reactive oxygen species. These are molecules that contain an unpaired electron. Because of our body's insistence on requiring oxygen to live, the formation of reactive *oxygen* species (ROS)* is an obligatory side product. From a molecular level, oxygen is required in a process called the *electron transport chain,* where it is the terminal electron receiver (electrons carry energy). Glucose is our body's energetic currency, and our bodies convert that glucose into adenosine triphosphate (ATP) by using oxygen** via aerobic metabolism.*** As a result of that process taking place literally tons of time while we are alive, ROS are created.

For the sake of brevity, from this point on, I will refer to free radicals and ROS collectively as ROS, though there is a distinction between the two as described.

**The priority of glucose conversion to energy is first from carbohydrates, then fat, then protein. This is the foundation of diets that eliminate carbohydrates from your diet, in essence forcing your body to turn fat into glucose for its energy needs.*

***Aerobic metabolism uses oxygen to make ATP. When we are oxygen-deprived for whatever reason or when we need short bursts of energy, anaerobic metabolism is utilized. Aerobic metabolism takes about 3 minutes to kick in, but is much more efficient in making ATP, creating 38 ATP molecules per molecule of glucose. Anaerobic metabolism kicks in at 10 seconds, lasts between 2-3 minutes normally, but only makes 2 ATP per*

> *molecule of glucose. It also makes the byproduct of lactic acid,*
> *which is what causes muscle soreness after intense exercise. If our*
> *cells are oxygen-deprived for extended periods of time and need to*
> *rely on anaerobic metabolism to make glucose, the accumulation*
> *of lactic acid causes other bad things like death.*

In addition to metabolism, ROS are generated externally by ionizing radiation, ozone, cigarette smoking, air pollutants, and industrial chemicals.[409] It turns out that people who smoke look older because they are older, and ultraviolet radiation does in fact age our skin. When there is an imbalance between our body's production of ROS and its ability to detoxify them, a state of *oxidative stress* is said to be present.[410] In general, it is believed that nature slightly favors ROS formation over its breakdown, resulting in a continuous low level of oxidative damage.[411] Why would nature do this? Keep reading.

The molecular feature whereby ROS cause cellular damage and the downstream effects of ageing is via the presence of an unpaired electron.[412] A stable molecule or atom has a neutral charge, and the presence of an unpaired electron gives it a negative charge and makes it highly unstable and reactive. ROS want to either contribute to or take away an electron from another molecule so that it can become electrically neutral. In so doing, ROS damage that molecule and compromise its function. By causing damage to lipids, proteins, and DNA, ROS can trigger a variety of human diseases.[413] These include two major causes of human death—cancer and atherosclerosis. In DNA, ROS can cause strand breakage and abnormal connections between its base pairs—referred to as protein cross-links.[414] This would interfere with the normal duplication or reading process of DNA, potentially leading to cancer via mutation.

And in atherosclerosis, ROS cause damage to the lipid components of cell membranes, which via a cascade of events leads to increased formation of plaques with subsequent tissue ischemia and organ damage.[415]

As a result of the cellular damage known to be caused by ROS and the fact that mitochondria are a significant source of ROS by virtue of their energy production duty, the Mitochondrial Free Radical Theory of Aging (MFRTA) was theorized by Denham Harman, an American biologist and physician (1916-2014) in the 1950s.[416]

Mitochondria are the energy plants in all of our cells and are thought to originally be bacteria that were phagocytosed (eaten) by cells and incorporated into a synergistic relationship. Mitochondria contain their own distinct DNA and are the largest (but not only) source of ROS in the cell as a result of their energy-producing activities. This is done via a process that involves the electron transport chain described earlier. During the process of making the main energy source our cells use (ATP), some electrons "leak" out and can create those nasty little ROS.[417] One might view this as codependency at the cellular level. These unfortunate mitochondria put themselves out there cell cycle after cell cycle to meet the energy demands of their cellular partners, only to be self-sabotaged by the very process by which they provide this care.

Evidence supporting the MFRTA include the observation that when the fruit fly *Drosophila* overexpress enzymes that destroy ROS, they live 30-40% longer than those that do not.[418] Another darling of geneticists, the nematode *C. elegans* also shows longer lifespan when it has greater amounts of ROS-destroying enzymes.[419] Alas, we are neither fruit fly nor nematode, and so the evidence is not as clear cut in humans or other mammals.

MFRTA predicts that calorie restriction will lead to decreased ROS production and longer lifespan—one reason being that there will be less food to convert to energy, subsequently producing fewer electrons flying around to generate ROS. This observation is in fact true, and we will explore it more in the next chapter. However, it is not necessarily true that lifespan is increased solely by reduction of ROS, because calorie restriction has other metabolic benefits that include decreasing insulin signaling and inducing a stress response.

One opposing theory to MFRTA proposes there is a therapeutic and necessary level of ROS that actually promotes health.[420,421] It is believed that ROS serve as molecular signals that activate stress responses beneficial to the organism. Basically, the very molecules that cause oxidative stress are what teach our cells how to deal with oxidative stress by upregulating its own antioxidants. Nature is clever. This type of phenomenon is referred to as hormesis and will be discussed more later.

Further evidence calling MFRTA into question includes observations that certain rodents that produce higher than average levels of ROS live as long or longer than other rodents.[422] A final confounding fact is that ROS are not just produced in mitochondria. They are produced throughout the cell in various locations and organelles.[423] So we cannot lay all the blame on our ageing on poor little mitochondria. That said, like many theories that prove to be incompletely accurate, research investigating MFRTA led to other findings that advanced the study of ageing.

Inflammation

Apart from their contribution to ROS formation, mitochondria are also believed to play a central role in our body's inflammatory response.[424] What's the deal with inflammation, and why is it one of the hot topics in ageing science? It just so happens that inflammation is believed to be *the* common risk factor for the most common non-communicable human diseases including but not limited to cardiovascular disease, diabetes, obesity and cancer. Taken together, mitochondrial dysfunction, oxidative stress and inflammation are "inextricably linked" in the human ageing process.[425] Oxidative stress leads to inflammation; inflammation leads to oxidative stress; and mitochondria are central players in both of these phenomena. Like ebony and ivory, one cannot exist without the others, and songs have been written about it.

In the end, ROS are obligatory byproducts of cellular processes and are likely the primary factors that contribute to ageing by their detrimental effects on lipids, proteins and DNA. However, our cells have the ability to repurpose ROS for other essential functions. Maybe they read my book. Therefore, there is not a black and white correlation between ROS levels and lifespan, and further study is required to more fully understand the complex relationships between ROS, cellular damage and longevity.

In the next section, we will look at a mitigator of DNA damage, the telomeres. These chromosomal structures act like a counterbalance to ROS and instead protect DNA from damage during cellular processes.

The Telomere: Longevity Predictor or Snake Oil?

In addition to damage via ROS, DNA detriment can also occur during the normal cellular replication process. One of the keys to preventing DNA damage during cell division lies in a structure called the telomere. The telomere is the region at the end of every chromosome consisting of repeating DNA sequences forming a loop that protects it from getting frayed, damaged or attached to something it shouldn't. Telomeres also prevent DNA ends from appearing like broken DNA strands and incurring the wrath of the DDR system.[426] The risk of aberrant DNA connections is especially high each time the cell divides and needs to unfurl it's entire 6-foot-long DNA sequence.

To appreciate the importance of the telomere's job, consider this analogy. If you've ever made one of those colorful braided and charmed bracelets—and if you have not, you should—you understand the importance of appropriately managing the ends of the strings each time you thread on a charm and when you are done, properly tying them off. If you fail to do so, you'll end up with a lot of charms and tears on the ground or a hopelessly tangled bracelet and in both cases, a distraught 6-year-old. In each of our cells, the telomere is what manages and protects the ends of DNA strings that contain 6.4 billion "charms" per copy so our cells can divide and replicate their colorful DNA bracelets incident-free. This is some heavy lifting.

With each cellular replication cycle* —i.e., as we age—the telomere end caps get a little bit shorter as a necessary result of how DNA duplicates itself.[427,428] As such, telomeres have been referred to as *molecular timers* that control the lifespan of a cell.[429] The length of a telomere simultaneously represents the cell's replicative history at the same time it imposes a replicative limit on the cell. The shorter telomeres become, the more likely they will fail to protect the ends of the chromosomes, potentially leading to DNA damage. When enough DNA damage occurs, a normal cell either dies or stops replicating (called *senescence*, to be discussed later), whereas an abnormal cell whose telomeres do not shorten may continue to divide and lead to carcinogenesis.[430,431]

> *Fun fact, Nobel prize winning Austrian physicist Erwin Schrödinger calculated in 1944 that only 50-60 successive cell divisions were necessary to make himself, which produced about 10^{15} cells, which takes into account cell turnover during his lifetime. Thus, he concluded, his body is approximately the 50th or 60th "descendant" of the original egg that was fertilized. (Schrodinger E. What Is Life? With, Mind and Matter and Autobiographical Sketches. Cambridge, United Kingdom: Cambridge University Press; 1992)*

There is a clear indirect relationship between telomere length and age—both chronological and biological. The shorter your telomere, the older you are. Just as with progeria conditions associated with defects in DNA repair mechanisms, accelerated telomere shortening leads to similar premature ageing diseases.[432]

The enzyme telomerase is tasked with the job of lengthening the telomere, but it is not active in every cell and is not perfect in its execution, and over time, cannot keep pace with the rate of shortening. The overall length or rate of telomere shortening has been shown to be associated with decreased life expectancy.[433,434] It has been shown that between 20-40% of longevity is heritable,[435,436] and this is likely associated in part with telomere length. Indeed, increased female longevity is associated with slower telomere shortening.[437] In addition, human cells infused with extra telomerase lived longer.[438]

In addition to being affected by cellular replication, telomeres are sensitive to a variety of environmental influences including oxidative stress, chronic inflammation, obesity, smoking, alcohol intake, psychological stress and physical activity.[439,440] In all of these situations, the cells whose telomeres are especially vulnerable are often those of our immune system, which in turn are linked with many chronic diseases and shorter lifespans.

Because of their properties and function, many researchers believe telomeres to be the holy grail of ageing biomarkers, representing both chronological age and biological age.[441,442] Whereas chronological age is simply how many birthdays we have seen, biological age denotes what the status of our individual tissues and cells are. Since chronological age does not directly correlate with biological age, a marker combining the two would serve very useful in research looking at ageing and the factors that influence it. If this is true, by assessing the status of someone's telomere, we can accurately say how old someone is. Who knows, telomere length might one day become standard data on someone's Bumble profile.

The declining function of our immune system is a significant factor associated with ageing[443] and represents an inheritable proxy for DNA ageing.[444] Research on telomere length in white blood cells shows that there is progressive shortening over time, and this loss is believed to partially account for the decline in our immune response as we age.[445] In one study, short telomeres were shown to be a risk factor for adverse COVID-19 outcomes.[446]

So if cells die when telomeres get too short, what happens when telomeres stay long? They don't die, which is good, right? Not so much. The popular belief is that telomere shortening is nature's means of suppressing tumor growth. Mutations add up over the course of an organism's lifespan, and the accumulation of these mutations can eventually lead to malignant transformation. Because the DDR system cannot keep up with the degree of DNA damage over time, an alternative method of tumor suppression developed in the form of programmed telomere shortening, leading to cessation of cell replication. Again, nature has thought this through.

In cells whose telomeres do not shorten, replication can continue uncontrollably,[447] leading to certain types of cancer.[448] This is the so-called "price of cellular immortality."[449] As such, biology defaults toward cessation of cell division, as most cells in our body do not contain telomerase, but it is found in 90% of tumor cells.[450] Accordingly, telomerase becomes an attractive target for certain cancer chemotherapies.[451] However, telomere shortening is a not a perfect system for cancer prevention, and unfortunately, short telomeres are also associated with increased cancer risk. This is referred to as the "telomere paradox."[452] The contradictory observation that short telomeres both predispose to cell death and unchecked cell replication exemplify one more pitfall of trying to oversimplify nature's complexity.

In general, however, telomere shortening past a certain point has been shown to lead to senescence (from Latin *sene* meaning "old"), or cessation of cellular replication without death of the cell.[453] When the telomere shortens past a certain point, the senescence pathway is activated.[454] Senescence can be thought of as an intermediary stage between normal cell function and apoptosis and is another failsafe to limit the risk of progression to uncontrolled cell growth. As such, the factors controlling senescence are critical, and we will explore this topic in the next section. Ultimately, it may not be possible to have your telomeric cake and eat it too. Telomere length preserves DNA replication capacity, but at the cost of malignant transformation over time. As we age, our physiology transitions from one that favors telomere length to one that allows progressive shortening.

Given the strong relationship between telomere length and cell viability, research is being done to determine if telomere length can be manipulated and maintained to extend cellular life. However, Chilton et.al (2017) warn that, "evolutionary pressures have fine-tuned telomere length" to optimize the risk of short- and long-telomere associated conditions. Too short, you age quicker; too long, you turn into a zombie. Therefore, telomere interventions should be approached with caution.

Cellular Senescence

Based on a seminal study by Hayflick and Moorhead from 1961, it is now generally accepted that all non-malignant somatic* cells have a replicative limit.[455] After about 50 divisions, they showed that human fibroblast cells stopped duplicating independent of any external influences, and therefore they concluded this was the result of internal factors they collectively referred to as *cellular senescence.*

> *In our bodies, cells can be divided into somatic and germline cells. Germline cells are what make sperm and eggs, and their DNA is passed on to our offspring. Moreover, they are immortal in that they can continue to replicate indefinitely. Somatic cells are those*

> *that are differentiated into specific tissues and organs. Once they have done this, their days are numbered, and they have a finite number of replication cycles possible. Mutations, if present are only passed onto offspring via germline cells, but not in somatic cells. Pluripotent stem cells are those that give rise to somatic cells in all the different tissue types in our body. They too have the capacity to divide indefinitely to produce more stem cells.*

Cessation of cell division is primarily in response to accumulated DNA damage from any cause.[456,457] This in turns activates the DDR system and the p53 pathway (the tumor suppressor gene that stops cell replication). We have reviewed the pathways by which cells with damaged and irreparable DNA either self-destruct from apoptosis or continue dividing and become risks for carcinogenesis. The third path that those cells with DNA damage may follow is senescence. This path was termed a "death mechanism" by evolutionary biologist August Weismann in the late 1800s.[458] He went on further to state that, "Death takes place because a worn-out tissue cannot forever renew itself, and because a capacity for increase by means of cell division is not everlasting but finite."

One might ask at this point why organisms have two seemingly competing methods of halting cell replication in apoptosis and senescence. A study by Childs et al. (2014)[459] suggested that each process evolved for different reasons with their own pros and cons. Apoptosis is cell-specific and does not bring an immune response with it other than that required to remove the dead cell itself. In contrast, senescence is more of a community event, where an immune response is triggered and where one senescent cell secretes factors that affect surrounding cells. As a result of this mass effect, senescence may be a more effective means of eliminating early tumor growth. They concluded that perhaps senescence holds an advantage over apoptosis due to its ability to communicate with other cells, despite the potential consequences of unchecked senescence, which will be addressed next.

Senescence can be thought of as the *ding* of the telomeric timer; once the telomere shortens enough, it's been a good run, and time is up for the cell. Senescent cells do not die but in fact remain metabolically active, but their persistence eventually results in pathology. The mechanism is thought to involve inflammatory chemicals secreted by senescent cells leading to dysfunction of nearby cells and the larger downstream effects of ageing, analogous to the metaphoric rotten apple.[460] In addition, persistence of senescent cells restricts the ability of our immune system to recognize and clear them out. The accumulation of senescent cells has been linked to ageing and a variety of chronic conditions including cancer, osteoporosis, osteoarthritis, pulmonary, cardiovascular and neurodegenerative diseases.[461]

For the above reasons, cellular senescence is suggested to be the ultimate indicator of the ageing process, because it bridges the molecular damage occurring to DNA and cells with the bigger, external appearance of ageing—referred to as the ageing phenotype.[462] In other words, people with a lot of senescent cells look old on the outside because they are old on the inside. Even though DNA damage is the root cause of ageing and telomeres are a proxy of measuring age, these two subcellular elements do not directly lead to the visible phenotypic appearance of ageing. Rather, it is the accumulation of senescent cells and their secreted chemicals that lead to tissue dysfunction and the appearance of an old organism.

That being said, senescence is a necessary phase of cellular housekeeping during processes like embryonic development, tissue regeneration, and wound healing, where old cells need to be cleared out to make room for new ones.[463] This is cellular-level Kondo-izing, if you will. In addition, cellular senescence is another means by which normal physiology prevents uncontrolled replication in DNA-damaged cells leading to cancer. Inducing cellular senescence is one critical function of the DDR system and is also one mechanism by which chemotherapy drugs work.[464] Unfortunately, cancer is tricky, and even cells induced into a senescent state can re-emerge into a malignant state.[465] Overall, just as with methylation, apoptosis, and telomere length, cellular senescence is both a beneficial and pathological phenomenon depending on context.

Once cells have entered into or been induced into senescence for a period of time, our immune system is charged with the task of removing them before they have overstayed their welcome, as over-accumulation of them and their pro-inflammatory byproducts in various organs systems leads to ageing and chronic conditions described previously.[466] As our immune system function declines with age—referred to as immunosenescence—so does its effectiveness in removal of senescent cells. Moreover, since our immune cells are those most vulnerable to telomere shortening from ROS, this creates a nasty one-two punch: a compromised immune system due to age leading to a vicious cycle of more compromised clearance of senescent cells leading to more ageing.

Accordingly, another hot area of research involves finding treatments to remove senescent cells or their harmful byproducts and enhancing our immune system's removal of them.[467,468] Collectively called senotherapeautics, the compounds are divided into *senolytics* (from Latin, *lysis*, meaning "a loosening") and *senomorphics* (from Latin *morph* for "form"). The senolytics target the senescent cells themselves by inducing apoptosis, while the senomorphics target inactivation or removal of the pro-inflammatory byproducts. Though still in the early phases of study, senolytic treatment has shown to be effective in improving physical function in patients with some types of kidney and lung disease.[469] In patients who have undergone chemotherapy, removal of senescent cells induced by treatment is thought to prevent relapse as well as alleviate sides effects of treatment such as fatigue.[470]

While senotherapeutics aim to manage senescence once it has appeared, researchers are also trying to prevent it from occurring altogether. *Metformin*—widely prescribed to treat type 2 diabetes—is one drug being looked at that inhibits cellular senescence and has the potential to be the first drug tested to slow ageing in humans.[471] First reported on in 2016, the trial is named TAME, standing for Targeting Aging with Metformin.[472] Pathways that metformin has an effect on include decreasing insulin levels and inhibiting the electron transport chain with reduction of ROS production and DNA damage.

Quite cleverly, one review article by Konopka and Miller (2019) is entitled, "Taming expectations of metformin as a treatment to extend healthspan."[473] They point out that the TAME study looks at how metformin may limit *progression* of chronic disease and not necessarily how it may increase lifespan. They suggest that a study looking to extend life should be done in patients before the onset of chronic disease, should be effective in delaying onset of those conditions, and should not be detrimental to healthier and younger people.

Adverse effects of metformin treatment should not be surprising given the listed mechanisms of action, which essentially slow down metabolic processes. You might live longer, but at the cost of being less alive from a metabolic standpoint. Moreover, metformin has been shown to cause vitamin B12 deficiency, lactic acidosis and gastrointestinal side effects.[474] In several studies, taking metformin in conjunction with doing exercise *blunted* the benefits of that exercise in terms of factors such as improvement in insulin sensitivity, skeletal muscle mass and overall cardiorespiratory fitness.[475,476] Thus, while metformin may be beneficial in older patients with pre-existing chronic disease, it may not be suitable for younger, healthier people.

Other drugs being looked at to slow or inhibit senescence include rapamycin and Beta-hydroxybutyrate, but these studies are still in their early stages.[477] Ongoing research continues to target multiple aspects of the senescence pathway as well as attempt to nip it at the bud altogether. Because of the potential to do harm to normal cells, senescence treatments are not without potentially significant adverse effects.

In the next section, we will look at actions outside the laboratory we can take that might limit or slow down the effects of ageing. The topics will be broken down into physical activities, dietary changes and supplements.

18

What Does Your DNA Good? Surprise, it's Exercise and Diet (and maybe Supplements).

I don't stop when I'm tired. I only stop when I'm done.
—Marshawn Lynch

In the previous chapter, we looked at molecular-level factors that influence the ageing process. Reactive oxygen species' detrimental effects on DNA are strongly believed to be the primary, unifying cause of intra-cellular ageing while cellular senescence is what leads to its recognizable, external manifestations. Additional elements such as methylation and telomere length and their effect on the cellular life cycle were also examined. Finally, dietary and medical treatments to counteract ROS and senescence are being studied and have already shown some success.

In this chapter, we will examine three lifestyle elements that are documented to have beneficial effects on the molecular pathways of ageing we have just investigated. Targeted drugs come with side effects and are currently scant and incompletely proven. Thus, optimizing our lifestyle is possibly the best current option to minimize DNA damage and chronic inflammation, preserve telomere length, and limit cellular senescence, thereby slowing the ageing process. The three lifestyle interventions we will discuss are exercise, calorie restriction and antioxidant supplements.

Exercise

And in breaking news, exercise is good for you. Apart from it being a great excuse to prance around in overpriced yoga pants, it has also been well established that moderate and regular exercise reduces the effects of ageing by decreasing oxidative stress levels[478] and chronic inflammation.[479] Although increased physical activity during exercise does increase ROS formation via its energy production requirements, our body responds by increasing its antioxidant response accordingly which improves its ability to deal with subsequent oxidative challenges.[480, 481] A review by Powers et al. (2020) weighed the double-edged sword that is vigorous exercise and concluded that it is unlikely to result in oxidative stress that is harmful to us.[482]

Other research, however, does recommend exercising caution with excessive physical activity. In the study by O'Keefe et al. (2020), researchers found that "chronic excessive endurance exercise" is associated with arrhythmias, myocardial fibrosis (stiffness of heart muscle), coronary artery calcification, and sudden cardiac death.[483] They suggest that the ideal amount of moderate or vigorous physical activity is 2.5-5 hours/week and that greater than 10 hours/week may be detrimental.

As a likely result of its ability to improve our ROS response, reduction in inflammation and possibly due to stimulation of increased telomerase activity, exercise has been associated with longer telomeres in many studies.[484, 485,486] In an article by Puterman et al. (2010), exercise was suggested to buffer the effect of chronic stress on shortening telomere length.[487]

Sounding a contrarian viewpoint, some researchers called into question the popular belief linking telomere length to exercise in their article, "Telomeres, Aging and Exercise: Guilty by Association?" (2017).[488] Note the lack of an Oxford comma. They point out that about 50% of studies show no relationship of physical activity to telomere length and suggest that telomere length may simply be the result of a healthier physiology and not the primary cause for it. Meaning, if the cell's DNA has sustained less damage via inflammation or ROS for other reasons, the telomeres will naturally be longer and not necessarily due to exercise. Ultimately, however, they state that the association between telomere length and exercise is "biologically plausible" given the preponderance of research supporting it.

Moving on, the social nature of exercise also seems to factor into its health benefits. In a study out of Copenhagen (2018) ,[489] it was observed that sports that involve more social interaction were associated with the best longevity improvement compared with the sedentary control group. Ranges of years gained were: tennis, 9.7 years; badminton, 6.2 years; soccer, 4.7 years; cycling, 3.7 years; swimming, 3.4 years; jogging, 3.2 years; calisthenics, 3.1 years; and health club activities, 1.5 years. This observation should not be surprising given the data presented earlier about the health benefits of relationships.

In addition to its association with improving our oxidative stress response and possibly our telomere length, there is abundant data that associates physical activity with healthier brains. Neuroscientist Wendy Suzuki gives very simple advice: "Do your brain a favor – move your body."[490] Physical activity has been shown to lower risk of diabetes, multiple sclerosis and neurodegenerative conditions such as Alzheimer's disease. Equally important, exercise improves our cognitive thinking and memory while increasing our sense of well-being.[491]

Although the pathway through which exercise affects brain health is not completely clear, it is known that factors released by contracting muscles—called myokines—do cross the blood brain barrier, stimulating specific neural pathways.[492] In particular, cathepsin B is believed to interact with the hippocampus, the area in the brain involved with learning and memory. There it enhances the production of Brain-Derived Neurotrophic Factor—BDNF (from Latin *troph-*, meaning "food"). BDNF is involved in most aspects of neuroplasticity, which is the ability of the brain to adapt to its changing environment via changes in its neuronal architecture and signaling pathways. Intensity, duration and frequency of exercise directly correlated with BDNF levels, with activities requiring more concentration or having a social aspect being associated with relatively higher elevations of BDNF. Interestingly, in animal models, stress caused decreased BDNF gene expression[493] while exercise led to demethylation (causing activation) of the BDNF gene.[494] These both represent epigenetic influences.

In contrast to exercise and its health benefits, leading a sedentary life and its risk of obesity is strongly associated with chronic inflammation and increased ROS formation in fat tissue. Both of these negative influences lead to DNA damage, telomere shortening and accelerated ageing.[495] More oxidative stress occurs with obesity due to the greater blood volume and its commensurately greater energy production and ROS formation.[496]

* * *

Though it is not surprising that exercise helps us be healthier, looking at how it specifically affects our DNA and cells adds context to this axiom and possibly motivates us to be more consistent in our physical practices and tailor them toward more social varieties of exercise. In the next section we will explore the other major means of managing our health: what we put in our mouths. This topic, like many others I have endeavored to cover in sections of each chapter, is a vast subject that normally comprises entire books. Thus, I will focus on a how a specific aspect of diet affects the health of our DNA.

Calorie Restriction

Calorie restriction (CR), also known as energy restriction, is defined as reduced caloric intake without malnutrition and was first noticed to increase lifespan in a study done on rats in 1939.[497] In 1993, researchers noted that mutations that reduced food intake in our trusty nematode *C. elegans* also demonstrated the "paradigm-shifting discovery" of life extension by up to 50%.[498] In mouse and rhesus monkey models, CR has been shown to be protective against age-associated DNA methylation patterns.[499,500] Although CR has yet to be shown to definitively increase human lifespan, it has been consistently demonstrated to decrease susceptibility to multiple age-related human conditions including cardiovascular disease, diabetes, cancer and naturally, obesity.[501,502] As a result of this research, CR is called "the most robust universal healthspan and lifespan-promoting intervention in species ranging from yeast to mammals"[503] and remains the only well-established method of improving health through diet.[504] In a broad sense, the ability of CR to improve lifespan and healthspan makes intuitive sense since less food equates with less overall metabolism, with a resultant decrease in metabolically-produced ROS and resultant oxidative DNA damage. However, the specific pathways by which this happens have yet to be fully described.

The first clinical trial of CR in non-obese people was started in 2007 and is called CALERIE, or Comprehensive Assessment of Long-Term Effects of Reducing Intake of Energy.[505] Do you get the sense someone was trying really hard to cleverly title this study? This was a 2-year randomized control trial by Ravussin et al. (2015), and it showed that CR was safe and feasible in nonobese people as well as effective in promoting weight loss. The study's CR goal was a 25% decrease over control diets; however, participants only achieved an average CR decrease of 11.7% over 2 years (19.5% reduction during the first 6 months and 9.1% over the remainder of the study). Baseline mean caloric intake was about 2,400 kcal/day for both groups. Though the length of the study was too short to draw conclusions about potential longevity benefits, CR did result in similar changes to longevity modulators seen in animal models and decreased risks factors for cardiovascular and metabolic disease. In addition, weight loss in the CR group was 7.6kg and predominantly due to body fat loss.

An offshoot study (referred to as a *post-hoc analysis*) using data from the CALERIE trial looked at DNA from the white blood cells of study participants.[506] For this analysis, the researchers developed something called a *bioclock*, which is a test that attempts to measure the pace of ageing from a single blood test. Their test, called DunedinPACE (catchy name, no?), and others like it are DNA methylation tests that are purported to be accurate clocks for assessing biological age that predict onset of various diseases and even forecast lifespan (what?!).[507] Using this test and the study data, researchers found that CR resulted in a 2-3% reduction in the pace of ageing, which is believed to translate to a 10-15% reduction in the risk of death. The results were not entirely conclusive though because they did not corroborate with the results of two other bioclock tests.

PhenoAge[508] and GrimAge[509] are two previously developed biomarker tests that were originally designed as research tools to test possible anti-ageing effects of laboratory interventions. However, as DNA decoding in the lab led to commercial offshoots such as 23andMe and Ancestry, these bioclocks have since been widely marketed to the public as direct-to-consumer biological ageing tests. These DNA methylation tests are claimed to be able to tell you such things as if you will have cancer or Alzheimer's disease, when you will have menopause, and finally, reveal your "time-to-death" and "time-to-coronary heart disease." Let's take a moment to disimpact this.

Even if we assume the claims of these biomarker tests' accuracy are true, my question about them is the following: What are you going to do with the results? What if it tells you that you are 10 years biologically older than your age? Easy, right? Change your lifestyle, eat better and exercise more. And if it tells you are you are the same biologic age as chronologic age? Would you not also try to live a healthier life? And finally, if it tells you that you are biologically younger than your chronologic age, after biomarker-shaming your buddies, are not going to continue to adopt healthy life habits? If the best and most obvious path is always going to be leading a healthy lifestyle, why get the test?

A more nuanced issue is that these tests represent a snapshot in time of whatever biomarkers are being looked at. Because of their newness, it is not clear yet how quickly if at all these markers might be affected by lifestyle changes and therefore how to interpret the data over time. In contrast, there are well-established blood tests that do not cost $300 a pop and that do assess health risk for the common causes of human disease and can be followed over time to determine whether your risk is increasing or decreasing. Although there is understandable excitement and individual curiosity about the use of these modern age crystal balls, the reality is that they are still in the early stages of development and generate conflicting results with each other,[510] all the while potentially creating anxiety or complacency in the tested individual.

Getting back to the health benefits of CR, though its ability to prolong human lifespan remains to be proven, it does play a role in recognized anti-ageing pathways. Overall, CR carries a potent anti-inflammatory effect[511] and by so doing, decreases the risk of inflammageing, a clever combination term incorporating inflammation and ageing.[512] No lie. Inflammageing is marked by chronically elevated levels of inflammatory markers that are thought to be causal factors in cardiovascular disease and risk factors for diabetes, kidney disease, cancer, depression and dementia. Many studies have also shown that CR decreases oxidative stress[513,514] and improves insulin* sensitivity,[515,516] both of which are associated with longevity. Finally, it is also hypothesized that CR may augment our DDR system,[517] and in mouse models, CR has been shown to suppress cellular senescence.[518]

**Endocrinology 101: Insulin is made by the pancreas to regulate glucose levels for all our body's organs. Since glucose is our cells' primary source of energy, glucose regulation is a big deal. When we eat carbohydrate-rich foods, glucose gets absorbed in our gut, passed into our bloodstream, and insulin gets secreted in order to lower our blood glucose. Insulin sensitivity is a good thing because that means our body's tissues readily take in glucose when insulin is secreted, limiting the deleterious effects of hyperglycemia. In contrast, insulin resistance causes all sorts of bad stuff because there is more glucose in our bloodstream. The combination of insulin resistance and decreased production of insulin is the cause of Type 2 diabetes, which affects 1 in 10 Americans and is typically due to obesity and physical inactivity.*

Another mechanism by which CR may benefit health is via inducing a short-lived stress response in the organism, which accordingly shows an associated increase in cortisol secretion.[519] This makes sense because if you are not ingesting glucose, cortisol is secreted to increase your blood glucose concentration for what your body assumes is a fight or flight situation. However, a prolonged stress response can lead to both muscle and bone breakdown, heart disease, diabetes, weight gain and suppression of your immune system.[520,521] So a little CR stress is a good thing; starvation is not.

Persistently high blood sugars also lead to greater production of advanced glycation end products (AGEs). AGEs are proinflammatory proteins, nucleic acids (DNA) or lipids that have sugars like glucose attached them.[522] They have been implicated in the ageing process, causing development or worsening of chronic conditions such as diabetes, cardiovascular and kidney disease and neurodegenerative disorders.[523,524,525] AGEs are believed to cause their deleterious effects by—you guessed it—increasing oxidative stress and causing formation of ROS. As a result, AGEs are also referred to as glycotoxins.

In addition to being made in our bodies, AGEs also are present in food, some more so than others and dependent on cooking and preservation methods. Notably, high temperature and low moisture drive AGE formation. Ingested AGEs have been shown to be absorbed into our bodies.[526] A study by Uribarri et al. (2010)[527] contains a comprehensive listing of AGE concentrations by food item, but be forewarned, it will likely cause low level panic to peruse it. Foods such as fish, legumes, low-fat milk products, vegetables, fruits, and whole grains are low in AGEs, while solid fats (yum!), fatty meats, full-fat dairy products, and highly processed foods are high in AGEs. In addition, boiling or stewing meats and adding acidic marinades such as lemon juice or vinegar lowers AGE concentration. On top of all the downsides presented to having high blood sugars, it also makes you look older.[528] The mechanism—you guessed it, again, ROS and their deleterious effects on the tissues making up your face literally add years to your appearance. So chew on that. Just don't broil it before you do.

Calorie restriction should not be equated with intermittent fasting—also referred to as time-restricted eating, another popular dieting trend. The distinction between CR and intermittent fasting (IF) is that IF does not equate with CR. One may consume the same or greater number of calories daily even while engaging in IF. In addition, most research has looked at the benefits of CR, not of IF.

That being said, there are still demonstrated benefits to IF even without CR. A study by Aksungar et al. (2017)[529] looked at a group of overweight (Body Mass Index 29-39) Muslim women aged 28-42 years. This group represents a unique model of IF in humans, and researchers followed a group of 23 participants over 2 years. They found that CR was almost 3 times more effective in promoting weight loss than IF (without CR). However, participants in the IF group still showed much of the same cellular and health benefits as those in the CR group.

Intermittent fasting may hold an advantage over CR in that it does not require a neurotic fixation on calorie counting. In a study by Lin et al. (2023),[530] they found that 8-hour IF without calorie counting still resulted in significant weight loss compared to controls and but not as much as in CR participants (10 lbs. in IF vs 12 lbs. in CR over one year). Perhaps the most interesting and encouraging fact was that the IF group also decreased their daily calorie consumption about the same as the CR group (about 400 calories) even though they were not instructed to do so. In this way, one might avoid laboriously counting their calories and instead engage in IF and have similar health benefits. For reference, the recommended daily intake is 2,000 calories for women and 2,500 calories for men. Therefore, a CR of 400 calories equates to 16-20% CR per day.

Because not eating is hard, people have looked at how to mimic the clear health benefits of CR with a pill. These are referred to as calorie or energy restriction mimetics (CRM/ERM) and include the previously discussed metformin and the about to be discussed resveratrol.[531] Spermidine—guess where that was harvested from?—is another CRM being studied.[532] One can only imagine the circumstances that led to *that* discovery. That being said, these should be approached with caution, though, as no CRM has been shown to mimic the positive properties of CR without adverse effects, e.g., metformin.

In conclusion, there is very convincing data linking CR with decreased risk of chronic conditions, better looks and improvement of healthspan, if not lengthening of lifespan. Ultimately, it may not ever be practical to prove that CR increases human longevity in a controlled clinical setting due to factors such as time, money, the duration of human lifespans and ethics. It's typically frowned upon to have interventional studies where one of the outcomes is death.

* * *

A personal health intervention I undertook was impaling my arm with a continuous glucose monitor (CGM) for 3 months. My father had type 2 diabetes, and I have a proclivity for sweets and carbs, so I thought it prudent get real time information on what foods, drinks and behaviors do to my blood glucose levels. I found that cereal is bad, and fats and protein are good. Cheese, no problem. Nuts, medium. Walking after lunch, very good. Getting dental procedures, bad. Sleeping early and consistently, good. Although the CGM provided extremely useful information, it also made me dysfunctionally neurotic. I really could not enjoy my meals or beverages without perpetually being worried about my next glucose spike. Ultimately, I used the knowledge I gained from wearing it, lowered my hemoglobin A1C (a blood test for glucose control that gives you a sense of your average blood sugar for the past 3 months), and then I ripped it off.

In the next and final section in this chapter, I will touch on the potential benefits antioxidant supplements have on our health. Although it is clear that lifestyle and diet are the best means of limiting the effects of chronic conditions and the manifestations of ageing, there is unquestionably an appeal to good health in pill-form.

Antioxidants in Foods and Supplements

Antioxidants are molecules that inactivate ROS in one of two ways: by enzymatically breaking them down or by combining with them and making them inert, a process also known as scavenging.[533] When our body's natural antioxidants are overwhelmed by ROS, oxidative stress ensues. In addition to cancer, oxidative stress is believed to contribute to such diverse conditions as inflammatory and ischemic diseases, AIDS, emphysema, organ transplantation complications, gastric ulcers, hypertension, preeclampsia, neurological disorders, alcoholism, and smoking-related diseases.[534]

Multiple nutrients from our diet have been shown to possess antioxidant activity. [535] Vitamin E,[536] Beta-carotene,[537] and vitamin C[538] are all believed to protect against cancer and other oxidative stress-induced conditions by their antioxidant and anti-inflammatory properties. They also specifically protect telomere length and in so doing, limit cellular apoptosis and senescence. Vitamin E is found in plant-based oils, nuts, seeds, fruits, and vegetables. The richest sources of beta-carotene are yellow, orange, and green leafy fruits and vegetables. Vitamin C is rich in citrus fruits (oranges, kiwi, lemon, grapefruit), bell peppers, strawberries, tomatoes, cruciferous vegetables (broccoli, Brussels sprouts, cabbage, cauliflower) and white potatoes.

A personal favorite of mine, dark chocolate (70%–85% cacao) has been identified in a number of studies to qualify as a legitimate health food due to its antioxidant properties and other health-promoting characteristics.[539] In addition to being both a ROS scavenger and an antioxidant defense upregulator, cacao constituents improve our immune response, limit inflammation in our nervous system and may also protect against diabetes by modulating insulin resistance. Most significantly, dark chocolate has been shown to consistently lower multiple risk factors for cardiovascular disease, the most common cause of human death and disability.

One additional health-promoting compound I will spend a bit more time reviewing is resveratrol due to its super-supplement status. Resveratrol is a naturally occurring polyphenol and is an intensely investigated bioactive compound found in many foods since its anti-cancer effects were first described in 1997.[540] These effects are mediated via multiple factors, with apoptosis induction being the significant one. Resveratrol also acts as a senomorphic, helping neutralize the harmful byproducts of senescent cells. Along with ginseng, resveratrol has been shown to inhibit stem cell senescence in the laboratory.[541] Finally, resveratrol is believed to be a key component accounting for the so-called "French paradox," where despite consuming a diet high in saturated fat, French people do not die off from coronary artery disease.[542] This is believed to be due mainly to resveratrol's strong antioxidant and anti-inflammatory properties as well as its ability to relax blood vessels.[543] As it turns out, red wine—loved by the French almost as much as cigarettes and not showering—contains high concentrations of resveratrol. But of course!* In a rodent study looking at heart muscle damage following ischemia, the optimized dose of resveratrol was extrapolated to be equivalent to a single glass of red wine per day.[544]

**More recently, the purported effects of red wine consumption on cardiovascular health in humans have been called into question, with some studies showing no benefit while others point out that achieving the resveratrol concentrations necessary would involve consuming more than 200 bottles of wine daily.[545] Check, please. Emphasis has been placed on other potentially health-beneficial behaviors French people exhibit such as exercising and other lifestyle factors. Clearly, there are some gaps to be filled in when attempting to scientifically account for the purported health benefits of drinking red wine, and therefore one might need to drink their cab with a grain of salt, enjoying it for what it is.*

In addition to its lowering of cancer and heart disease risk, resveratrol also possesses pro-immunologic, anti-obesity, anti-diabetic, and cholesterol-lowering properties. It has moreover been shown to protect against liver disease and neurodegenerative disorders such as Alzheimer's and Parkinson's Disease[546] and cognitive decline in general.[547] Resveratrol has truly earned its title as a "miraculous natural compound."[548] Can I get an OMG?!

Resveratrol is detectable in over 70 plants species but is most concentrated in the skin of red grapes and Japanese Itadori tea. In addition, pomegranates, nuts, blueberries, and dark chocolate are also reported to contain resveratrol in varying concentrations.[549] Historically, the issues with attempts to ingest resveratrol were its low absorption and short half-life in blood. However, resveratrol can be produced in mass quantities in the lab using fungus or E. coli,[550] and a study done in 2016 showed that taking just 500mg daily was sufficient in providing a therapeutic level of it.[551] Currently, you can buy one hundred and eighty 800 mg capsules of resveratrol on Amazon for $24.99 with free one-day Prime delivery.

It should be noted that many of the studies looking at resveratrol's biologic effects have not been done on humans or even in live animals.[552] In addition, many of the human studies showed no significant benefit. An article by Meng (2020) et al. provides a comprehensive and fairly current review of resveratrol's effects in the lab and in humans.[553]

Though generally thought to be safe, resveratrol does have potential adverse effects.[554] For instance, it demonstrates a specific type of dose-dependent effect—referred to as *hormesis* (Greek for, "to set in motion"), which describes the varying effects of a toxin or stressor on an organism, whereby it is actually beneficial in small doses but harmful in high doses.[555] This concept might be summarized by 19th century German philosopher Friedrich Nietzsche's aphorism, *What doesn't kill you makes you stronger*. Indeed, this effect exists for most things in our environment, including water and oxygen. However, there are particular substances and phenomena of interest that display this behavior.

The mechanism whereby chemicals or stressors have a hormetic effect is thought to be via induction of adaptive responses at the cellular and organism level. Indeed, hormesis is a key idea in evolutionary theory; organisms need to be exposed to toxic stressors in order to evolve mechanisms to more efficiently deal with them.[556] Our discussion of the beneficial role of low levels of ROS is a prime example of hormesis. In addition, carbon monoxide, fatal in high concentrations, is necessary in small amounts for neural signaling.

And on the organism level, exercise and intellectual pursuits both demonstrate hormetic benefits by generating cellular stress and ROS formation, making those muscle cells and neurons better adapted for subsequent stresses and possibly making them more resistant to ageing. Caloric restriction is also thought to benefit health via its hormetic effects that slightly increase cortisol secretion. In conclusion, with hormesis, a little stress goes a long way, and this may be one of the behavioral keys to mitigate the cellular causes of ageing.

Back to resveratrol, at low doses, resveratrol exerts a protective effect on cardiovascular and neurologic diseases. However, at high doses, it worsens those same conditions (bad thing) while it inhibits tumor growth (good thing).[557] It is theorized that the same *pro*-oxidative properties lead to both health side effects and tumor inhibition. These results have been observed in the lab and in animal models, but not humans as of yet.[558] Thus, in resveratrol's case, more is not necessarily better, and it seems resveratrol is what one study calls, "A double-edged sword in health benefits."[559]

The daily beneficial ranges of resveratrol dose vary but has been reported to be between 1-5 mg/kg of body weight. For example, if you weigh 150 pounds (68 kg), you should take between 70-350 mg of resveratrol per day. In rats fed greater than 25 mg/kg daily, resveratrol induced a cellular death signal in their heart tissue.[560] I hate it when that happens. That would amount to 1700 mg in the 150-pound person. So why does the resveratrol bottle I bought on Amazon recommend I take 1600 mg daily? Next question. In seriousness, studies in humans have shown that doses up to 5000 mg daily are safe.[561]

Although it likely does have health-promoting properties, resveratrol—

or any other supplement for that matter—are not the only answers to living long and prospering. Accordingly, reservation with resveratrol or any other hot new pill must be taken, and it behooves all of us to exercise our due diligence before putting them in our bodies. As discussed earlier, ROS do play an important stress-adapting biologic role and therefore bombing our bodies with antioxidants may not be prudent, with resveratrol hormesis serving as a cautionary tale.

In conclusion, resveratrol and dark chocolate are just two representatives of the many purported health ingestibles being touted. Rather than trying to provide an exhaustive list of them, my intention was to provide a scientific foundation upon which how to understand their common actions and make individual decisions going forward.

Alcohol and Caffeine

Before wrapping up this section on the potential health effects of things we take in orally, I need to address two last consumable elephants in the room: alcohol and caffeine. Despite playing a pivotal role in the history of humanity and human rituals since it was first made from rice in 7000 B.C. in China[562], alcohol is known to be toxic to cells and is causally linked to a number of cancers, including those affecting the esophagus, liver, breast, colon, oral cavity, rectum and probably the pancreas.[563] The carcinogenic mechanisms include direct DNA damage, inhibition of DNA repair, and DNA methylation disruption leading to oncogene activation.[564] In addition, alcohol can induce inflammation and cause oxidative stress.

On the other hand, it might be overly harsh to judge humanity's addiction to this toxic substance without recognizing its significance to human history. Indeed, some archaeologists believe that alcohol and the other chief human substance addiction—caffeine—were essential in the development of modern civilization.[565] Yang to alcohol's Yin, caffeine was cultivated later in human history and is a stimulant as opposed to a depressant. As such, caffeine and coffee spurred activity and innovation and was called by Thomas Jefferson, "the favorite drink of the civilized world." Moreover, caffeine has antioxidant and anti-inflammatory properties and is associated with decreased cancer risk.[566]

In light of the resveratrol data, some people might ask if there is there any amount of alcohol ingestion that may be healthy. Sorry, party people, the World Health Organization has declared that "No level of alcohol consumption is safe for our health."[567] Moreover, a study from the United Kingdom in March 2022 by Daviet et al. entitled, "Associations between alcohol consumption and gray and white matter volumes in the UK Biobank" concluded that even moderate amounts of alcohol ingestion (1-2 drinks/day) is associated with brain shrinkage.[568] However, the researchers did acknowledge that their study design did not allow for a cause-effect conclusion to be made.

But what about hormesis?! In one last desperate attempt to quell your cognitive dissonance with alcohol consumption, you might ask if it is possible that the intake of a small amount of alcohol may also provide health benefits by mildly stressing our bodies. One study looked at this and concluded that indeed one drink increased serum antioxidant activity, while three drinks increased pro-oxidant activity. It should be noted that this study was partially funded by Labatt and Guinness brewing.[569] No conflict of interests there.

Nevertheless, an inverse association between light to moderate consumption of alcohol (1-2 drinks/day) and cardiovascular risk has been consistently noted in a large number of epidemiologic studies.[570] In one article by Cui et al. that looked at patients with prediabetes or type 2 diabetes (2023),[571] researchers found that light consumption (less than 1 drink/week) decreased risk of all-cause mortality by almost 50% while heavy drinking (≥30 g/day for men and ≥15 g/day for women) increased stroke risk by 2.5 times. For reference, 30g of alcohol roughly correlates with 2 beers, 2 glasses of wine or a heavy shot of liquor. In the end, there is perhaps some protective effect of mild alcohol consumption. Researchers state this effect, however, does not warrant becoming a drinker for the sake of health if you are not currently one. Nice try.

Moving on, what about alcohol's influence on the creative process? Over the ages, from Socrates to Sinatra to *Bridesmaids*, alcohol has made its mark in human history's inspirational moments. Hemingway said, "Write drunk. Edit sober." Check.

Austrian psychologists looked at this perceived phenomenon in their cleverly titled study, "Creativity on tap? Effects of alcohol intoxication on creative cognition" (2017).[572] This was a randomized control trial that compared cognitive and creative performance between sober participants and those with an average blood alcohol concentration of 0.026. Importantly, all participants reported feeling "a little bit intoxicated." Researchers found that participants with mild intoxication performed worse in a test of executive control but better in a test of creative potential.* They concluded that "small attenuations of cognitive control may facilitate certain aspects of creative cognition" and that "higher cognitive control is not always equivalent to better cognitive performance."

> **Participants with mild intoxication scored higher in the Remote Associates Test (RAT), which is a test of creative potential. It was developed in 1962 and has since been considered as a valid measure of creativity. For example, the RAT presents three unrelated words (e.g., cottage, blue, cake) and asks for a solution word that provides an unexpected connection between them (answer: cheese) https://www.remote-associates-test.com/*

In the end, the health case against alcohol is quite strong with, at best, questionable objective benefits to humanity. Although abstention may be in our body's best interests, like my 1600 mg resveratrol capsules, it may be a hard pill to swallow for some of us. Because of the unlikely probability of universal abstinence, some research has looked at potential mitigating behaviors to offset alcohol's known detrimental effects. For instance, it has been suggested that pretreatment with antioxidants such as vitamins E and C may limit some of the oxidative stress brought on by alcohol.[573] Maybe that's why they put limes on cocktails. And in a study by Baglietto et al. (2005), researchers found that taking folate supplements might protect against the increased risk of breast cancer caused by alcohol. [574] Finally, if Saturday night moderation is unlikely, coffee and electrolyte supplements have been shown to reduce alcoholic hangover symptoms.[575]

Closing thoughts on DNA damage and Ageing

Reactive oxygen species and other products of chronic inflammation unquestionably cause DNA damage. There are clear pathways that lead to increased generation of these detrimental molecules, and specific lifestyle circumstances and behaviors may limit or augment them. Although it is very likely that DNA damage plays a central role in ageing, the evidence as yet is not solidified. First, it has not been convincingly shown that improving DNA repair extends lifespan.[576] Second, it is not yet possible to quantify DNA damage. Without knowing how much damage occurs, research cannot prove an association between damage and longevity and how much damage can be prevented by interventions. Lastly, studies have only identified a small number of DNA repair genes in ageing-related diseases or organisms with extreme longevity.

The counter for the above arguments against DNA damage being a driver of ageing is simply that genes and ageing are inordinately complicated, and deciphering the evolutionary intricacy of all the processes involved may not be in our wheelhouse currently. Moreover, most research supports and most researchers believe DNA damage to be the primary molecular cause of ageing, since no other physiological repair defect has the same deleterious effect on ageing. This makes the most sense since during the time of primordial soup, the main ingredient in that broth was DNA, and its preservation was the one and only goal.

* * *

Remember when there was all the rage with Sudoku—that logic-based number grid game—with hordes of people everywhere perpetually burying their faces in those 5" x 8" paperbacks? Peoples' obsession turned so extreme that in one instance, a drug-related jury trial in Australia was stopped because some jurors had been playing Sudoku instead of listening to the evidence.[577] I object! The purported benefits ranged from improving concentration to reducing stress and anxiety to growing your gray matter. Sound familiar? Turns out it doesn't, at least according to one study looking at the effect of so-called "brain-training games." [578] Alas, the study concludes, doing the *New York Times'* crossword or Sudoku doesn't stave off Alzheimer's disease; it only makes you better at doing the *New York Times'* crossword or Sudoku, respectively. As it turns out, saying "Hi!" to the person sitting next to you on the plane, train or automobile may be healthier for you than figuring out what number goes in what box. And so it goes.

In similar fashion, I would caution against going all in on the biohacks I reviewed. Following research is great, but following people is better. That didn't come out right. Anyway, although it is indeed exciting, and science may be on the cusp of developing age-defying treatments, pumping our expectation brakes may be in order. Science moves at the speed of, well, science, and the fountain of youth is not likely to be discovered before your next birthday. There's a stock expression in experimental biology: *from the bench to the bedside.* This refers to results obtained while seated on a lab bench (really it's a stool or comfortable chair, not a bench, but I didn't make this up) being quickly translated to treatments for patients at the bedside. At this point, I'd say we're still trying to find out what floor our patient is on.

Though there is certainly evidence that science can at least partially outwit nature and time, remember that many of the changes that are being measured on the molecular level are the result what we do with ourselves on a daily basis. Focusing too much on what is happening to our DNA and trying to alter it at the cellular level without also looking at how our environment and the choices we make are possibly the causative factors is failing to see the forest for the trees.

The reality is that many people who are interested in the science of how to live better and age slower are already living better and likely aging slower as a result of their lifestyle choices. Understandably we might want to eke out as many good years as we can with our bodies, but this is best done in tandem with the psychosocial and awareness work described previously. While you are popping your supplement horse pills, make sure you are getting consistent sleep and minimizing your stress. Before you start metformin or another drug du jour, consider putting regular trail playdates on your calendar. Finally, you might benefit from alternating between falling into the rabbit hole of basic science reading and spending those twenty minutes before bedtime meditating. Of course, these two sets of goals are not mutually exclusive. However, time and energy are limited, and as always, finding balance remains the elusive objective.

Nostalgia: It's all in your mind

It's been a whirlwind two chapters, and I have presented a lot of information looking at the complex relationship between the effect of environment on our DNA and the resultant manifestation known as ageing. Alas, in 2023, there is still no cure for living. Even if you happen to hit the healthy disposition lottery and dutifully execute the longevity hacks being touted, at some point, your body will start to decline. Our tickets will still get punched sooner or later. If you are lucky (or unlucky, depending on your perspective), you will still be able to remember when the days were sunny, the grass was green, and you had a full head of hair with someone to stroke it. When we get too old to do the things we used to, we may yet reap the benefits of those activities in the form of nostalgia. One could think of this as a mental repurposing of past accomplishments and adventures that are no longer possible.

It turns out that taking trips down memory lane are in fact good for us. In a study by Naidu et al. entitled, "Reliving the Good Old Days: Nostalgia Increases Psychological Wellbeing Through Collective Effervescence" (2023),[579] researchers found that although nostalgia involves an oftentimes melancholic longing, it still increases psychological well-being. This is mediated by our old friend, collective effervescence (discussed in the chapter about having fun), whereby the positive effects of the events are renewed when they are recalled and relived. This is because the moments we choose to nostalgize (yes, it's a legit word) about are typically those when we were connected to others and life felt special. Our days and these moments with our companions are numbered though, so rack up those nostalgic episodes while you can, because they will come in real handy when you are getting disimpacted. Seize the day, before the day seizes you.

The *carpe diem* message is executed to lyrical perfection in one of my favorite poems. Written by 17th century English poet Andrew Marvell and entitled, "To His Coy Mistress," it is a classic seduction poem in which he writes:

... But at my back I always hear
  Time's wingèd chariot hurrying near;
  And yonder all before us lie
  Deserts of vast eternity.
  ... Let us roll all our strength and all
  Our sweetness up into one ball,
  And tear our pleasures with rough strife
  Through the iron gates of life:

Thus, though we cannot make our sun
Stand still, yet we will make him run.

Now, should nostalgia not be your cup of awareness tea, and you seek unlimited refills of your chalice, the next chapter is for you.

19

I'll Take Immortality Please.

Our overblown intellectual faculties seem to be telling us both that we are eternal and that we are not.
—Stephen Cave

I don't want to achieve immortality through my work. I want to achieve it through not dying
—Woody Allen

Ageing and death are polarizing topics. In one camp, there are those who accept these as necessary consequences to being born, perhaps realizing that the opposite to the great truth of life is of course death. And then there is the other camp who have set their sights on the loftiest goal of physical well-being, living forever. For most of human history, immortality has been the promise of mythology and religion. However, with advances in the understanding of ageing we reviewed in the previous chapter, there are some people who believe eternal life is within reach.

Even though money cannot buy happiness, numerous Silicon Valley billionaires have bet that maybe it can buy immortality. These business giants, including the likes of Peter Thiel, PayPal co-founder and Jeff Bezos, who undeniably have the most materially abundant lives in the world are also the people who want to live forever, [580] putting their money where their mouths are and investing billions into research for immortality.

Larry Ellison ponders, "Death has never made any sense to me. How can a person be there and then just vanish, just not be there?", Mark Zuckerberg wants an answer to the question, "What will enable us to live forever?"[581] In contrarian fashion, Elon Musk states, "I can't think of a worse curse than living forever…having a good life, for longer, is better."[582,583] Musk's opinion is partially founded on his belief that if people in positions of influence do not die, new ideas will not be birthed, and society will stagnate. In the same camp, celebrity astrophysicist Neil deGrasse Tyson opines:

It is the knowledge that I am going to die that creates the focus that I bring to being alive. The urgency of accomplishment. The need to express love — now, not later. If we live forever, why even get out of bed in the morning? Because we always have tomorrow. That's not the type of life I want to lead.[584]

The cognitive conflict that is {not} literally slapping Mr.'s Ellison, Zuckerberg and various other super rich techies in the face is the *Mortality Paradox*. Coined by Cambridge University philosopher Stephen Cave, it is summarized thus:

On the one hand, our powerful intellects come inexorably to the conclusion that we, like all other living things around us, must one day die. Yet on the other, the one thing that these minds cannot imagine is the very state of nonexistence; it is literally inconceivable. Death therefore presents itself as both inevitable and impossible.[585]

Renaissance philosopher Michel de Montaigne writes that "to lament that we shall not be alive a hundred years hence, is the same folly as to be sorry we were not alive a hundred years ago."[586]

English moral philosopher Bernard Williams[587] is decidedly not a fan of living forever and argues that immortality would result in an "intolerable boredom." Critics call Williams and his proponents "Immortality Curmudgeons," and state there is no reason that someone who enjoys life as a mortal would not want to enjoy it forever.[588]

In the cult classic movie, *Groundhog Day*, newscaster Phil Connors, played by the perfectly droll Murray, is blessed with immortality and forced to re-live Groundhog Day countless times, awakening every morning on February 2 to "I Got You Babe." Initially in disbelief but realizing there are no consequences to his actions, he embarks on a course of entertaining hedonism. Seeing no end to the repeated day and falling into despair—as a result of his happiness set point—he commits various comical acts of literal self-destruction in an attempt to escape, one involving kidnapping the groundhog and driving off a cliff while berating the animal, "Don't drive angry! Don't drive angry!" Ultimately, he takes the high road and betters himself by learning piano and French, ice-sculpting, being kind, inspiring others, and even saving people's lives. The cycle is finally broken after Phil falls in love—of course—with his producer played by the enchanting Andie MacDowell and wakes up on February 3, still to "I Got You Babe" but now with MacDowell next to him.

* * *

Perhaps a healthier psychological mindset about our mortality straddles the multiple perspectives I have presented. While unbounded immortality optimism may be unrealistic, seeing tedium and boredom with unlimited life may be too pessimistic. Indeed, staying positive may lead to living longer. One study found that people having positive self-perceptions of ageing lived 7.5 years more than those who did not.[589] Thus, while incessant preoccupation with mortality may distract you from living life, being aware of death may motivate you to live a fuller life. In the end, since living forever is not on the menu today, making the most of the time we do have seems the only reasonable path for us mere mortals without astronomical disposable incomes. This all-in approach to life may have been best penned by twentieth century Welsh poet Dylan Thomas (1914-1953):

> *Do not go gentle into that good night,*
> *Old age should burn and rave at close of day;*
> *Rage, rage against the dying of the light.*

* * *

Really, I'll Take Immortality

Moving on from the philosophical aspects of immortality, let's look at the current state of realistically achieving it. Here I think it's important to make a distinction between living forever and not ageing, as the former without the latter would an unpleasant existence make. So, any reasonable entertaining of immortality must be accompanied with drastically minimized ageing (see previous chapters). Having said this, let's proceed.

Biological immortality does exist in nature, and it is seen in unicellular organisms such as bacteria and yeast. When it comes to multicellular organisms, the list becomes shorter. The previously cited 19th century evolutionary biologist August Weismann noted that the cells of *Pandorina Morum*, a type of green algae, were immortal and divided without limit.[590] The reason he hypothesized for their immortality was their lack of differentiation, which ended up being exactly right. This distinction was previously alluded to when discussing stem cells versus somatic cells. The former cells are undifferentiated and retain the capacity for unlimited replication while the latter are differentiated and do not. The underlying reason that differentiated cells are unable to continue dividing seems to be linked to their limited and diminishing telomerase activity. As discussed earlier, this is an enzyme that re-grows telomeres after each cell division, effectively resetting the cell's biological timer. Without telomerase, each cell division ticks down the time to cellular senescence or apoptosis. In contrast, embryonic stem cells retain telomerase activity and in so doing, are functionally immortal.[591] (Cellular immortality has been defined as replication in excess of the Hayflick[592] limit, which is about 50 cellular divisions in vitro.[593])

So if one key to cellular immortality is persistent telomerase activity, what can't you buy jars of it on Amazon? Cancer. Recall that cells die or become senescent for a reason—mainly due to accumulated DNA damage. Uncontrolled cellular division is the definition of cancer, and indeed, telomerase activation is thought to be a mandatory step in carcinogenesis. OK, what about those stem cells that are functionally immortal? Why don't they cause cancer? It turns out that all the theories of how cancer develops point to involvement of aberrant stem cells.[594] Doh!

The history of research looking at human cellular immortality had a pivotal and egregious moment in 1951. That is the year that Henrietta Lacks, a 31-year-old African-American mother of five, came to Johns Hopkins Hospital in Baltimore, the only institution that would provide free care to black Americans in that area. Henrietta was diagnosed with an aggressive cervical cancer, and two months after her admission, she died.[595,596,597] As was the custom of the time, without her permission or knowledge, her treating providers harvested cells from her cancer. They quickly discovered the remarkable ability of her cancer cells to replicate quickly and seemingly infinitely. Henrietta's cells became the first immortal human *cell line*.

A cell line is a lineage of cells that all derive from a common parent cell, serve the same function and have the ability to be stably duplicated over time. In basic science research, having a cell line is the equivalent of having unlimited twins for study. Both have identical DNA that are identically expressed, and as a result, it enables researchers to carry out experiments and draw conclusions more readily since everything is controlled for except the intervention being studied.

Naming Henrietta's cell line *HeLa,* researchers continued to duplicate these cells, use them for studies and even publish the entire genome for decades before the family was made aware of it. The HeLa cell line was used subsequently to develop the polio vaccine and treatments for cancer, HIV/AIDS, leukemia and Parkinson's disease. In 2009, it was reported that more than 60,000 articles had been published about research done using the HeLa cell line.[598] In August 2023, the Lacks' estate settled a lawsuit against Thermo Fisher Scientific, alleging the company continued to mass produce HeLa and profit from it even after it was revealed her tissue was taken without her consent.

So we have seen that cellular immortality in a multicellular organism is typically bad for its health due to malignant transformation from accumulated DNA damage. However, what if you coupled cellular immortality with a souped-up DNA repair mechanism? Enter the hydra. One of the earliest purported examples of an immortal multicellular organism is this little guy.[599] Hydra are simple freshwater animals, measuring from 10 to 30 mm tall to 1 mm wide, that possess the ability to regenerate and form 2 new hydra when cut in half. They contain between 50,000 to 100,000 cells (humans contain 30,000,000,000,000) and are visually reminiscent of the many-headed beast from Greek mythology.

The secret behind hydra's immortality success is multi-fold. First, they have the ability to both maintain their cellular telomere length while simultaneously having efficient DNA repair mechanisms.[600] Recall that telomere shortening is one failsafe against cancer due to ac-cumulated DNA damage. As a result of telomere length maintenance, it is believed that hydra cells do not undergo senescence. Another reason for hydra's age-defying behavior is by virtue of its high level of cell proliferation and renewal. Rolling stones gather no moss. In other words, if cells are being constantly renewed, senescence and its effects—even if present—cannot do their damage. Finally, hydra's immune system is also thought to be very efficient in protecting it against environmental stress and pathogens, both of which can lead to cellular damage and ageing.

So multicellular immortality in nature does exist, albeit in an organism with about 400 million times fewer cells than we have and likely fewer end of year projects and less access to fast food than we do. However, by studying hydra's clever ageing workarounds, although we may not be able to achieve immortality, it is possible to devise methods to stave off both cellular senescence and its after-effects.

As discussed in the previous chapter, one target of treatments such as metformin and supplements such as resveratrol are senescent cells and their ageing byproducts. The goal of these interventions is to create a state of so-called *negligible senescence*. In nature, there are multiple species that demonstrate this and resultantly exhibit both extended longevity and show few if any of the negative effects of ageing. Examples of these species include the naked mole rat, giant tortoise, ocean quahog clam, rockfish and Greenland shark, whose lifespans range between 200 to 500 years.[601]

Accordingly, research has looked at the mechanisms by which these organisms mitigate senescence.[602] What seems consistently true across these long-lived species is their enhanced ability to deal with oxidative stress. The picture is not completely clear, however. For instance, naked mole rats show more oxidative damage and possess less robust repair mechanisms, but still live longer than their rodent cousins; this is inconsistent with the free radical theory of ageing. In addition, the quahog clam's longevity seems to be independent of its telomere length, again not in line with the previously discussed mechanism for cellular longevity.

Studies have also looked at the shortest-lived vertebrates, such as the African turquoise killfish, whose maximum lifespan is 13 weeks. The idea is instead of trying to duplicate the longevity mechanisms found in longer-lived species, to alternatively try to prolong the lives of shorter-lived animals. What this research points to is the key role of the mitochondrion in lifespan. In addition, diet supplementation with the super-supplement resveratrol[603] (thought to act as a calorie restriction mimetic) and recolonizing the gut of older killifish with bacteria from younger killifish[604] (strengthening the proposed link between the gut microbiome and longevity) both resulted in lifespan extension.

Now before you rush off and ingest gobs of probiotics, it should be noted that in the study with killfish, antibiotics were given prior to recolonization in order to kill off the existing old-fish gut microbiome. In addition, the type of bacteria used and the specific timing of recolonization were critical components in increasing lifespan. Moreover, it was found that colonization of young killfish with older killfish microbiota did not result in decreased lifespan. The researchers concluded that the younger killfish's immune system was also a protective factor. Finally, there is not yet any study to date that demonstrates increases in human lifespan with microbiome manipulation.

Benefits of gut recolonization in humans has mainly been shown to be of benefit in cases of intestinal infections, commonly caused by *Clostridium difficile* (commonly known as *C.diff* colitis).[605] The technique in which this is performed, known as *fecal microbiota transplantation*, involves, you guessed it, transferring one person's poop into another person's intestines, typically from the bottom, using a colonoscope (camera that gets put where the sun don't shine). However, for those who do not fancy this invasion of their privates, in May 2023, the FDA approved a capsule with a near 90% success rate at eliminating *C.diff* infections.[606,607] Initially marketed as *Poop-in-a-Pill* (artistic license at play here), that got nixed by experts, and it is now known by the catchy name *SER-100*.

There is one other relatively new and exciting strategy to indirectly decrease the effects of ageing by acting as a senolytic treatment (removal of senescent cells). Known as *chimeric antigen receptor T-cell therapy*, (CAR T-cell), the treatment has been shown to successful in mice, increasing their survival and limiting the other adverse effects of senescent cells.[608] Originally developed to combat certain types of cancer such as leukemia, CAR T-cell treatment's first successful application came in 2011. The process involves harvesting the patient's T-cells, genetically programming them to recognize specific markers on cancer (or senescent) cells, making millions of copies of them, then re-injecting them back into the patient to do their job eliminating these cells.[609] Though promising, this type of treatment is extremely expensive—costing upwards of $500,000—and is not without significant side effects including confusion, seizures and a potentially fatal condition called cytokine release syndrome.

In summary up to this point, non-cancerous immortality for our 30 trillion cells is perhaps far from attainment, but extension of healthspan by various current and not too far-off options seems realistic. By limiting collateral damage in the form of oxidative damage and mitochondrial dysfunction using novel treatments and supplements, cellular senescence and its ageing manifestations may be delayed.

* * *

There is one last, possibly best hope for finding the path to forever. For this, let's journey to the Italian Riviera circa 1988, when acid-washed jeans were all the craze and Sophia Loren at age 54 might have been undergoing her midlife crisis. While summering and soaking in the heavenly waters, a German and Italian student discovered that the jellyfish, *Turritopsis dohrnii*, was ostensibly immortal.[610,611] What they noticed was that in response to environmental stressors, the adult forms of the jellyfish—called medusas—could age in reverse, becoming their infant versions—called polyps. They could then develop back into adult medusas and then return to their younger selves multiple times. Rinse and repeat. This has been observed to occur up to 10 consecutive times in controlled conditions over 2 years, making this jellyfish seemingly immortal.[612]

The mechanism by which *Turritopsis* performs this ageing sleight of hand is via a process called *transdifferentiation*.[613] This is where cells at any stage of development can turn into cells in a different stage of development. Normally, stem cells become differentiated somatic cells, and never the twain shall meet. However, with transdifferentiation, somatic cells can turn back into stem cells, making them immortal and that organism effectively young again, ala Benjamin Button (originally a short story by F. Scott Fitzgerald, it describes the life of a man who at birth appears 70 years-old, then continues to age in reverse).

Transdifferentiation represents the holy grail of ageing science and occupies the dreams and I daresay the nocturnal admissions of tech billionaires. Mind you, *Turritopsis* are about 4.5 mm x 4.5 mm—the size of your little fingernail—and similar to hydra, their feats of ageing trickery are performed on a scale magnitudes smaller than mammals and primates. While in *Turritopsis* and other jellyfish species, transdifferentiation is common, in vertebrates, it is extremely rare.

Eighteen years after the Riviera discovery, Japanese researcher Shinya

Yamanaka discovered what some have called the fountain of youth cocktail. In 2006, he published a landmark article that detailed a biochemical process that was able to cause differentiated mouse cells to turn back into stem cells using a special concoction of only 4 proteins, aptly referred to as the Yamanaka factors.[614] One year later, he was able to achieve the same results in human cells.[615] For this discovery, he rightly earned the 2012 Nobel Prize.[616]

Since this discovery, there have been several key experiments using the Yamanaka factors as a possible means of age reversal in mice. One of the first studies was in 2013 by Serrano et.al, and although it did indeed cause differentiated mouse cells to revert to stem cells, they also grew a bunch of tumors called teratomas.[617] This is the price of immortality referred to earlier. A second study from January 2023 (which has not undergone peer review) showed that elderly mice (124 weeks) injected with 3 of the Yamanaka factors lived another 18 weeks, compared to mice without the factors who lived only 9 weeks more.[618] No negative effects were reported in this study. In one last study, a team from Harvard showed that the Yamanaka factors could reverse some age-associated DNA methylation changes.[619]

As stated before, science moves at the pace of science, or at least it should. Accordingly, some critics have voiced concerns about the pace at which these Yamanaka factor studies are being done. Biologist Alejandro Ocampo points out that the number of studies published about the use of Yamanaka factors in a living organism is the same as the number of companies doing it.[620] This is understandable though as billions of dollars are being poured into research to fund these companies, and the temptation to jump in is justifiably high.

One such company is California based Altos Labs, backed by Russian billionaire Yuri Milner and Jeff Bezos and consulted on by Shinya Yamanaka himself. It's founder and chief scientist is Richard Klausner, former director of the U.S. National Cancer Institute. Klausner states Yamanaka's discovery represents "the biggest revolution in medicine, health, maybe even society, that humanity has ever experienced" and that it is even more important than the discovery of the structure of DNA.[621]

Despite the hype and money, critics remind us that there are major obstacles that need to be overcome before any conceivable human therapy is developed. First, Yamanaka factors involve the induction of genes, some of which cause cancer, and treatment without death is widely considered important. Second, gene therapy is not something that you can just walk into your doctor's office and get. Third, there needs to be way to monitor treatment outcomes that do not involve waiting for someone to die.

Because humans live much longer than mice or African killfish, determining if a specific intervention has successfully made someone younger is logistically difficult from a survival or purely visual standpoint. This is where the various biomarker tests we discussed in the previous chapter *may* come in handy. For instance, by looking at someone's epigenetic DNA methylation patterns, it may be possible to assign an accurate biological age before and after treatment with Yamanaka factors or any other intervention to determine if it worked. This is of course assuming the biomarker tests are accurately measuring biological age *and* will predictably change with treatment, both of which remain controversial.

All of this being said, proponents will remind us that the ability to make old cells young again is indisputable and reproducible in the laboratory. Moreover, far from being an outlandish technology, cellular reprogramming occurs each time mom and dad make a baby, as their adult DNA with all its years of epigenetic ageing imprints are wiped clean and a fresh, albeit slimy-faced baby is born. It remains to be seen when and if these interventions are optimized for and available to the population at large. Until then, exercise and diet remain decent options.

* * *

Before concluding the discussion on immortality hacking, let's take a moment to explore some of the logistical and ethical considerations that will arise if and when this advancement occurs. In an article in the *Financial Times* by Anjana Ahuja, she asks if life extension becomes the default, will refusal equate to suicide?[622] Furthermore, she wonders if it will it be possible to stay happily married to someone for 200 years!? Echoing Musk's concerns, Ahuja questions whether there will be stagnation of ideas and progress if old people don't kick the bucket. Another stark reality is what happens when your friends or family do not decide to prolong their lives? What kind of mind trip exists for those who stay young while their children and everyone else they knew grow old and die? Of similar import is the question will dating profiles read, "...enjoy walks on the beach, the Oxford comma and partners under 400 years-old?"

A more subtle stagnation issue with markedly prolonged life is that it would result in humanity's retaining the same gene pool over a long period of time. This might effectively stale our species' evolution by eliminating natural selection. That said, one could argue this phenomenon already exists with the abundance of resources and food we have had available since the industrial revolution, making survival and procreation a foregone conclusion for much of the world's population.

Another moral dilemma with radical life extension is how old is enough? How much time should each person be allotted, and how will this be decided? Will life be like an arcade game, when you can you add time by flicking in another quarter? The rich are already known to outlive the poor,[623] and life extension treatment would not conceivably play out differently.

As to the question of if it is ethical to radically prolong life, philosopher John Davis reminds us that the historic goal of much of medicine has been the prolongation of life, so extreme life extension should not be considered differently.[624] Point taken. Davis also justifies the disparity in those who will want life extension and those who might not get it by comparing it to modern-day organ transplant recipients and non-recipients. Perhaps Davis is basing his opinion on the truism that two wrongs make a right.

Ingemar Linden is another philosopher and author of the upcoming book, *The Case Against Death.*[625] You might be able to guess his stance on extended lifespan. He writes, "If our life and future is valuable, then dying is one of the worst things that could possibly befall us…I am a death abolitionist and a life prolongevist." Ingemar might do well to hire a new prose editor.

And in the other corner, Venki Ramakrishnan, chemistry Nobel laureate, minces no words when he states that "the older generation has to get out of the way" and that radical life extension is "advocated by California billionaires who are having such a good time at the party of life that they don't want it to stop. They don't want to go out into the cold night at their appointed time."[626]

Polarizing opinions aside, overpopulation and all of its demands on our planet's resources are already upon us, and radical life extension flies in the face of that reality. One could argue that life prolongation might allow great minds more time to develop technology to offset the impact of an even greater population. I guess we shall see.

* * *

In the next chapter, the final one, we will move from eternal life to a discussion of what has always been and remains a reality of being born: death. I am going to try to make light of Thomas' *good night*. By framing death as a necessary price for the gift of life, we might allow ourselves a measure of dignity and peace whenever our time should come. I consider myself fortunate, as I have been in the presence of one birth and two deaths of family members, all of which occurred at home, with loved ones, outside the confines of fluorescent lights and beeping monitors. These personal experiences as well as those I have been witness to in my profession have given shape to the type of death I envision for myself.

It's been a good run, and I'm happy you've hung in here until now.

20

You Might Want a Death Plan

I've reached the point where I hardly care whether I live or die. The world will keep on turning without me, and I can't do anything to change events anyway.
—Anne Frank

We are here to laugh at the odds and live our lives so well that Death will tremble to take us. —Charles Bukowski

As an orthopedic surgeon, though I do not often witness death in my practice, I do attend to physical disability on a daily basis. For almost twenty-five years, I have treated patients ranging from a few months old to beyond 100 years young. I remember a particularly spry 95-year-old lady whose hip fracture I fixed with a titanium rod. When she walked in for her 6-week postoperative visit—having driven herself—she was accompanied by her 89-year-old boyfriend, and both of them were dressed to the nines, seemingly ready for a night out on the town. They had each been around long enough to be widowed twice, and I felt so inspired to see they were still living so fully. I checked her x-rays, examined her, and gave her a clean bill of health. She thanked me, and as she was leaving, I commented to her that some people might say she was robbing the cradle.

Over the years, I have seen many examples of patients like her who remained healthy and independent into their 80s and beyond. By seeing what is possible in my patients, I formed an intention to age as well as they did, often asking them what their pro tips are. Their common answer to how to stay independent for as long as possible was: stay independent for as long as possible. What they meant by this is to take care of yourself and don't rely on others to manage your life affairs for you. Singer and songwriter Paul Anka succinctly summarizes this approach by saying, "If you don't stay moving, they will throw dirt on you." Pauly started his career at age 14 and continues performing to this day at age 82.

All this being said, no matter how well we take care of ourselves, disability and death do come for all of us eventually. And despite death being the only certainty in our lives following the moment we are born, not many people like to think about it, let alone talk about it, let alone make a plan for it. Yet we make plans for everything else in our lives, little and big, but not death. The answer to *Why not?* is obvious. It is the answer to *Why should we?* that I will attempt to make a case for. Incidentally, talking about a death plan does not make for good first date banter.

Of course, I am referring to formulating a plan for death that we can anticipate, occurring by "natural causes" or chronic conditions, and not those due to unexpected trauma or violence. However, even with death that we can predict, it is often not until we or someone we care for is near or at the precipice of it that we finally address it. And at that point, there are all sorts of other items hitting the fan, both logistical and psychological, which must necessarily detract from our emotional bandwidth.

What is more problematic than death itself is the disability that often precedes it. It is the rate of progression of disability that is the key determinant to our quality of life as we round that last corner. The following graph schematically represents two extremes of disability progression at the end of our lives. The line with the steeper drop-off corresponds with a fairly short period of disability preceding death. The second line shows a gradual descent over time and represents a protracted period of disability. Excluding immortality, it is reasonable to presume that most people would prefer the shortest possible duration of disability to precede their death. It may be that some combination of the health hacks I discussed in the preceding chapters may allow us to live with maximal function for as long as possible. In addition, there may be other mechanisms that allow us to call our death shot, as it were, which I will get to later.

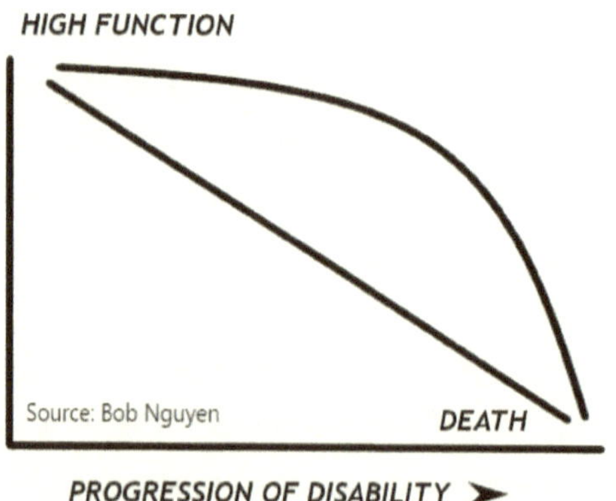

There were two personal death experiences I witnessed that planted the seed for and then solidified my intention to have a death plan. The first death experience—my ex-grandma-in-law's—followed the more abrupt decline, and the second—my father's—followed the more protracted path. Let's start in Russia.

* * *

It was November, and my ex-wife and I had just arrived at her grandma's *dacha*, which was their small exurban home on the outskirts of Moscow. It had two small rooms and running—but not hot— water, and the bathroom was outside. Though not yet snowing, the temperatures hovered around freezing during the day, which made each latrine excursion an exercise in maximal efficiency. In total, with other family and a family friend, there were six of us staying in this modest home.

My ex's grandmother had just turned eighty and had survived the harshness of a Soviet Russia with all of her wits about her. She had a head of cropped, white hair that required little or no maintenance, stood about 4'11", and had kind blue eyes. To cut to the chase, upon being introduced to me, her only granddaughter's new husband, she sized me up, smiled, and said, "Nice to meet you." She hugged and kissed me, and after some pause said, "I believe my granddaughter is in good hands. So I can die now." Hearing the translation, I laughed uncomfortably.

That evening, I suggested we go out and eat in Moscow to celebrate. These being simple folk, going out for dinner was something they had done a handful of times in their lives. To her credit, my ex's grannie partied it up, drinking wine and dancing to the string-heavy, dreamy Turkish music that was playing in the restaurant.

Early the next morning, I was awoken by my ex who frantically told me her grandma had just collapsed while having her morning tea. I found her down, went through the checklist of basic life support—checking her ABCs (airway, breathing, circulation). Her airway was open, but she was not breathing, and she had no pulse. I started CPR. This continued for about 45 minutes before paramedics arrived, at which point I stopped CPR and stepped aside. They did not take over. Instead, they stood there and simply said, "What do you want us to do? She's old." Although initially shocked, as a physician, I of course saw the sense in this approach. Even if they were successful in reviving her, the most likely outcome after such a long period of cerebral oxygen deprivation would be severe brain damage, with her languishing and unresponsive in an intensive care unit for days or weeks, never regaining consciousness, with her family burdened with the decision of when to withdraw care.

* * *

Fast forward 15 years to 2016. My dad had retired at age 82 from the private practice that he and my mother opened about 25 years prior. At the time, my siblings and I were happy that our parents could finally enjoy retirement. However, because he had dedicated his whole life to work in order to provide for us, at the time he retired, he did not have any hobbies or relationships to fall back on. He had not repurposed himself. My mom, on the other hand, remained intellectually active after retirement by managing the multiple rental properties they owned, and to this day she remains sharp and physically independent as a result.

About three years into his retirement, my dad was at home with my mom and my sister. Being diabetic, he was prone to hypoglycemic events, and so on this particular morning, feeling those pangs, he was rapidly and haphazardly stuffing food into his mouth. One of these items was called bánh tét, a type of Vietnamese cake consisting of a sticky rice exterior with a core of various fillings, some savory, some sweet. And believe you me, these are delicious! Unfortunately, he failed to adequately chew one prior to swallowing it, and it completely blocked his airway. As he frantically inhaled, he drew the sticky rice right into his lungs and came very close to choking to death right there. My sister had the presence of mind to recognize this and attempt a Heimlich maneuver, but this was unsuccessful due to the sticky consistency of the food. Using her fingers, she manually scooped out as much of the rice as possible, and after he collapsed, initiated CPR, while my mom called 911. Once the paramedics arrived, they employed a non-Russian approach and resuscitated my father, taking him to the closest hospital which was only 2 miles away.

Admitted to the ICU, the medical term for my dad's condition was aspiration pneumonia, whereby instead of going down the esophagus, food or liquid contents take the path into the lungs. We've all had this experience to minor degrees, but imagine instead of just one bit of that crème brulet going down the wrong hole, the entire piece goes in there. The ensuing inflammatory response to the foreign material coupled with whatever bacterial load is in that piece of food leads to this very severe type of lung infection. That same evening, the ICU attending came in to discuss what advanced medical directives we had in place for my dad. Basically, he was communicating that there was a more than small probability my dad would not survive his ICU admission.

For context, in pre-COVID times, the mortality rate of patients over the age of 80 admitted to the ICU or hospital ranged close to 50%.[627] (During COVID, 6-month mortality went up to 72%.[628]) My brother and I implicitly understood this, but it was still hard to take in. My dad's ICU neighbor in fact passed away, and to keep the statistics true, my dad willed himself to survive, and he was discharged from the hospital and back home 4 days later.

This sounds like a happy ending, right? Not so much. Data shows that in patients over 80 years-old discharged from the ICU after pneumonia, there is a 3.6 to 10.1-fold increase in mortality over the next 2 years.[629] And so, for the next four years, my dad's level of function took that path of gradual decline shown in my graph. He never regained his pre-ICU level of strength, cognition, or ability to take care of himself. More than once after his ICU discharge, my dad needed to be brought back into the hospital because he had failed to stay properly nourished and hydrated at home. These were short admissions though, and he would be sent home tanked up.

We get to March 2020, shortly after the COVID-19 pandemic officially started in the U.S., and my dad was nearing his 89th birthday. For the past eighteen months, he had gradually lost the ability to independently get up and walk, toilet and feed himself. Even his communication dwindled to uttering only a few words at a time. My 80-year-old mom had become his full-time caretaker, and it was obviously exacting a toll on her both emotionally and physically. It's impossible for me to describe the tragedy of seeing this man who had escaped his war-torn home and worked so hard with my mom to rebuild their lives from scratch, providing for my siblings and I with all the opportunities we had, decline to this level. Sprinkled into this tragedy, though, were sweet moments such as watching my 6-year-old daughter spoon feed him and me tucking him in at night, kissing his forehead, telling him I love him, with him thanking me.

In the week preceding his birthday, my dad had once again stopped taking in food, even when fed by hand. When he also stopped taking in liquid, this was a much graver sign. With this being COVID times, no one was allowed to be with their family members in the hospital. So as a family, we had a decision to make. We could send my dad to the ER where COVID was spiking and where he would be alone, unable to communicate for himself, where at best he would be resuscitated and discharged home. And at worst, he would be admitted for an indeterminate amount of time and undergo any number of invasive and resuscitative measures. There would the ever-present risk of COVID infection and realistically, death, and all of this with none of us able to be at his side. Even should he escape the hospital again, to what quality of life would he be returning? My dad's present condition did not represent an abrupt change to his state of health. He had not been drinking wine and dancing the evening before. Even though he no longer communicated verbally to any significant degree, I believe he continued to be aware of his reality. I believe his cessation of taking in liquids was a choice, the only one left he could make himself. It was a choice that said that he had had enough and that he was ready to be done.

As a family, we continued to deliberate our options over the following hours. Dad was sat up in a chair and for the most part unresponsive, taking agonal* breaths. However, there was a brief moment when we were all in the same room, where he abruptly opened his eyes, looked around, and seemed to take us all in. This was his moment of clarity, sometimes referred to as terminal lucidity, in which there is a sudden and unexpected return of awareness occurring shortly before death.[630] Less than an hour after this moment, we watched my dad take his last breath.

> *Agonal breathing is a distinct form of abnormal and erratic breathing mediated by the primitive part of our brain in response to a life-threatening condition. If the underlying condition is not corrected, agonal breathing eventually leads to cessation of breathing and death.*

* * *

While both my ex-grannie and dad had lived full lives into their 80s, the manner in which they spent their final moments and years were markedly different. Witnessing both of their deaths made a lasting impact on me that I naturally came back to once I started contemplating my own mortality. I believe the most pivotal factors in my grannie being able to let go were that she felt she had lived a full life and that she knew her loved ones were taken care of. She retained her agency until her last sip of black tea with honey, while my dad slowly lost his bit by bit over the course of years.

To me, my grannie's passing could not have been better scripted. I witnessed it at the beginning of my career, and at the time, it was difficult for me to fully take in and understand how someone's mind could exert ultimate and immediate control over their body. I chalked it up to coincidence. However, over the course of my career since then, I have seen first-hand the influence someone's expectations and intentions have on their return to health following surgery or injury. In comparable patients with the same injury and in whom I have performed the same surgery, there is often striking inconsistency in their recovery patterns.

Indeed, psychological factors are known to be associated with surgical outcomes. In one study from the journal *Anesthesia* (2019),[631] it was demonstrated that surgical patients with pre-existing anxiety, depression and low self-efficacy consistently had more postoperative pain with worse physiological surgical outcomes and postoperative quality of life.

Given that a person's level of well-being or lack thereof has been shown to have measurable and multiple effects on their physical health as we discussed earlier,[632] it's not hard to imagine that one's mind can consciously or undeliberately exert an influence on their physical recovery from surgery, and not just their subjective experience of it. Taken to the extreme, our minds might even be able to cause our own deaths. In fact, there is a recognized phenomenon of thinking yourself to death, referred to as *psychogenic death*, and it is just beginning to be understood.

British psychologist and researcher John Leach has devoted his career to the study of survival psychology. His research looked at historical life and death events from colonial Jamestown to slave ships to Auschwitz to the Vietnam War and cites examples where some people seemed to die at will while others survived.[633] In addition to Leach's investigations, there have been numerous subsequent and similar reports of death occurring soon after a terminal diagnosis is given to a patient. [634] Leach collectively groups these behavioral phenomena into what he calls *Dysexistential syndrome.* For more than 20 years, he failed to find a biological explanation for this until he realized he was barking up the wrong psychological tree. Instead of asking what allowed some people to survive while others died, he should have asked what makes some people die when there is no external cause for it?

To put this self-initiated death phenomenon into a bigger context, we need to reference the work of Walter Cannon, a pioneering physiologist of human emotions. In 1915, he first described the phrase *flight or fight,* which is an animal's emergency response to a perceived threat.[635] This response involves dramatic and rapid shifts in such things as the secretion of adrenaline and cortisol, organ-specific changes in blood supply, glucose availability, and clotting capacity, all in an effort to limit harm and increase survivability. Since Cannon's initial description of this basic animal survival response, two other "F's" have been added: freeze and fawn.[636] These two responses occur when an animal is unable to escape a threat and represent forms of our *passive* coping response. In contrast, flight or fight are types of our *active* coping response.

Leach hypothesized that psychogenic death may be the result of an unchecked passive coping response—basically, when the *freeze* reaction goes on too long. In his study from 2018, he refers to psychogenic death as *give-up-itis* (this term makes a play on the medical suffix *-itis,* meaning inflammation) and suggests one biological mechanism by which it can occur.[637] The pathway he homed in on involves the prefrontal cortex and the basal ganglia and our favorite neurotransmitter dopamine. Disequilibrium of these dopamine pathways results in persistently decreased production of it, with the resultant emotion of hopelessness.* If this goes on too long, the person takes a cerebral dive-bombing run referred to as a "spiral of disengagement."[638] This process starts with withdrawal, progresses to apathy, and ends in psychogenic death unless the person adapts to their situation and snaps out of it.

> *Recall the varied roles of dopamine in our nervous system, including pleasure and our perception of time. With prolonged disruption of specific dopamine pathways, researchers such as psychiatrist David Kissane suggest the resultant emotional consequence is demoralization, which is the feeling that pleasure will not be experienced over an extended period of time, not just in the present. Unchecked, this may be one mechanism for psychogenic death.*

Although Leach's research and hypotheses center around mortality that occurs in otherwise physically healthy people in circumstances of extreme psychological stress, psychogenic death could conceivably be in play during end-of-life situations when a person has decided they are done with living, like my grannie. Many of us may have known lifelong couples who passed away within a short time period of each other. The context may be different, but the neural mechanisms may be similar. Instead of overwhelming turmoil leading to hopelessness, it may be the absence of regret and a feeling of completion that lead to conscious resignation with the similar end result of death. To my knowledge, no study has been published to look at this, so I grant it is solely my conjecture.

In another one of his insightful books, *Being Mortal: Medicine and What Matters in the End,*[639] Atul Gawande writes, "The only way death is not meaningless is to see yourself as part of something greater:

a family, a community, a society. If you don't, mortality is only a horror." I imagine for my grannie, she absolutely saw herself as part of something greater and as a result, rather than being horrified by death, she opened herself to it once she felt complete in her life.

Though he does not call it a death plan, Gawande does emphasize the importance of identifying what is important to each individual as they approach the end of their lives. Options range from living at home to nursing homes to assisted care facilities; oftentimes this is determined based on the individual's medical needs and personal finances. Perhaps more important than where a person spends their last days is what aspects of life they consider optional and what they consider hard stops. Do they need to be able to communicate, feed themselves and not be hooked up to machines? How much pain is too much? When considering the loved ones they leave behind, what cost is too much to keep themselves alive? None of these are easy questions to answer, but they are necessary to ask.

Answering all these questions does not translate to being able to manifest our own death. However, it does spell out our intentions and wishes for the end of life. In so doing, it psychologically paves our yellow brick road home and facilitates decision-making for those involved in our care.

* * *

If manifesting your own death is one side of the death plan coin, the other side is physician-assisted suicide (PAS), or medical aid in dying. In this situation, physicians set up terminally ill patients to self-administer lethal doses of medication. This is currently legal in eleven jurisdictions: California, Colorado, District of Columbia, Hawaii, Montana, Maine, New Jersey, New Mexico, Oregon, Vermont, and Washington.[640] In the U.S., PAS is legal only on those patients who have a life expectancy of six months or fewer. Europe has historically been more progressive in this regard, and in countries such as Germany, Switzerland, Spain, Italy, Austria, Belgium and the Netherlands, patients need not have a terminal diagnosis, and voluntary euthanasia is also legal.[641]

Oregon was the first state to legalize PAS with its Death with Dignity Act of 1994. The three most commons reasons that people chose to end their lives were the loss of ability to enjoy life (96.2%), the loss of autonomy or independence of thought (92.4%), and the loss of dignity (75.4%).[642] Notably absent from this list is pain as a reason to end life. Also of note, as of early 2022, Oregon is now the first state to allow its doctors to prescribe life-ending drugs to out of state residents.[643]

I will not attempt to fully analyze the arguments for and against taking this active approach to death, but I will offer the following. On the one hand, no one would argue that retaining our personal liberty is paramount throughout our lives, including at the end of them. And on the other hand, opponents will argue that a slippery slope exists with PAS—in that its application might be eugenically expanded to disabled or chronically ill people and other vulnerable populations who may not understand or be given full informed consent. Preposterous? Recall that in this country, forced sterilization was carried out on people with Down's Syndrome and other disabilities until 1969.[644] Moreover, just as with the prospect of radical life extension, there is a potentially equal and opposite disparity between those who will have the privilege to live longest and what groups might be driven to curtail their existence.

Humanity is a curious species. Our dominant ability to survive had led to a paradoxical conflict of when to call our lives done, and the expression *first species problems* comes to mind. I do not believe there is a universally acceptable answer to this struggle, but I am sure that, if we allow it, there is a natural wisdom that can guide each of us in our passage from this world to whatever awaits us in the next.

* * *

After my father passed, my mother, my siblings and I, and my daughter were all able to stay with him. There were no beeping machines, no glaring lights, no interruptions by medical staff telling us our time with him was up. It was just us and my dad. We simply sat around next to his reposed body, recounting our favorite stories together, combing his hair and flattening out his wrinkles to make him as presentable as possible for his next journey. There was very little crying, as we all recognized that this man, who had provided for us his whole life and without whom none of us would be there, was finally free of his failed body and mind and would now exist forever in our hearts as the husband, father and grandfather we loved.

21

Conclusion

Not everyone goes through a midlife crisis, but this book was never really just about midlife. Rather, it's more about our shared human experience. But I needed a hook. Writing it has been an enriching exploration into some of the quirks and features of human behavior and biology. In lieu of a relationship, it has given me a consistent and healthy reason to wake up early and stay up late. Equally important, it has been a thoughtful means of connecting and sharing what I have learned along the way with people in my life, and now, with you the reader. There were so many times that something came up in conversation, and I would say, "That's in my book!"

I believe that at our core, we all want to connect with our fellow human beings, and that connection is the central source of joy during our time going around the sun. Throughout our lives, these opportunities for connection present themselves and we can choose whether or not to engage in them. I believe that if each of us looks at our lives, we can devise and realize our own personal journey of self-exploration that simultaneously connects us to others.

Crisis is a crucible, and I have always been someone who responds with my best self when I feel challenged. Maybe you are too. Since you have made it here, I challenge you to rethink your purpose, to cultivate the important relationships in your life, to do uncomfortable things, to break a sweat and have fun. Surround yourself with people whom you care for and who care for you. And though it may not be easy to believe at times, always remember that you have been and will always be worthy of love.

Our main opponent in the pursuit for individual growth is of course our own selves, and accordingly, each person's approach will need to be different. Each of us has diverse backgrounds and different obstacles –be it our hedonic set point, where we sit on the expectations spectrum or our specific life circumstances. I have tried to introduce a variety of psychological concepts and research-based findings in the hope that any reader may curate their personalized well-being and longevity strategies. I invite you to pick one or two health or happiness hacks I presented, publicly espouse them, and thereby allow yourself to become knowing devotees.

Life keeps coming, often requiring us to self-evaluate and recalibrate. In the words of Ram Dass, it's "as if you came into the kingdom of heaven and you saw how it all was and you felt these new states of awareness, and then you got cast out again."[645] At some point, personal crisis causes us to come down from our awareness peaks. Each time, we need to rediscover what will get us back there.

Timing is everything. I wrote this book because I felt I needed to write it. After the impulse to document my *a-ha!* moment occurred, it only grew stronger, and ignoring it was not an option. In my life, I have learned to recognize pivotal instants and realize that I have no choice but to pursue them to their logical endpoint.

I'll close with words that, as I reach my own midlife, are simultaneously prescient, urgent and clear.

Life moves pretty fast. If you don't stop and look around once in a while, you could miss it.

Crater Lake

Notes

INTRODUCTION

1   Blanchflower DG, Oswald AJ. Is well-being U-shaped over the life cycle? Soc Sci Med. 2008 Apr;66(8):1733-49. doi: 10.1016/j.socscimed.2008.01.030.

2   Rauch, Jonathan (2018). The Happiness Curve: Why Life Gets Better After 50. New York: Picador.

SAYING F*CK IT! WHEN YOU'RE 50

3   Ducharme, Jamie. Why the COVID-19 Pandemic Has Caused a Widespread Existential Crisis. Time Magazine online. DECEMBER 29, 2020 .

4   Galinsky, Adam and Kray, Laura. Op-Ed: How COVID created a universal midlife crisis. The Los Angeles Times. May 15, 2022.

5   Widdicombe, Lizzie. The Rise of the COVID Midlife Crisis: Why are so many women leaving corporate America? The New Yorker. August 14, 2021.

6   https://freakonomics.com/podcast-tag/commitment-devices/

7   Aronson, E. (1999). Dissonance, hypocrisy, and the self-concept. In E. Harmon-Jones & J. Mills (Eds.), *Cognitive dissonance: Progress on a pivotal theory in social psychology* (pp. 103–126). American Psychological Association.

8   Nordgren, Loran and Schonthal, David. The Human Element: Overcoming Resistance That Awaits New Ideas. (2021) New York: Wiley.

9   Milkman, Katy. (2021). How to Change: The Science of Getting from Where You Are to Where You Want to Be. New York: Penguin Random House.

THE MIDLIFE CRISIS PANDEMIC

10   Fontinelle, A. "What Is The Great Resignation? Causes, Statistics, and Trends." Reviewed by Potters, C. November 30, 2022. https://www.investopedia.com/the-great-resignation-5199074#:~:text=The%20Great%20Resignation%20describes%20the,of%20the%20COVID%2D19%20pandemic.

11   Cook, Ian (2021-09-15). "Who Is Driving the Great Resignation?". Harvard Business Review.

12   Epstude K, Roese NJ. The functional theory of counterfactual thinking. Pers Soc Psychol Rev. 2008 May;12(2):168-92. doi: 10.1177/1088868308316091. PMID: 18453477; PMCID: PMC2408534.

13   Nicuță, E.G., Constantin, T. Take Nothing for Granted: Downward Social Comparison and Counterfactual Thinking Increase Adolescents' State Gratitude for the Little Things in Life. J Happiness Stud **22**, 3543–3570 (2021).

14   Emmons, R. A., & McCullough, M. E. (2003). Counting blessings versus burdens: An experimental investigation of gratitude and subjective well-being in daily life. Journal of Personality and Social Psychology, 84(2), 377–389.

15   Broomhall AG, Phillips WJ, Hine DW, Loi NM. Upward counterfactual thinking and depression: A meta-analysis. Clin Psychol Rev. 2017 Jul;55:56-73. doi: 10.1016/j.cpr.2017.04.010. Epub 2017 Apr 27. PMID: 28501706.

16   Jaques E. Death and the mid-life crisis. Int J Psychoanal. 1965 Oct;46(4):502-14.

17   https://wilewomen.com/blogs/journal/why-isnt-there-a-female-midlife-crisis-and-why-were-calling-it-an-awakening

18   Lieblich A. Successful career women at midlife: crises and transitions. Int J Aging Hum Dev. 1986;23(4):301-12.

19   Hedgeman, E., Hasson, R.E., Karvonen-Gutierrez, C.A. et al. Perceived stress across the midlife: longitudinal changes among a diverse sample of women, the Study of Women's health Across the Nation (SWAN). womens midlife health 4, 2 (2018).

20   Carol Graham & Julia Ruiz Pozuelo, 2017. "Happiness, stress, and age: how the U curve varies across people and places," Journal of Population Economics, Springer;European Society for Population Economics, vol. 30(1), pages 225-264, January.

21   Weiss, Alexander; King, James E.; Inoue-Murayama, Miho; Oswald, Andrew J. "Evidence for a midlife crisis in great apes consistent with the U-shape in human well-being" Proceedings Of The National Academy Of Sciences Of The USA, Volume: 109 Issue: 49 Pages: 19949-19952.

22   Van Gennep, Arnold. Les Rites de Passage, 1909.

23   Campbell, Joseph. The Hero with a Thousand Faces (1949). Princeton: Princeton University Press.

24   Kondo, Marie. The Life-Changing Magic of Tidying Up: The Japanese Art of Decluttering and Organizing (2014). Berkeley: Clarkson Potter/Ten Speed.

YOUR 20S: ON YOUR MARKS...

25   Gail Sheehy, Passages: Predictable Crises of Adult Life (1974). Toronto: Clarke, Irwin and Co.

26   https://markmanson.net/

27   Jay, Meg. The Defining Decade (2012). New York: Twelve.

28   Sharot, Tali. The Optimism Bias: A Tour of the Irrationally Positive Brain. (2012). New York: Vintage.

29   Sharot, Tali. The Science of Optimism: Why We're Hard-Wired for Hope. (2012). TED book.

30   Matheson, SM, Asher, L, Bateson, M. Larger, enriched cages are associated with 'optimistic' response biases in captive European starlings (Sturnus vulgaris). Appl. Anim. Behav. Sci., 109 (2008), pp. 374-383.

31   Jennings, Will. Why costs overrun: risk, optimism and uncertainty in budgeting for the London 2012 Olympic Games. Construction Management and Economics 30 Apr 2012.

32   Cay M, Ucar C, Senol D, Cevirgen F, Ozbag D, Altay Z, Yildiz S. Effect of increase in cortisol level due to stress in healthy young individuals on dynamic and static balance scores. North Clin Istanb. 2018 May 29;5(4):295-301.

33   Justin B. Echouffo-Tcheugui, Sarah C. Conner, Jayandra J. Himali, Pauline Maillard, Charles S. DeCarli, Alexa S. Beiser, Ramachandran S. Vasan, Sudha Seshadri Circulating cortisol and cognitive and structural brain measures. The Framingham Heart Study. Neurology Nov 2018, 91 (21) e1961-e1970

34   Kim JK, Crimmins EM. How does age affect personal and social reactions to COVID-19: Results from the national Understanding America Study. PLoS One. 2020 Nov 10;15(11):e0241950.

35   Duell N, Steinberg L, Icenogle G, Chein J, Chaudhary N, Di Giunta L, Dodge KA, Fanti KA, Lansford JE, Oburu P, Pastorelli C, Skinner AT, Sorbring E, Tapanya S, Uribe Tirado LM, Alampay LP, Al-Hassan SM, Takash HMS, Bacchini D, Chang L. Age Patterns in Risk Taking Across the World. J Youth Adolesc. 2018 May;47(5):1052-1072.

36   Mather, Mark. Life on Hold: How the coronavirus is affecting young people's major life decisions. Population Reference Bureau. July 23, 2020.

37   Bellotti L, Zaniboni S, Balducci C, Grote G. Rapid Review on COVID-19, Work-Related Aspects, and Age Differences. Int J Environ Res Public Health. 2021 May 13;18(10):5166.

38   Walsh, Colleen. Young Adults Hardest Hit by Loneliness During Pandemic. The Harvard Gazette. February 17, 2021.

39   Frueh, Sara. The Pandemic 'Baby Bust' and Rebound. National Academies online. June 17, 2022

40   Frueh, Sara. The Pandemic 'Baby Bust' and Rebound. Jun 2022. https://www.nat ionalacademies.org/news/2022/06/the-pandemic-baby-bust-and-rebound

YOUR 30S: THE HEDONIC TREADMILL AND HAPPINESS SET POINT

41   Gail Sheehy, Passages: Predictable Crises of Adult Life (1974). Toronto: Clarke, Irwin and Co.

42   Bhattacharya K, Ghosh A, Monsivais D, Dunbar RI, Kaski K. Sex differences in social focus across the life cycle in humans. R Soc Open Sci. 2016 Apr 6;3(4):160097.

43   Bhattacharya K, Ghosh A, Monsivais D, Dunbar RI, Kaski K. Sex differences in social focus across the life cycle in humans. R Soc Open Sci. 2016 Apr 6;3(4):160097.

44   Miller, Claire. Where Young College Graduates Are Choosing to Live. New York Times online. Oct 20, 2014.

45   Rawlins, William. Friendship Matters: Communication, Dialectics, and the Life Course. (1992). New York: Transaction Publishers.

46   Shellnutt, Kate. Why 30 is the decade friends disappear — and what to do about it. Jul 12, 2016. Vox.com

47   Senthilingam, Meera. This is the age when you start losing friends. CNN online. June 6, 2016

48   Brickman, P., & Campbell, D. T. (1971). Hedonic relativism and planning the good society. In M. H. Appley (Ed.), Adaptation-level theory (pp. 287-305). New York: Academic Press.

49   Frederick S, Loewenstein G (1999) Hedonic adaptation. Well-Being: The Foundations of Hedonic Psychology, eds Kahneman D, Diener E, Schwarz N (Russell Sage Foundation, New York), pp 302–329

50   Diener, Ed; Lucas, Richard E.; Scollon, Christie Napa (2006). "Beyond the hedonic treadmill: Revising the adaptation theory of well-being". American Psychologist. 61 (4): 305–314.

51   Brickman, P., & Campbell, D. T. (1971). Hedonic relativism and planning the good society. In M. H. Appley (Ed.), Adaptation-level theory (pp. 287-305). New York: Academic Press.

52   Lykken, David; Tellegen, Auke (1996). "Happiness Is a Stochastic Phenomenon". Psychological Science. 7 (3): 186–189.

53   Brickman, Philip; Coates, Dan; Janoff-Bulman, Ronnie (1978). "Lottery winners and accident victims: Is happiness relative?" Journal of Personality and Social Psychology. 36 (8): 917–927.

54   Jachimowicz, J. M., Frey, E. L., Matz, S. C., Jeronimus, B. F., & Galinsky, A. D. (2022). The Sharp Spikes of Poverty: Financial Scarcity Is Related to Higher Levels of Distress Intensity in Daily Life. Social Psychological and Personality Science, 13(8), 1187–1198.

55   Jachimowicz, J. M., Mo, R., Greenberg, A. E., Jeronimus, B., & Whillans, A. V. (2021). Income More Reliably Predicts Frequent Than Intense Happiness. Social Psychological and Personality Science, 12(7), 1294–1306.

56   https://www.urban.org/urban-wire/real-homeownership-gap-between-todays-young-adults-and-past-generations-much-larger-you

57   Scheibe S, De Bloom J, Modderman T. Resilience during Crisis and the Role of Age: Involuntary Telework during the COVID-19 Pandemic. Int J Environ Res Public Health. 2022 Feb 4;19(3):1762.

58   Linkov, I., Galaitsi, S., Klasa, K., Wister, A. "Resilience and Healthy Aging." July 26, 2021. Psychiatric Times.

59   Jeste DV, Savla GN, Thompson WK, Vahia IV, Glorioso DK, Martin AS, Palmer BW, Rock D, Golshan S, Kraemer HC, Depp CA. Association between older age and more successful aging: critical role of resilience and depression. Am J Psychiatry. 2013 Feb;170(2):188-96.

60   https://www.wsj.com/story/from-twitter-to-meta-tech-layoffs-by-the-numbers-0afd8714

61   Contreras, Brian and Ding, Jamie. "In the wake of massive layoffs, tech workers reconsider their future." JAN. 24, 2023. The Los Angeles Times.

YOUR 40S: WAIT FOR IT…

62   Terkel, Studs. Working. (1972) New York: Ballantine Books.

63   Gail Sheehy, Passages: Predictable Crises of Adult Life (1974). Toronto: Clarke, Irwin and Co.

64   Brown, Noah. "Alcohol consumption during the COVID-19 pandemic projected to cause more liver disease and deaths." Massachusetts General Hospital, PRESS RELEASE DEC 2021

65   Barbosa C, Dowd WN, Barnosky A, Karriker-Jaffe KJ. Alcohol Consumption During the First Year of the COVID-19 Pandemic in the United States: Results From a Nationally Representative Longitudinal Survey. J Addict Med. 2023 Jan-Feb 01;17(1):e11-e17

66 Farberman, Rhea. "U.S. Experienced Highest Ever Combined Rates of Deaths Due to Alcohol, Drugs, and Suicide During the COVID-19 Pandemic." May 2022. The Trust for America's Health website.

67 Calls to suicide hotlines rise during COVID-19 pandemic by Michael Krafcik. Newschannel 3. Friday, July 17th 2020

68 Hannes Schwandt, Hannes. Unmet aspirations as an explanation for the age U-shape in wellbeing. Journal of Economic Behavior & Organization. Volume 122, 2016, Pages 75-87, ISSN 0167-2681

69 Carol Graham & Julia Ruiz Pozuelo, 2017. "Happiness, stress, and age: how the U curve varies across people and places," Journal of Population Economics, Springer;European Society for Population Economics, vol. 30(1), pages 225-264, January.

70 Sharot, Tali. The Optimism Bias: A Tour of the Irrationally Positive Brain. (2012). New York: Vintage.

71 Gail Sheehy, Passages: Predictable Crises of Adult Life (1974). Toronto: Clarke, Irwin and Co.

EMOTIONAL WELL-BEING: THE LAY OF THE LAND

72 Brooks, Arthur. From Strength to Strength: Finding Success, Happiness, and Deep Purpose in the Second Half of Life. (2022) New York: Penguin Random House.

73 Hollis, James. (2005). Finding Meaning in the Second Half of Life: How to Finally, Really Grow Up (2005). New York: Penguin Random House

74 Gail Sheehy, Passages: Predictable Crises of Adult Life (1974). Toronto: Clarke, Irwin and Co.

75 Welwood, John. On Spiritual Bypassing and Relationship. https://www.scienceandnonduality.com/article/on-spiritual-bypassing-and-relationship

76 https://thriveworks.com/help-with/self-improvement/self-worth-vs-self-esteem/

77 Svedberg P, Hallsten L, Narusyte J, Bodin L, Blom V. "Genetic and environmental influences on the association between performance-based self-esteem and exhaustion: A study of the self-worth notion of burnout." Scand J Psychol. 2016 Oct;57(5):419-26.

78 Winch, Guy, Ph.D. Emotional First Aid: Healing Rejection, Guilt, Failure, and Other Everyday Hurts. (2014). New York: Plume.

DO NOT PURSUE HAPPINESS

79   What Einstein meant by 'God does not play dice'https://aeon.co/ideas/what-einstein-meant-by-god-does-not-play-dice, edited by Nigel Warburton

80   Jiang Y, Zou D, Li Y, Gu S, Dong J, Ma X, Xu S, Wang F, Huang JH. Monoamine Neurotransmitters Control Basic Emotions and Affect Major Depressive Disorders. Pharmaceuticals (Basel). 2022 Sep 28;15(10):1203.

81   https://www.laphamsquarterly.org/happiness/impossible-dream

82   Gruber J, Mauss IB, Tamir M. A Dark Side of Happiness? How, When, and Why Happiness Is Not Always Good. Perspect Psychol Sci. 2011 May;6(3):222-33.

83   Mauss IB, Tamir M, Anderson CL, Savino NS. Can seeking happiness make people unhappy? [corrected] Paradoxical effects of valuing happiness. Emotion. 2011 Aug;11(4):807-15.

84   Carver CS, Scheier MF. Attention and self-regulation: A control theory approach to human behavior. New York, NY: Springer-Verlag; 1981.

85   McGuirk L, Kuppens P, Kingston R, Bastian B. Does a culture of happiness increase rumination over failure? Emotion. 2018 Aug;18(5):755-764.

86   Mike Rucker, The Fun Habit: How The Disciplined Pursuit of Joy And Wonder Can Change Your Life, 2023. New York: Atria Books

87   Kim A, Maglio SJ. Vanishing time in the pursuit of happiness. Psychon Bull Rev. 2018 Aug;25(4):1337-1342.

88   Klein MO, Battagello DS, Cardoso AR, Hauser DN, Bittencourt JC, Correa RG. Dopamine: Functions, Signaling, and Association with Neurological Diseases. Cell Mol Neurobiol. 2019 Jan;39(1):31-59. doi: 10.1007/s10571-018-0632-3. Epub 2018 Nov 16. PMID: 30446950.

89   Simen P, Matell M. Why does time seem to fly when we're having fun? Science. 2016 Dec 9;354(6317):1231-1232.

90   Soares S, Atallah BV, Paton JJ. Midbrain dopamine neurons control judgment of time. Science. 2016 Dec 9;354(6317):1273-1277. doi: 10.1126/science.aah5234. PMID: 27940870.

91   Eid M, Diener E. Norms for experiencing emotions in different cultures: inter- and intranational differences. J Pers Soc Psychol. 2001 Nov;81(5):869-85.

92   Ford, B. Q., Dmitrieva, J. O., Heller, D., Chentsova-Dutton, Y., Grossmann, I., Tamir, M., Uchida, Y., Koopmann-Holm, B., Floerke, V. A., Uhrig, M., Bokhan, T., & Mauss, I. B. (2015). Culture shapes whether the pursuit of happiness predicts higher or lower well-being. Journal of Experimental Psychology: General, 144(6), 1053–1062.

93 Wilson, T. D., & Gilbert, D. T. (2003). "Affective forecasting." Advances in Experimental Social Psychology, 35, 345-411.

94 Wenze, S. J., Gunthert, K. C., & German, R. E. (2012). Biases in affective forecasting and recall in individuals with depression and anxiety symptoms. Personality and Social Psychology Bulletin, 38(7), 895-906.

95 Lyubomirsky, S., Sheldon, K. M., & Schkade, D. (2005). Pursuing happiness: The architecture of sustainable change. Review Of General Psychology,9, 111–131.

96 Diener, Ed; Lucas, Richard E.; Scollon, Christie Napa (2006). "Beyond the hedonic treadmill: Revising the adaptation theory of well-being". American Psychologist. 61 (4): 305–314.

97 Lykken, D. T. (2007). "Beyond the hedonic treadmill: Revising the adaptation theory of well-being": Comment on Diener, Lucas, and Scollon (2006). American Psychologist, 62(6), 611–612.

98 Wilson, T. D., & Gilbert, D. T. (2003). Affective forecasting. Advances in Experimental Social Psychology, 35, 345-411.

99 https://en.wikipedia.org/wiki/Loss_aversion#cite_note-:0-4

100 Kahneman, D. & Tversky, A. (1992). "Advances in prospect theory: Cumulative representation of uncertainty". Journal of Risk and Uncertainty. 5 (4): 297–323.

101 Kahneman, Daniel; Tversky, Amos (1979). "Prospect Theory: An Analysis of Decision under Risk" (PDF). Econometrica. 47 (2): 263–291.

102 Kahneman, D., & Tversky, A. (1984). Choices, values, and frames. American Psychologist, 39(4), 341–350.

103 Kahneman, D., & Snell, J. (1992). Predicting a changing taste: Do people know what they will like? Journal of Behavioral Decision Making, 5(3), 187-200.

104 Kahneman, D., & Thaler, R. H. (2006). "Anomalies: Utility maximization and experienced utility." Journal of Economic Perspectives, 20(1), 221-234.

105 Jeffrey D. Green, Jody L. Davis, Laura B. Luchies, Anthony E. Coy, Daryl R. Van Tongeren, Chelsea A. Reid, Eli J. Finkel,
Victims versus perpetrators: Affective and empathic forecasting regarding transgressions in romantic relationships,
Journal of Experimental Social Psychology, Volume 49, Issue 3, 2013, Pages 329-333, ISSN 0022-1031,

106 https://www.americanbar.org/groups/bar_services/publications/bar_leader/20 03_04/2801/malpracticecaps/

107 Duggan C, Wilson C, DiPonio L, Trumpower B, Meade MA. Resilience and Happiness After Spinal Cord Injury: A Qualitative Study. Top Spinal Cord Inj

Rehabil. 2016 Spring;22(2):99-110.

108 Mansour C, Tamirisa KP, Lundberg G, Sharma G, Mehta LS, Mehran R, Volgman AS, Parwani P. Sexual Harassment, Victim Blaming, and the Potential Impact on Women in Cardiology. JACC Case Rep. 2021 May 19;3(6):978-981.

109 Halpern, J., & Arnold, R. M. (2008). "Affective forecasting: An unrecognized challenge in making serious health decisions." Journal of General Internal Medicine, 23(10), 1708-1712.

WINNING THE EXPECTATIONS GAME

110 Hannes Schwandt, Hannes. Unmet aspirations as an explanation for the age U-shape in wellbeing. Journal of Economic Behavior & Organization. Volume 122, 2016, Pages 75-87, ISSN 0167-2681

111 Rutledge, Robb B.; Skandali,Nikolina; Dayan, Peter; and Dolan, Raymond J. A computational and neural model of momentary subjective well-being. Proceedings of the National Academy of Sciences (PNAS) August 4, 2014, 111 (33) 12252-12257.

112 Norem, J. K., & Cantor, N. (1986b). Defensive pessimism: Harnessing anxiety as motivation. Journal of Personality and Social Psychology, 51, 1208–1217.

113 Norem, J. K. (2008). Defensive pessimism, anxiety, and the complexity of evaluating self-regulation. Social and Personality Psychology Compass, 2, 121-134.

114 Norem, Julie. The Positive Power Of Negative Thinking. (2002) New York: Basic Books.

115 Singer, J. D., & Willett, J. B. (2003). Applied longitudinal data analysis: Modeling change and event occurrence. Oxford, UK: Oxford University Press.

116 Brower, A. M., & Ketterhagen, A. (2004). Is there an inherent mismatch between how black and white students expect to succeed in college and what their college expects from them? Journal of Social Issues, 60, 95–116

117 Sanna, L. J. (1998). Defensive pessimism and optimism: The bitter–sweet influence of mood on performance and prefactual and counterfactual thinking. Cognition and Emotion, 12, 635–665.

118 Koo M, Algoe SB, Wilson TD, Gilbert DT. It's a wonderful life: mentally subtracting positive events improves people's affective states, contrary to their affective forecasts. J Pers Soc Psychol. 2008 Nov;95(5):1217-24.

119 Norem, J. K., & Cantor, N. (1986b). Defensive pessimism: Harnessing anxiety as motivation. Journal of Personality and Social Psychology, 51, 1208–1217.

120 Norem, J. K. (2008). Defensive pessimism, anxiety, and the complexity of evaluating self-regulation. Social and Personality Psychology Compass, 2, 121-134.

121 Elliot, A. J., & Church, M. A. (2003). A motivational analysis of defensive pessimism and self-handicapping. Journal of Personality, *71*(3), 369–396.

122 Martin, Andrew J, Marsh, Herbert W, Debus, Raymond L. Self-handicapping and defensive pessimism: A model of self-protection from a longitudinal perspective. Contemporary Educational Psychology. Volume 28, Issue 1, 2003, Pages 1-36, ISSN 0361-476X

123 Jones, E., & Berglas, S. (1978). Control of attributions about the self through self-handicapping strategies: The appeal of alcohol and the role of underachievement. Personality and Social Psychology Bulletin, 4, 200–206.

124 Zuckerman, M., Kieffer, S., & Knee, C. (1998). Consequences of selfhandicapping: Effects on coping, academic performance, and adjustment. Journal of Personality and Social Psychology, 74, 1619–1628.

AWARENESS AND SELF-CARE

125 Tsering, Geshe Tashi. The Four Noble Truths: The Foundation of Buddhist Thought, Volume 1. (2005) Somerville: Wisdom Publications.

126 https://tricycle.org/article/haemin-sunim-awareness/#:~:text=Buddhism%20tea ches%20us%20that%20all,only%20of%20your%20own%20awareness.

127 https://www.lionsroar.com/the-fullness-of-emptiness/#:~:text=%E2%80%9CFo rm%20is%20not%20other%20than,Because%20one%20exists%2C%20everything %20exists.

128 https://tricycle.org/beginners/buddhism/what-do-buddhists-mean-when-they-talk-about-emptiness/

129 https://www.snibbe.com/art/emptiness

130 https://www.lionsroar.com/the-fullness-of-emptiness/#:~:text=%E2%80%9CFo rm%20is%20not%20other%20than,Because%20one%20exists%2C%20everything %20exists.

131 Bhikkhu, Thanissaro. Hang on to Your Ego. Although many believe that the ego is just a source of trouble, Thanissaro Bhikkhu teaches that a healthy, functioning ego is a crucial tool on the path to Awakening. (Summer 2007).

132 https://jackkornfield.com/self-hatred/

133 Bhikkhu, Thanissaro. Hang on to Your Ego. Although many believe that the ego is just a source of trouble, Thanissaro Bhikkhu teaches that a healthy, functioning

ego is a crucial tool on the path to Awakening. (Summer 2007). https://tricycle.or g/magazine/healthy-ego/

134 Cherry, Kendra. Id, Ego, and Superego: Freud's Elements of Personality. Sept 2022. https://www.verywellmind.com/the-id-ego-and-superego-2795951#:~:te xt=and%20socially%20acceptable.-,The%20Ego,responsible%20for%20dealing%2 0with%20reality.

135 https://www.dhammatalks.org/books/SelvesNot-self/Section0009.html

136 Bhikkhu, Thanissaro. Hang on to Your Ego. Although many believe that the ego is just a source of trouble, Thanissaro Bhikkhu teaches that a healthy, functioning ego is a crucial tool on the path to Awakening. (Summer 2007). https://tricycle.or g/magazine/healthy-ego/

137 Epstein, Mark. Does your ego serve you, or do you serve it? What Buddhism and Freud say about self-slavery. Feb 2018. https://bigthink.com/big-think-books/m ark-epstein-advice-not-given-freud-buddhism-ego/#:~:text=Neither%20Buddhi sm%20nor%20psychotherapy%20seeks,demands%20of%20self%20and%20other.

138 Reolfi, Elaine. Mindfulness at work: cliché or common sense? Jun 2019. https://w ww.linkedin.com/pulse/mindfulness-work-clich%C3%A9-common-sense-elain e-russell-reolfi

139 Randles, Orla. Mindfulness: crucial or cliché? Jul 2017. https://medium.com/@o rla_randles/mindfulness-crucial-or-clich%C3%A9-9e0db57dca0b

140 Raab, Diana. Calming the Monkey Mind:Do you have an inner voice that hinders your success? Sep 2017. https://www.psychologytoday.com/us/blog/the-empo werment-diary/201709/calming-the-monkey-mind

141 https://en.wikipedia.org/wiki/Ram_Dass

142 https://www.ramdass.org/about-ram-dass/

143 Pahnke, Walter N. Drugs and Mysticism. The International Journal of Parapsy-chology.Vol VIII (No. 2) Spring 1966; 295-313

144 Doblin, R. (1991). Pahnke's "Good Friday experiment": A long-term follow-up and methodological critique. Journal of Transpersonal Psychology, 23(1), 1–28.

145 Dass Ram. Be Here Now. (1971). San Cristobal: Lama Foundation.

146 https://www.lionsroar.com/mindful-living-thich-nhat-hanh-on-the-practice-of -mindfulness-march-2010/

147 https://nalandabodhi.org/path/meditation/

148 https://en.wikipedia.org/wiki/Richard_Davidson

149 Davidson RJ, Kabat-Zinn J, Schumacher J, Rosenkranz M, Muller D, Santorelli SF, Urbanowski F, Harrington A, Bonus K, Sheridan JF. Alterations in brain and

immune function produced by mindfulness meditation. Psychosom Med. 2003 Jul-Aug;65(4):564-70.

150 Lutz A, McFarlin DR, Perlman DM, Salomons TV, Davidson RJ. Altered anterior insula activation during anticipation and experience of painful stimuli in expert meditators. Neuroimage. 2013 Jan 1;64:538-46.

151 Lutz A, McFarlin DR, Perlman DM, Salomons TV, Davidson RJ. Altered anterior insula activation during anticipation and experience of painful stimuli in expert meditators. Neuroimage. 2013 Jan 1;64:538-46.

152 Siegel, Dan. Aware: The Science and Practice of Presence. (2020) New York: TarcherPerigee

153 Kabat-Zinn J (2013). Full Catastrophe Living: Using the Wisdom of Your Body and Mind to Face Stress, Pain, and Illness. New York: Bantam Dell.

154 Gotink RA, Meijboom R, Vernooij MW, Smits M, Hunink MG. 8-week Mindfulness Based Stress Reduction induces brain changes similar to traditional long-term meditation practice - A systematic review. Brain Cogn. 2016 Oct;108:32-41.

155 Kral TRA, Imhoff-Smith T, Dean DC, Grupe D, Adluru N, Patsenko E, Mumford JA, Goldman R, Rosenkranz MA, Davidson RJ. Mindfulness-Based Stress Reduction-related changes in posterior cingulate resting brain connectivity. Soc Cogn Affect Neurosci. 2019 Jul 31;14(7):777-787.

156 Hölzel BK, Carmody J, Vangel M, Congleton C, Yerramsetti SM, Gard T, Lazar SW. Mindfulness practice leads to increases in regional brain gray matter density. Psychiatry Res. 2011 Jan 30;191(1):36-43.

157 https://positivepsychology.com/mindfulness-based-stress-reduction-mbsr/

158 Niazi AK, Niazi SK. Mindfulness-based stress reduction: a non-pharmacological approach for chronic illnesses. N Am J Med Sci. 2011 Jan;3(1):20-3.

159 Kral TRA, Davis K, Korponay C, Hirshberg MJ, Hoel R, Tello LY, Goldman RI, Rosenkranz MA, Lutz A, Davidson RJ. Absence of structural brain changes from mindfulness-based stress reduction: Two combined randomized controlled trials. Sci Adv. 2022 May 20;8(20):eabk3316.

160 Welwood, John. On Spiritual Bypassing and Relationship. https://www.scienceandnonduality.com/article/on-spiritual-bypassing-and-relationship

161 Raab, Ph.D., D. (2019, January 23). What is Spiritual Bypassing? John Welwood, who coined the term, died this week. Psychology Today.

162 https://www.mantrayogacollective.com/blog/spiritual-bypassing

163 Wildhood, Megan. There's Something Spreading Faster Than COVID-19, and It's Not Fear. It's Toxic Positivity. April 2020. https://www.madinamerica.com/2

020/04/toxic-positivity/

164 Burford, Molly. Pandemic Toxic Positivity Isn't Just Annoying. It's Dangerous. Dec 2020. https://www.self.com/story/pandemic-toxic-positivity

165 Croft, A., Dunn, E. W., & Quoidbach, J. (2014). From Tribulations to Appreciation: Experiencing Adversity in the Past Predicts Greater Savoring in the Present. Social Psychological and Personality Science, 5(5), 511–516.

166 Calhoun, L. G., & Tedeschi, R. G. (2001). Posttraumatic growth: The positive lessons of loss. In R. A. Neimeyer (Ed.), Meaning reconstruction & the experience of loss (pp. 157–172). American Psychological Association.

167 Joseph S., Linley P. A. (2006). Growth following adversity: Theoretical perspectives and implications for clinical practice. Clinical Psychology Review, 26, 1041–1053.

168 Frankl, Viktor. Man's Search for Meaning: An Introduction to Logotherapy. (1946)

169 https://iep.utm.edu/fouc-eth/#SH4a

170 Harris, Aisha. A History of Self-Care: From its radical roots to its yuppie-driven middle age to its election-inspired resurgence. April 2017. https://www.slate.com/articles/arts/culturebox/2017/04/the_history_of_self_care.html

171 https://en.wikipedia.org/wiki/Self-love

172 https://en.wikipedia.org/wiki/Audre_Lorde

173 https://trends.google.com/trends/explore?date=2010-10-01%202023-04-20&geo=US&q=self-care

174 Yan BW, Hsia RY, Yeung V, Sloan FA. Changes in Mental Health Following the 2016 Presidential Election. J Gen Intern Med. 2021 Jan;36(1):170-177.

175 https://trends.google.com/trends/explore?date=2010-10-01%202023-04-20&geo=US&q=self-care

176 Neff, Kristin and Germer, Christopher. The Mindful Self-Compassion Workbook: A Proven Way to Accept Yourself, Build Inner Strength, and Thrive. (2018) New York: Guilford Publications, Inc.

177 Clark, Alicia. Why Does Self-Care Sometimes Feel So Hard? Feb 2020. https://www.psychologytoday.com/us/blog/hack-your-anxiety/202002/why-does-self-care-sometimes-feel-so-hard

178 Rozin, P., & Royzman, E. B. (2001). Negativity Bias, Negativity Dominance, and Contagion. Personality and Social Psychology Review, 5(4), 296–320.

179 Baumeister, R. F., Bratslavsky, E., Finkenauer, C., & Vohs, K. D. (2001). Bad is Stronger than Good. Review of General Psychology, 5(4), 323–370.

180 Vaish A, Grossmann T, Woodward A. Not all emotions are created equal: the negativity bias in social-emotional development. Psychol Bull. 2008 May;134(3):383-403.

181 Soroka, S., Fournier, P., & Nir, L. (2019). Cross-national evidence of a negativity bias in psychophysiological reactions to news. Proceedings of the National Academy of Sciences, 116(38), 18888-18892.

182 Hibbing, J. R., Smith, K. B. and Alford, J. R. (2014) "Differences in negativity bias underlie variations in political ideology," Behavioral and Brain Sciences. Cambridge University Press, 37(3), pp. 297–307.

183 Kiken, L. G., & Shook, N. J. (2011). Looking Up: Mindfulness Increases Positive Judgments and Reduces Negativity Bias. Social Psychological and Personality Science, 2(4), 425-431.

184 Joinson C. Coping with compassion fatigue. Nursing. 1992 Apr;22(4):116, 118-9, 120. PMID: 1570090.

185 Figley CR, Roop RG. Compassion fatigue in the animal-care community. Washington DC: Humane Society Press; 2006.

186 Cocker F, Joss N. Compassion Fatigue among Healthcare, Emergency and Community Service Workers: A Systematic Review. Int J Environ Res Public Health. 2016 Jun 22;13(6):618.

187 Lluch C, Galiana L, Doménech P, Sansó N. The Impact of the COVID-19 Pandemic on Burnout, Compassion Fatigue, and Compassion Satisfaction in Healthcare Personnel: A Systematic Review of the Literature Published during the First Year of the Pandemic. Healthcare (Basel). 2022 Feb 13;10(2):364.

188 Lambros A. Compassion fatigue: The cost some workers pay for caring. 2014. [Last accessed July 8, 2019]. Available from: https://theconversation.com/compassion-fatigue-the-cost-some-workers-pay-for-caring-30865.

189 Gawande, Atul. Complications: A Surgeon's Notes on an Imperfect Science (2003). New York: Metropolitan Books.

190 Salzberg, Sharon. Lovingkindness: The Revolutionary Art of Happiness (2002). Boulder: Shambhala Publications.

KINDNESS, GRATEFULNESS AND AWE

191 East, Elizabeth. What's the problem with 'literally'? The Spectator online. 2 June 2021.

192 Lyubomirsky, S., Sheldon, K. M., & Schkade, D. (2005). Pursuing happiness: The architecture of sustainable change. Review Of General Psychology,9, 111–131.

193 Lyubomirsky, S., King, L. A., & Diener, E. (2004). Is happiness a strength?: An examination of the benefits and costs of frequent positive affect. Manuscript submitted for publication.

194 Trivers, R. (1971). The evolution of reciprocal altruism. Quarterly Review of Biology, 46, 35–57.

195 Buss D. M. (1989). Sex differences in human mate preferences: Evolutionary hypotheses tested in 37 cultures. Behavioral and Brain Sciences, 12(1), 1–14.

196 Baumeister, R. F., & Leary, M. R. (1995). The need to belong: Desire for interpersonal attachments as a fundamental human motivation. Psychological Bulletin, 117, 497–529.

197 Rutledge, Robb B., Skandalia, Nikolina, Dayanc, Peter and Dolana, Raymond J. A computational and neural model of momentary subjective well-being. Proceedings of the National Academy of Sciences (PNAS) August 4, 2014, 111 (33) 12252-12257

198 Simen P, Matell M. Why does time seem to fly when we're having fun? Science. 2016 Dec 9;354(6317):1231-1232.

199 Soares S, Atallah BV, Paton JJ. Midbrain dopamine neurons control judgment of time. Science. 2016 Dec 9;354(6317):1273-1277.

200 Emmons, R. A., & McCullough, M. E. (2003). Counting blessings versus burdens: An experimental investigation of gratitude and subjective wellbeing in daily life. Journal of Personality and Social Psychology, 84, 377–389.

201 Kaufman, Scott Barry. The Opposite of Toxic Positivity. (Aug 2021). The Atlantic.com. https://www.theatlantic.com/family/archive/2021/08/tragic-optimism-opposite-toxic-positivity/619786/

202 Nelson, Kristi. https://grateful.org/

203 Jans-Beken, L. G. P. J., & Wong, P. T. P. (2019). Development and preliminary validation of the Existential Gratitude Scale (EGS). Counselling Psychology Quarterly.

204 Eisenberg N, Fabes RA, Spinrad TL. Prosocial behavior. In: Eisenberg N, Damon W, Lerner RM, editors. Handbook of child psychology: Vol. 3. Social, emotional, and personality development. 6th ed. New York: Wiley; 2006. pp. 646–718.

205 Grant AM, Gino F. A little thanks goes a long way: Explaining why gratitude expressions motivate prosocial behavior. J Pers Soc Psychol. 2010 Jun;98(6):946-55..

206 Epley, N., Kumar, A., Dungan, J., & Echelbarger, M. (2023). A Prosociality Paradox: How Miscalibrated Social Cognition Creates a Misplaced Barrier to Prosocial

Action. Current Directions in Psychological Science, 32(1), 33–41.

207 Sheldon KM, Boehm JK, Lyubomirsky S. Variety is the spice of happiness: The hedonic adaptation prevention (HAP) model. In: Boniwell I, David S, editors. Oxford handbook of happiness (2013). Oxford: Oxford University Press

208 Jachimowicz, J. M., Mo, R., Greenberg, A. E., Jeronimus, B., & Whillans, A. V. (2021). Income More Reliably Predicts Frequent Than Intense Happiness. Social Psychological and Personality Science, 12(7), 1294–1306.

209 Lyubomirsky S, Dickerhoof R, Boehm JK, Sheldon KM. Becoming happier takes both a will and a proper way: an experimental longitudinal intervention to boost well-being. Emotion. 2011 Apr;11(2):391-402.

210 Sheldon KM, Lyubomirsky S. Is it possible to become happier? (And, if so, how?) Social and Personality Psychology Compass. 2007;1:129–145.

211 Jordan Etkin, Cassie Mogilner, Does Variety Among Activities Increase Happiness?, Journal of Consumer Research, Volume 43, Issue 2, August 2016, Pages 210–229.

212 https://knowledge.wharton.upenn.edu/article/does-variety-fuel-happiness-at-work-and-in-life-it-depends/

213 Pearsall, Paul. AWE: The Delights and Dangers of Our Eleventh Emotion. (2017)Deerfield Beach: Health Communications, Inc.

214 Dacher Keltner, Awe: The New Science of Everyday Wonder and How It Can Transform Your Life (2023). London: Penguin Press.

215 Rudd M, Vohs KD, Aaker J. Awe expands people's perception of time, alters decision making, and enhances well-being. Psychol Sci. 2012 Oct 1;23(10):1130-6. doi: 10.1177/0956797612438731. Epub 2012 Aug 10. PMID: 22886132.

216 Bai Y, Ocampo J, Jin G, Chen S, Benet-Martinez V, Monroy M, Anderson C, Keltner D. Awe, daily stress, and elevated life satisfaction. J Pers Soc Psychol. 2021 Apr;120(4):837-860. doi: 10.1037/pspa0000267. PMID: 33764120.

217 Dacher Keltner, Awe: The New Science of Everyday Wonder and How It Can Transform Your Life (2023). London: Penguin Press.

218 O'Leary, John. In Awe: Rediscover Your Childlike Wonder to Unleash Inspiration, Meaning, and Joy. (2020) Sydney: Currency Publishers.

BEFORE YOU WRECK YOURSELF, REPURPOSE YOURSELF.

219 Hooker SA, Masters KS. Purpose in life is associated with physical activity measured by accelerometer. Journal of Health Psychology. 2016;21(6):962-971.

220 Burrow, Anthony L. and Hill, Patrick L., Editors. (2020). The Ecology of Purposeful Living Across the Lifespan: Developmental, Educational, and Social Perspectives. Switzerland: Springer International Publishing

221 Boyle PA, Barnes LL, Buchman AS, Bennett DA. Purpose in life is associated with mortality among community-dwelling older persons. Psychosom Med. 2009 Jun;71(5):574-9.

222 Boyle, P. A., et al. "Purpose in life is associated with a reduced risk of Alzheimer's disease and Mild Cognitive Impairment among community based older persons." Archives of General Psychiatry 71 (2009): 574-9.

223 Sharf, Zack. (2023). Variety. https://variety.com/2023/tv/news/marie-kondo-stops-tidying-up-home-messy-1235504610/

224 Smith, Sean (2002). *J.K. Rowling: A Biography*. Arrow Books. ISBN 0-09-944542-5.

225 https://en.wikipedia.org/wiki/J._K._Rowling#CITEREFCruz2008

226 Watson, Julie; Kellner, Tomas (26 February 2004). "J.K. Rowling and the billion-dollar empire". *Forbes*.

227 Executives in the U.S.: average age at hire 2018 | Statista

228 Physicians' average age by specialty (beckersasc.com)

229 https://www.pgpf.org/blog/2022/07/why-are-americans-working-longer#:~:text=Why%20Has%20the%20Average%20Retirement,health%20insurance%20features%20and%20costs.

230 https://www.pewresearch.org/short-reads/2021/11/04/amid-the-pandemic-a-rising-share-of-older-u-s-adults-are-now-retired/

231 https://www.health.harvard.edu/staying-healthy/working-later-in-life-can-pay-off-in-more-than-just-income

232 Brooks, Arthur. From Strength to Strength: Finding Success, Happiness, and Deep Purpose in the Second Half of Life. (2022) New York: Penguin Random House.

233 Sansone, C., & Harackiewicz, J. M. (Eds.). (2000). Intrinsic and extrinsic motivation: The search for optimal motivation and performance. Academic Press.

234 Nickerson, Charlotte. "Differences of Extrinsic and Intrinsic Motivation." Dec 2021. Simply Psychology online.

235 Ryan R. M., Deci E. L. (2000). Intrinsic and extrinsic motivations: classic definitions and new directions. Contemp. Educ. Psychol. 25, 54–67 10.1006/ceps.1999.1020

236   https://en.wikipedia.org/wiki/Self-determination_theory

237   Ryan, R. M., & Deci, E. L. (2017). Self-determination theory: Basic psychological needs in motivation, development, and wellness. New York, NY: Guilford Press.

238   Deci, E. L., & Ryan, R. M. (1985). The general causality orientations scale: Self-determination in personality. Journal of Research in Personality, 19(2), 109-134.

239   Deci, E.L. (1971) Effects of Externally Mediated Rewards on Intrinsic Motivation. Journal of Personality and Social Psychology, 18, 105-115.

240   Lepper, M. R., & Greene, D. (1975). Turning play into work: Effects of adult surveillance and extrinsic rewards on children's intrinsic motivation. Journal of Personality and Social Psychology, 31(3), 479–486.

241   Medic, N., Mack, D. E., Wilson, P. M., Starkes, J. L. (2007). The effects of athletic scholarships on motivation in sport. Journal of Sport Behavior, 30, 292–306.

242   Moller, A. C., & Sheldon, K. M. (2020). Athletic scholarships are negatively associated with intrinsic motivation for sports, even decades later: Evidence for long-term undermining. Motivation Science, 6(1), 43–48.

243   Vallerand, R. J. (2012). Intrinsic and extrinsic motivation in sport and physical activity: A review and a look at the future. In G. Tenenbaum & E. Eklund (Eds.), Handbook of sport psychology (3rd ed., pp. 59–83). New York, NY: Wiley.

244   Inguglia, C., Liga, F., Lo Coco, A. et al. Satisfaction and frustration of autonomy and relatedness needs: Associations with parenting dimensions and psychological functioning. Motiv Emot 42, 691–705 (2018).

245   Guay, F. (2022). Applying Self-Determination Theory to Education: Regulations Types, Psychological Needs, and Autonomy Supporting Behaviors. Canadian Journal of School Psychology, 37(1), 75–92.

246   Mallett, Clifford and Hanrahan, Stephanie (2004). Elite athletes: Why does the 'fire' burn so brightly?. Psychology of Sport and Exercise 5 (2) 183-200.

247   Moran, Christina and Diefendorff, James M. and Kim, Tae-Yeol and Liu, Zhi Qiang, A Profile Approach to Self-Determination Theory Motivations at Work. (December 1, 2012).

248   Vallerand, R. J.; Reid, G. (1984). "On the causal effects of perceived competence on intrinsic motivation: A test of cognitive evaluation theory". Journal of Sport Psychology. 6: 94–102.

249   https://en.wikipedia.org/wiki/Three-act_structure#:~:text=The%20three%2Dact%20structure%20is,the%20Confrontation%2C%20and%20the%20Resolution.

250   https://www.cnbc.com/2017/08/02/what-amazon-billionaire-jeff-bezos-was-doing-in-his-20s.html

251 https://hbr.org/2019/03/facing-your-mid-career-crisis

252 https://www.npr.org/2023/02/27/1159858537/can-i-afford-to-quit-my-job

253 Arkes, H and Blumer, C.The psychology of sunk cost. Organ. Behav. Hum. Decis., 35 (1) (1985), pp. 124-140.

254 Negrini, Marcello and Riedl, Arno M. and Wibral, Matthias and Wibral, Matthias, Sunk cost in investment decisions (June 21, 2022). Journal of Economic Behavior and Organization.

255 https://en.wikipedia.org/wiki/Sunk_cost

256 Arkes, Hal R, and Peter Ayton. 1999. "The Sunk Cost and Concorde Effects: Are Humans Less Rational Than Lower Animals?" Psychological Bulletin 125 (5): 591–600.

257 Rego, Sara; Arantes, Joana; Magalhães, Paula (2016-11-29). "Is there a Sunk Cost Effect in Committed Relationships?". Current Psychology. 37 (3): 508–519.

258 Volf, Miroslav. Croasmun, Matthew. McAnnally-Linz, Ryan. Life Worth Living: A Guide to What Matters Most (2023). New York: The Open Field

BREAK OUT OF YOUR COMFORT ZONE: FINDING OPTIMAL ANXIETY

259 Tugend, Alina (11 February 2011). "Tiptoeing Out of One's Comfort Zone (and of Course, Back In)". The New York Times. Retrieved 11 December 2014.

260 Bardwick, J. (1991). Danger in the comfort zone: From boardroom to mailroom – How to break the entitlement habit that's killing American business. American Management Association.

261 Yerkes, R., & Dodson, J. (1907). The dancing mouse, A study in animal behavior, Journal of Comparative Neurology & Psychology, 18, 459–482.

262 Beck, Melinda. "Anxiety Can Bring Out the Best." The Wall Street Journal. Dow Jones & Company, 18 June 2012. Web. 22 Jan. 2017.

263 Siegel, D. J. (1999). The developing mind: Toward a neurobiology of interpersonal experience. Guilford Press.

264 Shellnutt, Kate. Why 30 is the decade friends disappear — and what to do about it. Jul 12, 2016. Vox.com

265 Schwartz, Christine R. (2013). "Trends and Variation in Assortative Mating: Causes and Consequences". Annual Review of Sociology. 39 (1): 451–470.

266 Aiello, Luca Maria; Barrat, Alain; Schifanella, Rossano; Cattuto, Ciro; Markines, Benjamin; Menczer, Filippo (2012-05-01). "Friendship prediction and homophily in social media". ACM Transactions on the Web. 6 (2): 1–33.

267 McPherson, Miller; Smith-Lovin, Lynn; Cook, James M. (2003-11-28). "Birds of a Feather: Homophily in Social Networks". Annual Review of Sociology. 27 (1): 415–444.

268 Ciampaglia, G.L., Menczer, F. Biases Make People Vulnerable to Misinformation Spread by Social Media. Jan. 10, 2019. The Conversation. Scientific American online.

269 https://www.axios.com/2017/12/15/sean-parker-unloads-on-facebook-god-only-knows-what-its-doing-to-our-childrens-brains-1513306792

270 https://www.npr.org/transcripts/1127249176

271 Rogers, E. M. (1962). Diffusion of innovations. New York, Free Press of Glencoe.

272 Kim C, Hyun-Soo Kim H. Network Ties, Upward Status Heterophily, and Unanticipated Health Consequences. J Health Soc Behav. 2023 Mar 18:2214652311555892.

273 https://en.wikipedia.org/wiki/Tuba_City_Regional_Health_Care_Corporation

274 Nickerson, R. S. (1998). Confirmation Bias: A Ubiquitous Phenomenon in Many Guises. Review of General Psychology, 2(2), 175–220.

275 https://en.wikipedia.org/wiki/Confirmation_bias

276 Bhatti A. Cognitive bias in clinical practice - nurturing healthy skepticism among medical students. Adv Med Educ Pract. 2018 Apr 10;9:235-237. doi: 10.2147/AMEP.S149558. PMID: 29692640; PMCID: PMC5901151.

277 Kunitomo, K., Harada, T. & Watari, T. Cognitive biases encountered by physicians in the emergency room. BMC Emerg Med 22, 148 (2022).

278 https://thedecisionlab.com/biases/cognitive-dissonance

279 Bacon, F. T. (1979). Credibility of repeated statements: Memory for trivia. Journal of Experimental Psychology: Human Learning and Memory, 5(3), 241–252.

280 Hassan, A., Barber, S.J. The effects of repetition frequency on the illusory truth effect. Cogn. Research 6, 38 (2021).

281 Taleb, N. N. (2012). Antifragile: Things that gain from disorder. New York, NY: Random House.

LAUGH AND HAVE FUN. BUT DON'T DIE.

282 C. D. Bryant and C. J. Forsyth, "The Fun God: Sports, Recreation, Leisure, and Amusement in the United States," Sociological Spectrum, Vol. 25, No. 2, 2005, pp. 197-211

283 Garber, Megan. "Are We Having Too Much Fun?" The Atlantic. April 27, 2017.

284 Kelly, Finn. Redefining Fun in a Post-Pandemic World. Dec 13, 2021. Forbes online. https://www.forbes.com/sites/forbesbusinesscouncil/2021/12/13/redef ining-fun-in-a-post-pandemic-world/?sh=14d74a265b75

285 https://en.wikipedia.org/wiki/Death_from_laughter

286 Provine RR. 2001 Laughter: a scientific investigation. London, UK: Penguin.

287 https://thegrandhealthcare.com/bridgeview/night-owls-fun-bad-health/

288 Reutrakul S, Knutson KL. Consequences of Circadian Disruption on Cardiometabolic Health. Sleep Med Clin. 2015 Dec;10(4):455-68.

289 Postman, Neil. Amusing Ourselves to Death: Public Discourse in the Age of Show Business (1985). New York: Viking Penguin.

290 Garber, Megan. "Are We Having Too Much Fun?" The Atlantic. April 27, 2017.

291 Frankl, Viktor. Man's Search for Meaning: An Introduction to Logotherapy. (1946)

292 Maslow, A. H. (1943). A theory of human motivation. Psychological Review, 50, 370–396.

293 Adler NE, Ostrove JM. Socioeconomic status and health: what we know and what we don't. Ann N Y Acad Sci. 1999;896:3–15.

294 Lindstrom M, Hanson BS, Ostergren PO. Socioeconomic differences in leisure-time physical activity: the role of social participation and social capital in shaping health related behaviour. Soc Sci Med. 2001;52:441–51.

295 He XZ, Baker DW. Differences in leisure-time, household, and work-related physical activity by race, ethnicity, and education. J Gen Intern Med. 2005;20:259–66.

296 Pressman SD, Matthews KA, Cohen S, Martire LM, Scheier M, Baum A, Schulz R. Association of enjoyable leisure activities with psychological and physical well-being. Psychosom Med. 2009 Sep;71(7):725-32.

297 Berk LS, Tan SA, Fry WF, Napier BJ, Lee JW, Hubbard RW, Lewis JE, Eby WC. Neuroendocrine and stress hormone changes during mirthful laughter. Am J Med Sci. 1989 Dec;298(6):390-6.

298 Sakurada K, Konta T, Watanabe M, Ishizawa K, Ueno Y, Yamashita H, Kayama T. Associations of Frequency of Laughter With Risk of All-Cause Mortality and Cardiovascular Disease Incidence in a General Population: Findings From the Yamagata Study. J Epidemiol. 2020 Apr 5;30(4):188-193.

299 Dunbar R. I. M., Baron Rebecca, Frangou Anna, Pearce Eiluned, van Leeuwen Edwin J. C., Stow Julie, Partridge Giselle, MacDonald Ian, Barra Vincent and van Vugt Mark (2012)Social laughter is correlated with an elevated pain thresholdProc. R. Soc. B.2791161–1167

300 Gervais, M. & Wilson, D. S. 2005 The evolution and functions of laughter and humor: a synthetic approach. Q. Rev. Biol. 80, 395 –430.

301 Dunbar R. I. M. 2022. Laughter and its role in the evolution of human social bonding. Phil. Trans. R. Soc.

302 Provine RR. 2001 Laughter: a scientific investigation. London, UK: Penguin.

303 Dunbar R. I. M. 2022. Laughter and its role in the evolution of human social bonding. Phil. Trans. R. Soc.

304 McManus IC, Furnham A. "Fun, fun, fun": Types of fun, attitudes to fun, and their relation to personality and biographical factors. *Psychology.* 2010;1:159–168.

305 Reis HT, O'Keefe SD, Lane RD. Fun Is More Fun When Others Are Involved. J Posit Psychol. 2017;12(6):547-557.

306 Keltner, Dacher. Awe: The New Science of Everyday Wonder and How It Can Transform Your Life (2023). London: Penguin Press.

307 Price, Catherine. (2021). The Power of Fun: How to Feel Alive Again. New York: The Dial Press.

308 https://www.nifplay.org/about-us/about-dr-stuart-brown/

309 Brown, Stuart. Play: How it Shapes the Brain, Opens the Imagination, and Invigorates the Soul (2010). New York: Avery.

310 Durkheim, Émile. The Elementary Forms of the Religious Life, (1912, English translation by Joseph Swain: 1915) The Free Press, 1965; HarperCollins, 1976.

311 Gabriel, S., Naidu, E., Paravati, E., Morrison, C. D., & Gainey, K. (2020). Creating the sacred from the profane: Collective effervescence and everyday activities. The Journal of Positive Psychology, 15(1), 129–154.

312 Xygalatas D, Konvalinka I, Bulbulia J, Roepstorff A. Quantifying collective effervescence: Heart-rate dynamics at a fire-walking ritual. Commun Integr Biol. 2011 Nov 1;4(6):735-8.

313 Csikszentmihalyi, Mihaly (1990). Flow: the psychology of optimal experience (1st ed.). New York: Harper & Row.

314 Geirland, John (1996). "Go With The Flow". Wired, September, Issue 4.09.

315 https://en.wikipedia.org/wiki/Mihaly_Csikszentmihalyi#cite_note-BBF-20

316 https://jamesclear.com/goldilocks-rule

317 Rucker, Mike. The Fun Habit: How The Disciplined Pursuit of Joy And Wonder Can Change Your Life, 2023. New York: Atria Books

318 Sheldon KM, Boehm JK, Lyubomirsky S. Variety is the spice of happiness: The hedonic adaptation prevention (HAP) model. In: Boniwell I, David S, editors. Oxford handbook of happiness (2013). Oxford: Oxford University Press

319 Jordan Etkin, Cassie Mogilner, Does Variety Among Activities Increase Happiness?, Journal of Consumer Research, Volume 43, Issue 2, August 2016, Pages 210–229.

320 https://michaelrucker.com/having-fun/variable-hedonics/

IT'S YOUR RELATIONSHIPS, STUPID.

321 Cohen, S. (2004). Social Relationships and Health. American Psychologist, 59(8), 676–684.]

322 https://en.wikipedia.org/wiki/Sheldon_Cohen

323 Cohen S, Janicki-Deverts D, Miller GE. 2007. Psychological stress and disease. J. Am. Med. Assoc. 298:1685–87

324 Cohen S, Alper CM, Doyle WJ, Treanor JJ, Turner RB. Positive emotional style predicts resistance to illness after experimental exposure to rhinovirus or influenza a virus. Psychosom Med. 2006 Nov-Dec;68(6):809-15.

325 Cohen S, Doyle WJ, Skoner DP, Rabin BS, Gwaltney JM Jr. Social ties and susceptibility to the common cold. JAMA. 1997 Jun 25;277(24):1940-4. PMID: 9200634.

326 Sheldon KM, Boehm JK, Lyubomirsky S. Variety is the spice of happiness: The hedonic adaptation prevention (HAP) model. In: Boniwell I, David S, editors. Oxford handbook of happiness (2013). Oxford: Oxford University Press

327 Holt-Lunstad J, Smith TB, Layton JB (2010) Social Relationships and Mortality Risk: A Meta-analytic Review. PLoS Med 7(7): e1000316. https://doi.org/10.1371/journal.pmed.1000316

328 Miller, G., Chen, E. & Cole, S.W. Health psychology: developing biologically plausible models linking the social world and physical health. Annu. Rev. Psychol. 60, 501–524 (2009).

329 Eisenberger, N., Cole, S. Social neuroscience and health: neurophysiological mechanisms linking social ties with physical health. Nat Neurosci 15, 669–674 (2012).

330 Waldinger, Robert and Schulz, Marc. (2023). The Good Life: Lessons from the World's Longest Scientific Study of Happiness. New York: Simon and Shuster.

331 Cohen S, Doyle WJ, Skoner DP, Rabin BS, Gwaltney JM Jr. Social ties and susceptibility to the common cold. JAMA. 1997 Jun 25;277(24):1940-4. PMID: 9200634.

332 Ward, Adrian F., et al. "Brain drain: The mere presence of one's own smartphone reduces available cognitive capacity." Journal of the Association for Consumer Research 2.2 (2017): 140-154.

333 Price, Catherine. How to Break Up With Your Phone: The 30-Day Plan to Take Back Your Life (2018). Berkeley: Ten Speed Press

334 Lembke, Anna. Dopamine Nation: Finding Balance in the Age of Indulgence (2021). New York: Dutton.

335 Lodge JM, Harrison WJ. The Role of Attention in Learning in the Digital Age. Yale J Biol Med. 2019 Mar 25;92(1):21-28.

336 Loh KK, Kanai R. How Has the Internet Reshaped Human Cognition? Neuroscientist. 2016 Oct;22(5):506-20.

337 https://www.psychologytoday.com/us/blog/high-octane-women/201201/6-reasons-you-should-spend-more-time-alone

338 https://www.cdc.gov/aging/publications/features/lonely-older-adults.html

339 Pimlott N. The ministry of loneliness. Can Fam Physician. 2018 Mar;64(3):166.

340 Khan MSR, Kadoya Y. Loneliness during the COVID-19 Pandemic: A Comparison between Older and Younger People. Int J Environ Res Public Health. 2021 Jul 25;18(15):7871.

341 Hawkley LC, Capitanio JP. Perceived isolation, evolutionary fitness and health outcomes: a lifespan approach. Philos Trans R Soc Lond B. 2015;370(1669):20140114.

342 Luo Y, Hawkley LC, Waite LJ, Cacioppo JT. Loneliness, health and mortality in old age: a national longitudinal study. Soc Sci Med. 2012;74(6):907–14. Epub 2012 Jan 25.

343 Gerst-Emerson K, Jayawardhana J. Loneliness as a public health issue: the impact of loneliness on health care utilization among older adults. Am J Pub Health. 2015;105(5):1013–9. Epub 2015 Mar 19.

344 https://mcc.gse.harvard.edu/reports/loneliness-in-america

345 Granovetter, Mark S. "The Strength of Weak Ties." American Journal of Sociology 78, no. 6 (1973): 1360–80.

346 https://officesnapshots.com/2012/07/16/pixar-headquarters-and-the-legacy-of-steve-jobs/

347 Törnberg P. Echo chambers and viral misinformation: Modeling fake news as complex contagion. PLoS One. 2018 Sep 20;13(9)

348 Sandstrom, G. M., & Dunn, E. W. (2014). Social Interactions and Well-Being: The Surprising Power of Weak Ties. Personality and Social Psychology Bulletin, 40(7), 910–922.

349 Moreton, J., Kelly, C.S., & Sandstrom G.M. (2023). Social support from weak ties: Insight from the literature on minimal social interactions. Social and Personality Psychology Compass, e12729.

350 Sandstrom, G.M., & Boothby, E.J. (2021). Why do people avoid talking to strangers? A mini meta-analysis of predicted fears and actual experiences talking to a stranger. Self and Identity, 20(1), 47-71.

351 Boothby, E. J., Cooney, G., Sandstrom, G. M., & Clark, M. S. (2018). The Liking Gap in Conversations: Do People Like Us More Than We Think? Psychological Science, 29(11), 1742–1756.

352 Sandstrom G.M.,* Boothby, E.J.*, & Cooney, G.* (2022). Talking to strangers: A week-long intervention reduces fear of rejection and increases conversational ability. Journal of Experimental Social Psychology, 102.

353 Cohen S, Doyle WJ, Skoner DP, Rabin BS, Gwaltney JM Jr. Social ties and susceptibility to the common cold. JAMA. 1997 Jun 25;277(24):1940-4.

354 Wilson, T. D., & Gilbert, D. T. (2003). "Affective forecasting." Advances in Experimental Social Psychology, 35, 345-411.

355 Wilson, T. D., & Gilbert, D. T. (2003). "Affective forecasting." Advances in Experimental Social Psychology, 35, 345-411.

356 Epley, N., Kumar, A., Dungan, J., & Echelbarger, M. (2023). A Prosociality Paradox: How Miscalibrated Social Cognition Creates a Misplaced Barrier to Prosocial Action. Current Directions in Psychological Science, 32(1), 33–41.

357 https://en.wikipedia.org/wiki/Human_microbiome

358 Sherwin E, Bordenstein SR, Quinn JL, Dinan TG, Cryan JF. Microbiota and the social brain. Science. 2019 Nov 1;366(6465):eaar2016.

359 Valles-Colomer M, Falony G, Darzi Y, Tigchelaar EF, Wang J, Tito RY, Schiweck C, Kurilshikov A, Joossens M, Wijmenga C, Claes S, Van Oudenhove L, Zhernakova A, Vieira-Silva S, Raes J. The neuroactive potential of the human gut microbiota in quality of life and depression. Nat Microbiol. 2019 Apr;4(4):623-632.

360 https://www.researchgate.net/publication/336939110_Microbiota_and_the_social_brain

361 Baião R, Capitão LP, Higgins C, Browning M, Harmer CJ, Burnet PWJ. Multi-species probiotic administration reduces emotional salience and improves mood in subjects with moderate depression: a randomised, double-blind, placebo-controlled study. Psychol Med. 2023 Jun;53(8):3437-3447.

362 Kao AC, Safarikova J, Marquardt T, Mullins B, Lennox BR, Burnet PWJ. Pro-cognitive effect of a prebiotic in psychosis: A double blind placebo controlled

cross-over study. Schizophr Res. 2019 Jun;208:460-461.

363 file:///C:/Users/q201360/Downloads/Kao.schiz.res.lett.pdf

364 Badal VD, Vaccariello ED, Murray ER, Yu KE, Knight R, Jeste DV, Nguyen TT. The Gut Microbiome, Aging, and Longevity: A Systematic Review. Nutrients. 2020 Dec 7;12(12):3759.

365 Mehta RS, Lochhead P, Wang Y, Ma W, Nguyen LH, Kochar B, Huttenhower C, Grodstein F, Chan AT. Association of midlife antibiotic use with subsequent cognitive function in women.

366 Folk D, Dunn E. A systematic review of the strength of evidence for the most commonly recommended happiness strategies in mainstream media. Nat Hum Behav. 2023 Jul 20.

367 https://www.sciencenews.org/article/nature-exercise-happiness-psychology

368 https://www.sciencemediacentre.org/expert-reaction-to-systematic-review-of-happiness-increasing-strategies-in-mentally-healthy-people/

369 Bakkevig MK, Nielsen R. Impact of wet underwear on thermoregulatory responses and thermal comfort in the cold. Ergonomics. 1994 Aug;37(8):1375-89.

WHAT DOES A BODY GOOD? IT'S YOUR DNA.

370 Mendelson, Anne (2023). Spoiled: The Myth of Milk as a Superfood. New York: Columbia University Press.

371 Miller, G., Chen, E. & Cole, S.W. Health psychology: developing biologically plausible models linking the social world and physical health. Annu. Rev. Psychol. 60, 501–524 (2009).

372 Eisenberger, N., Cole, S. Social neuroscience and health: neurophysiological mechanisms linking social ties with physical health. Nat Neurosci 15, 669–674 (2012).

373 Cookson W, Liang L, Abecasis G, Moffatt M, Lathrop M. Mapping complex disease traits with global gene expression. Nat Rev Genet. 2009;10:184–194.

374 Cole SW (2014) Human Social Genomics. PLoS Genet 10(8): e1004601. https://doi.org/10.1371/journal.pgen.1004601

375 Slavich GM, Mengelkoch S, Cole SW. Human social genomics: Concepts, mechanisms, and implications for health. Lifestyle Med (Hoboken). 2023 Apr;4(2):e75. doi: 10.1002/lim2.75. Epub 2023 Feb 25.

376 Cole, Steve W.; Hawkley, Louise C.; Arevalo, Jesusa M.; Sung, Caroline Y.; Rose, Robert M.; Cacioppo, John T. (2007-01-01). "Social regulation of gene expression in human leukocytes". Genome Biology. 8 (9): R189.

377 Idaghdour Y, Storey JD, Jadallah SJ, Gibson G. A genome-wide gene expression signature of environmental geography in leukocytes of Moroccan Amazighs. PLoS Genet. 2008 Apr 11;4(4):e1000052.

378 Idaghdour, Youssef; Czika, Wendy; Shianna, Kevin V.; Lee, Sang H.; Visscher, Peter M.; Martin, Hilary C.; Miclaus, Kelci; Jadallah, Sami J.; Goldstein, David B. (2010-01-01). "Geographical genomics of human leukocyte gene expression variation in southern Morocco". Nature Genetics. 42 (1): 62–67.

379 Maleszka, Ryszard (27 October 2014). "Epigenetic integration of environmental and genomic signals in honey bees: the critical interplay of nutritional, brain and reproductive networks". Epigenetics. 3 (4): 188–192.

380 https://en.wikipedia.org/wiki/Royal_jelly#cite_note-Maleszka,_R_2008-3

381 Federal Government Seizes Dozens of Misbranded Drug Products: FDA warned company about making medical claims for bee-derived products". Food and Drug Administration. Apr 5, 2010.

382 Morita H, Ikeda T, Kajita K, Fujioka K, Mori I, Okada H, Uno Y, Ishizuka T. Effect of royal jelly ingestion for six months on healthy volunteers. Nutr J. 2012 Sep 21;11:77. doi: 10.1186/1475-2891-11-77.

383 Kucharski, R.; Maleszka, J.; Foret, S.; Maleszka, R. (13 March 2008). "Nutritional Control of Reproductive Status in Honeybees via DNA Methylation". Science. 319 (5871): 1827–1830.

384 Johnson AA, Akman K, Calimport SR, Wuttke D, Stolzing A, de Magalhães JP. The role of DNA methylation in aging, rejuvenation, and age-related disease. Rejuvenation Res. 2012 Oct;15(5):483-94.

385 Bin-Jumah MN, Nadeem MS, Gilani SJ, Al-Abbasi FA, Ullah I, Alzarea SI, Ghoneim MM, Alshehri S, Uddin A, Murtaza BN, Kazmi I. Genes and Longevity of Lifespan. Int J Mol Sci. 2022 Jan 28;23(3):1499.

386 Miller JL, Grant PA. The role of DNA methylation and histone modifications in transcriptional regulation in humans. Subcell Biochem. 2013;61:289-317.

387 Miller JL, Grant PA. The role of DNA methylation and histone modifications in transcriptional regulation in humans. Subcell Biochem. 2013;61:289-317.

388 Deaton AM, Bird A. CpG islands and the regulation of transcription. Genes Dev. 2011 May 15;25(10):1010-22.

389 Johnson AA, Akman K, Calimport SR, Wuttke D, Stolzing A, de Magalhães JP. The role of DNA methylation in aging, rejuvenation, and age-related disease. Rejuvenation Res. 2012 Oct;15(5):483-94.

390 Suzuki H, Toyota M, Sato H, Sonoda T, Sakauchi F, Mori M. Roles and causes of abnormal DNA methylation in gastrointestinal cancers. Asian Pac J Cancer Prev. 2006 Apr-Jun;7(2):177-85.

391 Kanwal R, Gupta S (April 2012). "Epigenetic modifications in cancer". Clinical Genetics. 81 (4): 303–311.

392 Jin B, Robertson KD (2013). "DNA methyltransferases, DNA damage repair, and cancer". Adv. Exp. Med. Biol. Advances in Experimental Medicine and Biology. 754: 3–29.

393 Ehrlich M. DNA hypomethylation in cancer cells. Epigenomics. 2009 Dec;1(2):239-59.

394 Li Y, Tollefsbol TO. Impact on DNA methylation in cancer prevention and therapy by bioactive dietary components. Curr Med Chem. 2010;17(20):2141-51.

395 Lam TK, Gallicchio L, Lindsley K, Shiels M, Hammond E, Tao XG, et al. Cruciferous vegetable consumption and lung cancer risk: a systematic review. Cancer Epidemiol Biomarkers Prev. 2009;18:184–95.

396 Wu X, Zhou QH, Xu K. Are isothiocyanates potential anti-cancer drugs? Acta Pharmacol Sin. 2009 May;30(5):501-12. doi: 10.1038/aps.2009.50. PMID: 19417730; PMCID: PMC4002831.

397 Verhoeven DTH, Verhagen H, Goldbohm RA, van den Brandt PA, van Poppel G. A review of mechanisms underlying anticarcinogenicity by brassica vegetables. Chem Biol Interact. 1997;103:79–129.

398 Kim Y. Folate and carcinogenesis: evidence, mechanisms, and implications. J Nutr Biochem. 1999;10:66–88.

399 Davis C, Uthus E, Finley J. Dietary selenium and arsenic affect DNA methylation in vitro in Caco-2 cells and in vivo in rat liver and colon. J Nutr. 2000;130:2903–9.

400 Elmore S. Apoptosis: a review of programmed cell death. Toxicol Pathol. 2007 Jun;35(4):495-516.

401 Khan N, Adhami VM, Mukhtar H. Apoptosis by dietary agents for prevention and treatment of cancer. Biochem Pharmacol. 2008 Dec 1;76(11):1333-9.

402 Ozaki T, Nakagawara A. Role of p53 in Cell Death and Human Cancers. Cancers (Basel). 2011 Mar 3;3(1):994-1013.

403 Meulmeester E, Jochemsen AG. p53: a guide to apoptosis. Curr Cancer Drug Targets. 2008;8:87–97.

404 Elmore S. Apoptosis: a review of programmed cell death. Toxicol Pathol. 2007 Jun;35(4):495-516.

405 Schumacher B The Mystery of Human Aging: Surprising Insights from a Science That's Still Young. (Algora Publishing, 2017).

406 Schumacher B, Pothof J, Vijg J, Hoeijmakers JHJ. The central role of DNA damage in the ageing process. Nature. 2021;592(7856):695-703.

407 Lindahl T Instability and decay of the primary structure of DNA. Nature 362, 709–715 (1993).

408 Gilbert SF. Developmental Biology. 6th edition. Sunderland (MA): Sinauer Associates; 2000. Aging: The Biology of Senescence. Available from: https://www.ncbi.nlm.nih.gov/books/NBK10041/

409 Bagchi K, Puri S. Free radicals and antioxidants in health and disease. East Mediterranean Health Jr. 1998;4:350–60.

410 Pizzino G, Irrera N, Cucinotta M, Pallio G, Mannino F, Arcoraci V, Squadrito F, Altavilla D, Bitto A. Oxidative Stress: Harms and Benefits for Human Health. Oxid Med Cell Longev. 2017;2017:8416763.

411 Di Meo S, Napolitano G, Venditti P. Physiological and Pathological Role of ROS: Benefits and Limitations of Antioxidant Treatment. Int J Mol Sci. 2019 Sep 27;20(19):4810.

412 https://www.cellgs.com/blog/free-radicals-vs-reactive-oxygen-species-whats-the-difference.html#:~:text=Free%20radicals%20are%20produced%20by,%2C%20Opollutants%2C%20and%20cigarette%20smoke.&text=Reactive%20oxygen%20species%2C%20or%20ROS,free%20radicals%20that%20contain%20oxygen.

413 Lobo V, Patil A, Phatak A, Chandra N. Free radicals, antioxidants and functional foods: Impact on human health. Pharmacogn Rev. 2010 Jul;4(8):118-26.

414 Lobo V, Patil A, Phatak A, Chandra N. Free radicals, antioxidants and functional foods: Impact on human health. Pharmacogn Rev. 2010 Jul;4(8):118-26.

415 Burtenshaw D, Kitching M, Redmond EM, Megson IL, Cahill PA. Reactive Oxygen Species (ROS), Intimal Thickening, and Subclinical Atherosclerotic Disease. Front Cardiovasc Med. 2019 Aug 2;6:89.

416 Harman, D (1956). "Aging: a theory based on free radical and radiation chemistry". Journal of Gerontology. 11 (3): 298–300.

417 Sanz A, Stefanatos RK. The mitochondrial free radical theory of aging: a critical view. Curr Aging Sci. 2008 Mar;1(1):10-21.

418 Orr W S , Sohal R S . Extension of lifespan by overexpression of superoxide dismutase and catalase in Drosophila melanogaster. Science. 1994;263:1128–1130.

419 Larsen P L . Aging and resistance to oxidative damage in C. elegans. Proc. Natl. Acad. Sci. USA. 1993;90:8905–8909.

420 Liu Y, Long J, Liu J. Mitochondrial free radical theory of aging: who moved my premise? Geriatr Gerontol Int. 2014 Oct;14(4):740-9.

421 Sergio Di Meo, Tanea T. Reed, Paola Venditti, Victor Manuel Victor, "Role of ROS and RNS Sources in Physiological and Pathological Conditions", Oxidative Medicine and Cellular Longevity, vol. 2016, Article ID 1245049, 44 pages, 2016. https://doi.org/10.1155/2016/1245049

422 Sanz A, Stefanatos RK. The mitochondrial free radical theory of aging: a critical view. Curr Aging Sci. 2008 Mar;1(1):10-21.

423 Di Meo S, Reed TT, Venditti P, Victor VM. Role of ROS and RNS Sources in Physiological and Pathological Conditions. Oxid Med Cell Longev. 2016;2016:1245049.

424 Missiroli S, Genovese I, Perrone M, Vezzani B, Vitto VAM, Giorgi C. The Role of Mitochondria in Inflammation: From Cancer to Neurodegenerative Disorders. J Clin Med. 2020 Mar 9;9(3):740.

425 Camps J, García-Heredia A. Introduction: oxidation and inflammation, a molecular link between non-communicable diseases. Adv Exp Med Biol. 2014;824:1-4.

426 Lee J, Pellegrini MV. Biochemistry, Telomere And Telomerase. [Updated 2022 Dec 11]. In: StatPearls [Internet]. Treasure Island (FL): StatPearls Publishing; 2023 Jan-. Available from: https://www.ncbi.nlm.nih.gov/books/NBK576429/

427 Griffith JD, Comeau L, Rosenfield S, Stansel RM, Bianchi A, Moss H, de Lange T. Mammalian telomeres end in a large duplex loop. Cell. 1999 May 14;97(4):503-14.

428 Demanelis K, Jasmine F, Chen LS, et al; GTEx Consortium. Determinants of telomere length across human tissues. Science. 2020; 369(6509):eaaz6876

429 Lee J, Pellegrini MV. Biochemistry, Telomere And Telomerase. [Updated 2022 Dec 11]. In: StatPearls [Internet]. Treasure Island (FL): StatPearls Publishing; 2023 Jan-. Available from: https://www.ncbi.nlm.nih.gov/books/NBK576429/

430 https://www.genome.gov/genetics-glossary/Telomere#:~:text=A%20telomere%20is%20a%20region,successfully%2C%20and%20the%20cell%20dies.

431 Bodnar AG, Ouellette M, Frolkis M, et al.. Extension of life-span by introduction of telomerase into normal human cells. Science. 1998;279(5349):349-352.

432 Decker M.L., Chavez E., Vulto I., Lansdorp P.M. Telomere length in hutchinson-gilford progeria syndrome. Mech. Ageing Dev. 2009;130:377–383.

433 Lansdorp PM. Telomeres, aging, and cancer: the big picture. Blood. 2022 Feb 10;139(6):813-821.

434 Vedder O., Moiron M., Bichet C., Bauch C., Verhulst S., Becker P.H., Bouwhuis S. Telomere length is heritable and genetically correlated with lifespan in a wild bird. Mol. Ecol. 2021.

435 Bin-Jumah MN, Nadeem MS, Gilani SJ, Al-Abbasi FA, Ullah I, Alzarea SI, Ghoneim MM, Alshehri S, Uddin A, Murtaza BN, Kazmi I. Genes and Longevity of Lifespan. Int J Mol Sci. 2022 Jan 28;23(3):1499.

436 Van den Berg N., Rodríguez-Girondo M., van Dijk I., Mourits R., Mandemakers K., Janssens A., Beekman M., Smith K., Slagboom P. Longevity defined as top 10% survivors and beyond is transmitted as a quantitative genetic trait. Nat Commun. 2019;10:35.

437 Öngel M.E., Yıldız C., Akpınaroğlu C., Yilmaz B., Özilgen M. Why women may live longer than men do? A telomere-length regulated and diet-based entropic assessment. Clin. Nutr. 2021;40:1186–1191.

438 Bodnar AG et al. Extension of life-span by introduction of telomerase into normal human cells. Science 279, 349–52 (1998).

439 Chilton W., O'Brien B., Charchar F. Telomeres, Aging and Exercise: Guilty by Association? Int. J. Mol. Sci. 2017;18:2573.

440 Epel ES. Psychological and metabolic stress: a recipe for accelerated cellular aging? Hormones (Athens). 2009 Jan-Mar;8(1):7-22.

441 Brown L., Needham B., Ailshire J. Telomere length among older U.S. Adults: Differences by race/ethnicity, gender and age. J. Aging Health. 2016;29:1350–1366.

442 Needham B.L., Adler N., Gregorich S., Rehkopf D., Lin J., Blackburn E.H., Epel E.S. Socioeconomic status, health behavior and leukocyte telomere length in the national health and nutrition examination survey, 1999–2002. Soc. Sci. Med. 2013;85:1–8.

443 Ahadi S., Zhou W., Schussler-Fiorenza Rose S.M., Sailani M.R., Contrepois K., Avina M., Ashland M., Brunet A., Snyder M. Personal aging markers and ageotypes revealed by deep longitudinal profiling. Nat. Med. 2020;26:83–90.

444 Li C, Stoma S, Lotta LA, Warner S, Albrecht E, Allione A, Arp PP, Broer L, Buxton JL, Da Silva Couto Alves A, Deelen J, et al. Genome-wide Association Analysis in Humans Links Nucleotide Metabolism to Leukocyte Telomere Length. Am J Hum Genet. 2020 Mar 5;106(3):389-404.

445 Yousefzadeh MJ, Flores RR, Zhu Y, et al. An aged immune system drives senescence and ageing of solid organs. Nature. 2021; 594(7861):100-105.

446 Wang Q, Codd V, Raisi-Estabragh Z, et al. Shorter leukocyte telomere length is associated with adverse COVID-19 outcomes: a cohort study in UK Biobank. EBioMedicine. 2021;70:103485.

447 Bejarano L, Bosso G, Louzame J, Serrano R, Gómez-Casero E, Martínez-Torrecuadrada J, Martínez S, Blanco-Aparicio C, Pastor J, Blasco MA. Multiple

cancer pathways regulate telomere protection. EMBO Mol Med. 2019 Jul;11(7):e10292.

448 Haycock PC, Burgess S, Nounu A, et al; Telomeres Mendelian Randomization Collaboration. Association between telomere length and risk of cancer and nonneoplastic diseases: a mendelian randomization study. JAMA Oncol. 2017;3(5):636-651.

449 McNally EJ, Luncsford PJ, Armanios M. Long telomeres and cancer risk: the price of cellular immortality. J Clin Invest. 2019;129(9):3474-3481.

450 Kim NW, Piatyszek MA, Prowse KR, Harley CB, West MD, Ho PL, Coviello GM, Wright WE, Weinrich SL, Shay JW. Specific association of human telomerase activity with immortal cells and cancer. Science. 1994 Dec 23;266(5193):2011-5.

451 Jäger K, Walter M. Therapeutic Targeting of Telomerase. Genes (Basel). 2016 Jul 21;7(7)

452 Nassour J, Schmidt TT, Karlseder J. Telomeres and cancer: resolving the paradox. Annu Rev Cancer Biol. 2021;5(1):59-77.

453 Lundblad V & Szostak JW A mutant with a defect in telomere elongation leads to senescence in yeast. Cell 57, 633–643 (1989).

454 d'Adda di Fagagna F, Reaper PM, Clay-Farrace L, Fiegler H, Carr P, Von Zglinicki T, Saretzki G, Carter NP, Jackson SP. A DNA damage checkpoint response in telomere-initiated senescence. Nature. 2003 Nov 13;426(6963):194-8.

455 HAYFLICK L, MOORHEAD PS. The serial cultivation of human diploid cell strains. Exp Cell Res. 1961 Dec;25:585-621.

456 https://www.cellsignal.com/science-resources/overview-of-cellular-senescence

457 Huang, W., Hickson, L.J., Eirin, A. et al. Cellular senescence: the good, the bad and the unknown. Nat Rev Nephrol 18, 611–627 (2022).

458 Lansdorp PM. Telomeres, aging, and cancer: the big picture. Blood. 2022 Feb 10;139(6):813-821.

459 Childs BG, Baker DJ, Kirkland JL, Campisi J, van Deursen JM. Senescence and apoptosis: dueling or complementary cell fates? EMBO Rep. 2014 Nov;15(11):1139-53.

460 Kaur J, Farr JN. Cellular senescence in age-related disorders. Transl Res. 2020 Dec;226:96-104.

461 Huang, W., Hickson, L.J., Eirin, A. et al. Cellular senescence: the good, the bad and the unknown. Nat Rev Nephrol 18, 611–627 (2022).

462 Bhatia-Dey N, Kanherkar RR, Stair SE, Makarev EO, Csoka AB. Cellular Senescence as the Causal Nexus of Aging. Front Genet. 2016 Feb 12;7:13.

463 Huang, W., Hickson, L.J., Eirin, A. et al. Cellular senescence: the good, the bad and the unknown. Nat Rev Nephrol 18, 611–627 (2022).

464 Rodier F et al. DNA-SCARS: Distinct nuclear structures that sustain damage-induced senescence growth arrest and inflammatory cytokine secretion. J. Cell Sci. 124, 68–81 (2011).

465 Saleh T, Tyutyunyk-Massey L, Murray GF, Alotaibi MR, Kawale AS, Elsayed Z, Henderson SC, Yakovlev V, Elmore LW, Toor A, Harada H, Reed J, Landry JW, Gewirtz DA. Tumor cell escape from therapy-induced senescence. Biochem Pharmacol. 2019 Apr;162:202-212.

466 Song P, An J, Zou MH. Immune Clearance of Senescent Cells to Combat Ageing and Chronic Diseases. Cells. 2020 Mar 10;9(3):671.

467 von Kobbe C. Targeting senescent cells: approaches, opportunities, challenges. Aging (Albany NY). 2019 Nov 30;11(24):12844-12861.

468 Lagoumtzi SM, Chondrogianni N. Senolytics and senomorphics: Natural and synthetic therapeutics in the treatment of aging and chronic diseases. Free Radic Biol Med. 2021 Aug 1;171:169-190.

469 Wissler Gerdes EO, Misra A, Netto JME, Tchkonia T, Kirkland JL. Strategies for late phase preclinical and early clinical trials of senolytics. Mech Ageing Dev. 2021 Dec;200:111591.

470 Wang, L., Lankhorst, L. & Bernards, R. Exploiting senescence for the treatment of cancer. Nat Rev Cancer 22, 340–355 (2022).

471 Glossmann H.H., Lutz O.M.D. Metformin and aging: A review. Gerontology. 2019;65:581–590.

472 Barzilai N, Crandall JP, Kritchevsky SB, Espeland MA. Metformin as a tool to target aging. Cell Metab. 2016;23:1060–1065.

473 Konopka AR, Miller BF. Taming expectations of metformin as a treatment to extend healthspan. Geroscience. 2019 Apr;41(2):101-108.

474 Soukas A.A., Hao H., Wu L. Metformin as anti-aging therapy: Is it for everyone? Trends Endocrinol. Metab. 2019;30:745–755.

475 Konopka AR, Laurin JL, Schoenberg HM, Reid JJ, Castor WM, Wolff CA, Musci RV, Safairad OD, Linden MA, Biela LM, Bailey SM, Hamilton KL, Miller BF (2018) Metformin inhibits mitochondrial adaptations to aerobic exercise training in older adults. Aging Cell e12880

476 Walton RG, Dungan CM, Long DE, Tuggle SC, Kosmac K, Peck BD, Bush HM, Villasante Tezanos AG, McGwin G, Windham ST, Ovalle F, Bamman MM, Kern PA, Peterson CA. Metformin blunts muscle hypertrophy in response to

progressive resistance exercise training in older adults: A randomized, double-blind, placebo-controlled, multicenter trial: The MASTERS trial. Aging Cell. 2019 Dec;18(6):e13039.

477 Song P, An J, Zou MH. Immune Clearance of Senescent Cells to Combat Ageing and Chronic Diseases. Cells. 2020 Mar 10;9(3):671.

    Glossmann H.H., Lutz O.M.D. Metformin and aging: A review. Gerontology. 2019;65:581–590.

WHAT DOES YOUR DNA GOOD? SURPRISE, IT'S EXERCISE AND DIET (AND MAYBE SUPPLEMENTS).

478 Sallam, N.; Laher, I. Exercise Modulates Oxidative Stress and Inflammation in Aging and Cardiovascular Diseases. Oxid. Med. Cell. Longev. 2016, 2016, 7239639.

479 Beavers KM, Brinkley TE, Nicklas BJ. Effect of exercise training on chronic inflammation. Clin Chim Acta. 2010 Jun 3;411(11-12):785-93.

480 Radak, Z.; Chung, H.Y.; Goto, S. Systemic adaptation to oxidative challenge induced by regular exercise. Free Radic. Biol. Med. 2008, 44, 153–159.

481 Powers, S.K.; Ji, L.L.; Leeuwenburgh, C. Exercise training-induced alterations in skeletal muscle antioxidant capacity: A brief review. Med. Sci. Sports Exerc. 1999, 31, 987–997.

482 Powers SK, Deminice R, Ozdemir M, Yoshihara T, Bomkamp MP, Hyatt H. Exercise-induced oxidative stress: Friend or foe? J Sport Health Sci. 2020 Sep;9(5):415-425.

483 O'Keefe EL, Torres-Acosta N, O'Keefe JH, Lavie CJ. Training for Longevity: The Reverse J-Curve for Exercise. Mo Med. 2020 Jul-Aug;117(4):355-361.

484 Arsenis N.C., You T., Ogawa E.F., Tinsley G.M., Zuo L. Physical activity and telomere length: Impact of aging and potential mechanisms of action. Oncotarget. 2017;8:45008–45019.

485 Balan E, Decottignies A, Deldicque L. Physical Activity and Nutrition: Two Promising Strategies for Telomere Maintenance? Nutrients. 2018 Dec 7;10(12):1942.

486 Ludlow AT, Zimmerman JB, Witkowski S, Hearn JW, Hatfield BD, Roth SM. Relationship between physical activity level, telomere length, and telomerase activity. Med Sci Sports Exerc. 2008 Oct;40(10):1764-71.

487 Puterman E, Lin J, Blackburn E, O'Donovan A, Adler N, Epel E. The power of exercise: buffering the effect of chronic stress on telomere length. PLoS One. 2010 May 26;5(5):e10837.

488 Chilton W., O'Brien B., Charchar F. Telomeres, Aging and Exercise: Guilty by Association? Int. J. Mol. Sci. 2017;18:2573. doi: 10.3390/ijms18122573.

489 Schnohr P, O'Keefe JH, Holtermann A, Lavie CJ, Lange P, Jensen GB, Marott JL. Various Leisure-Time Physical Activities Associated With Widely Divergent Life Expectancies: The Copenhagen City Heart Study. Mayo Clin Proc. 2018 Dec;93(12):1775-1785.

490 Wendy Suzuki, Do your brain a favor — move your body, January 13, 20239:22 AM ET, Heard on TED Radio Hour

491 Di Liegro CM, Schiera G, Proia P, Di Liegro I. Physical Activity and Brain Health. Genes (Basel). 2019 Sep 17;10(9):720.

492 Pedersen BK. Physical activity and muscle-brain crosstalk. Nat Rev Endocrinol. 2019 Jul;15(7):383-392.

493 Tsankova N.M., Berton O., Renthal W., Kumar A., Neve R.L., Nestler E.J. Sustained hippocampal chromatin regulation in a mouse model of depression and antidepressant action. Nat. Neurosci. 2006;9:519–525. doi: 10.1038/nn1659.

494 Gomez-Pinilla F., Zhuang Y., Feng J., Ying Z., Fan G. Exercise impacts brain-derived neurotrophic factor plasticity by engaging mechanisms of epigenetic regulation. Eur. J. Neurosci. 2011;33:383–390.

495 Lee J, Pellegrini MV. Biochemistry, Telomere And Telomerase. [Updated 2022 Dec 11]. In: StatPearls [Internet]. Treasure Island (FL): StatPearls Publishing; 2023 Jan-. Available from: https://www.ncbi.nlm.nih.gov/books/NBK576429/

496 McGrath M, Wong JY, Michaud D, Hunter DJ, De Vivo I. Telomere length, cigarette smoking, and bladder cancer risk in men and women. Cancer Epidemiol Biomarkers Prev. 2007 Apr;16(4):815-9.

497 McCay CM, Maynard LA, Sperling G & Barnes LL Retarded Growth, Life Span, Ultimate Body Size and Age Changes in the Albino Rat after Feeding Diets Restricted in Calories. J. Nutr. (1939). doi: 10.1093/jn/18.1.1

498 Kenyon C, Chang J, Gensch E, Rudner A & Tabtiang R A C. elegans mutant that lives twice as long as wild type. Nature 366, 461–464 (1993).

499 Hahn, O. et al. Dietary restriction protects from age-associated DNA methylation and induces epigenetic reprogramming of lipid metabolism. Genome Biol. 18, 56 (2017).

500 Maegawa, S., Lu, Y., Tahara, T. et al. Caloric restriction delays age-related methylation drift. Nat Commun 8, 539 (2017).

501 Omodei D, Fontana L. Calorie restriction and prevention of age-associated chronic disease. FEBS Lett. 2011 Jun 6;585(11):1537-42.

502 Flanagan EW, Most J, Mey JT, Redman LM. Calorie Restriction and Aging in Humans. Annu Rev Nutr. 2020 Sep 23;40:105-133.

503 Schumacher B, Pothof J, Vijg J, Hoeijmakers JHJ. The central role of DNA damage in the ageing process. Nature. 2021;592(7856):695-703.

504 Mattson MP. Dietary factors, hormesis and health. Ageing Res Rev. 2008 Jan;7(1):43-8.

505 Ravussin E, Redman LM, Rochon J, Das SK, Fontana L, Kraus WE, Romashkan S, Williamson DA, Meydani SN, Villareal DT, Smith SR, Stein RI, Scott TM, Stewart TM, Saltzman E, Klein S, Bhapkar M, Martin CK, Gilhooly CH, Holloszy JO, Hadley EC, Roberts SB; CALERIE Study Group. A 2-Year Randomized Controlled Trial of Human Caloric Restriction: Feasibility and Effects on Predictors of Health Span and Longevity. J Gerontol A Biol Sci Med Sci. 2015 Sep;70(9):1097-104. doi: 10.1093/gerona/glv057. Epub 2015 Jul 17. Erratum in: J Gerontol A Biol Sci Med Sci. 2016 Jun;71(6):839-40.

506 Waziry, R., Ryan, C.P., Corcoran, D.L. et al. Effect of long-term caloric restriction on DNA methylation measures of biological aging in healthy adults from the CALERIE trial. Nat Aging 3, 248–257 (2023).

507 He X, Liu J, Liu B, Shi J. The use of DNA methylation clock in aging research. Exp Biol Med (Maywood). 2021 Feb;246(4):436-446.

508 Levine ME, Lu AT, Quach A, Chen BH, Assimes TL, Bandinelli S, Hou L, Baccarelli AA, Stewart JD, Li Y, Whitsel EA, Wilson JG, Reiner AP, Aviv A, Lohman K, Liu Y, Ferrucci L, Horvath S. An epigenetic biomarker of aging for lifespan and healthspan. Aging (Albany NY). 2018 Apr 18;10(4):573-591.

509 Lu AT, Quach A, Wilson JG, Reiner AP, Aviv A, Raj K, Hou L, Baccarelli AA, Li Y, Stewart JD, Whitsel EA, Assimes TL, Ferrucci L, Horvath S. DNA methylation GrimAge strongly predicts lifespan and healthspan. Aging (Albany NY). 2019 Jan 21;11(2):303-327.

510 https://www.cnn.com/2023/02/10/health/restricting-calories-longevity-wellness/index.html

511 Opalach K, Rangaraju S, Madorsky I, Leeuwenburgh C, Notterpek L. Lifelong calorie restriction alleviates age-related oxidative damage in peripheral nerves. Rejuvenation Res. 2010;13:65–74.

512 Ferrucci L, Fabbri E. Inflammageing: chronic inflammation in ageing, cardiovascular disease, and frailty. Nat Rev Cardiol. 2018 Sep;15(9):505-522.

513 Sohal RS, Weindruch R. Oxidative stress, caloric restriction, and aging. Science. 1996 Jul 5;273(5271):59-63.

514 Walsh ME, Shi Y, Van Remmen H. The effects of dietary restriction on oxidative stress in rodents. Free Radic Biol Med. 2014 Jan;66:88-99.

515 Lamming DW, and Anderson RM (2014). Metabolic Effects of Caloric Restriction In eLS (Chichester: John Wiley & Sons, Ltd;).

516 Johnson ML, Distelmaier K, Lanza IR, Irving BA, Robinson MM, Konopka AR, Shulman GI, Nair KS. Mechanism by Which Caloric Restriction Improves Insulin Sensitivity in Sedentary Obese Adults. Diabetes. 2016 Jan;65(1):74-84.

517 Vermeij WP et al. Restricted diet delays accelerated ageing and genomic stress in DNA-repair-deficient mice. Nature 537, 427–431 (2016).

518 Wang C., Maddick M., Miwa S., Jurk D., Czapiewski R., Saretzki G., et al. (2010). Adult-onset, short-term dietary restriction reduces cell senescence in mice. Aging (Albany NY) 2 555–566.

519 Tomiyama AJ, Mann T, Vinas D, Hunger JM, Dejager J, Taylor SE. Low calorie dieting increases cortisol. Psychosom Med. 2010 May;72(4):357-64.

520 Cay M, Ucar C, Senol D, Cevirgen F, Ozbag D, Altay Z, Yildiz S. Effect of increase in cortisol level due to stress in healthy young individuals on dynamic and static balance scores. North Clin Istanb. 2018 May 29;5(4):295-301.

521 Justin B. Echouffo-Tcheugui, Sarah C. Conner, Jayandra J. Himali, Pauline Maillard, Charles S. DeCarli, Alexa S. Beiser, Ramachandran S. Vasan, Sudha Seshadri Circulating cortisol and cognitive and structural brain measures. The Framingham Heart Study. Neurology Nov 2018, 91 (21) e1961-e1970.

522 Prasad C, Davis KE, Imrhan V, Juma S, Vijayagopal P. Advanced Glycation End Products and Risks for Chronic Diseases: Intervening Through Lifestyle Modification. Am J Lifestyle Med. 2017 May 15;13(4):384-404.

523 Schumacher B, Pothof J, Vijg J, Hoeijmakers JHJ. The central role of DNA damage in the ageing process. Nature. 2021;592(7856):695-703.

524 Chaudhuri J, Bains Y, Guha S, Kahn A, Hall D, Bose N, Gugliucci A, Kapahi P. The Role of Advanced Glycation End Products in Aging and Metabolic Diseases: Bridging Association and Causality. Cell Metab. 2018 Sep 4;28(3):337-352.

525 Richard D. Semba and others, Does Accumulation of Advanced Glycation End Products Contribute to the Aging Phenotype?, The Journals of Gerontology: Series A, Volume 65A, Issue 9, September 2010, Pages 963–975.

526 Koschinsky T, He CJ, Mitsuhashi T, Bucala R, Liu C, Bueting C, Heitmann K, Vlassara H. Orally absorbed reactive advanced glycation end products (glycotoxins): An environmental risk factor in diabetic nephropathy. Proc Natl Acad Sci USA. 1997;94:6474–6479.

527 Uribarri J, Woodruff S, Goodman S, Cai W, Chen X, Pyzik R, Yong A, Striker GE, Vlassara H. Advanced glycation end products in foods and a practical guide to their reduction in the diet. J Am Diet Assoc. 2010 Jun;110(6):911-16.e12.

528 Noordam R, Gunn DA, Tomlin CC, Maier AB, Mooijaart SP, Slagboom PE, Westendorp RG, de Craen AJ, van Heemst D; Leiden Longevity Study Group. High serum glucose levels are associated with a higher perceived age. Age (Dordr). 2013 Feb;35(1):189-95.

529 Aksungar FB, Sarıkaya M, Coskun A, Serteser M, Unsal I. Comparison of Intermittent Fasting Versus Caloric Restriction in Obese Subjects: A Two Year Follow-Up. J Nutr Health Aging. 2017;21(6):681-685.

530 Lin S, Cienfuegos S, Ezpeleta M, Gabel K, Pavlou V, Mulas A, Chakos K, McStay M, Wu J, Tussing-Humphreys L, Alexandria SJ, Sanchez J, Unterman T, Varady KA. Time-Restricted Eating Without Calorie Counting for Weight Loss in a Racially Diverse Population : A Randomized Controlled Trial. Ann Intern Med. 2023 Jul;176(7):885-895.

531 Nikolai, S., Pallauf, K., Huebbe, P., & Rimbach, G. (2015). Energy restriction and potential energy restriction mimetics. Nutrition Research Reviews, 28(2), 100-120.

532 Singh S, Kumar R, Garg G, Singh AK, Verma AK, Bissoyi A, Rizvi SI. Spermidine, a caloric restriction mimetic, provides neuroprotection against normal and D-galactose-induced oxidative stress and apoptosis through activation of autophagy in male rats during aging. Biogerontology. 2021 Feb;22(1):35-47.

533 https://www.cellgs.com/blog/free-radicals-vs-reactive-oxygen-species-whats-the-difference.html#:~:text=Free%20radicals%20are%20produced%20by,%2C%20Opollutants%2C%20and%20cigarette%20smoke.&text=Reactive%20oxygen%20species%2C%20or%20ROS,free%20radicals%20that%20contain%20oxygen.

534 Stefanis L, Burke RE, Greene LA. Apoptosis in neurodegenerative disorders. Curr Opin Neurol. 1997;10:299–305.

535 Lobo V, Patil A, Phatak A, Chandra N. Free radicals, antioxidants and functional foods: Impact on human health. Pharmacogn Rev. 2010 Jul;4(8):118-26.

536 Sokol RJ. Vitamin E deficiency and neurologic diseses. Annu Rev Nutr. 1988;8:351–73.

537 Poppel GV, Golddbohm RA. Epidemiologic evidence for β – carotene and cancer prevention. Am J Clin Nutr. 1995;62:1393–5.

538 Glatthaar BE, Horing DH, Moser U. The role of ascorbic acid in carcinogenesis. Adv Exp Med Biol. 1986;206:357–77.

539 Katz DL, Doughty K, Ali A. Cocoa and chocolate in human health and disease. Antioxid Redox Signal. 2011 Nov 15;15(10):2779-811.

540 Jang M, Cai L, Udeani GO, Slowing KV, Thomas CF, Beecher CW, Fong HH, Farnsworth NR, Kinghorn AD, Mehta RG, Moon RC, Pezzuto JM. Cancer chemopreventive activity of resveratrol, a natural product derived from grapes. Science. 1997 Jan 10;275(5297):218-20.

541 Tousian H, Razavi BM, Hosseinzadeh H. Looking for immortality: Review of phytotherapy for stem cell senescence. Iran J Basic Med Sci. 2020 Feb;23(2):154-166.

542 Renaud S, de Lorgeril M. Wine, alcohol, platelets, and the French paradox for coronary heart disease. Lancet. 1992 Jun 20;339(8808):1523-6.

543 Meng X, Zhou J, Zhao CN, Gan RY, Li HB. Health Benefits and Molecular Mechanisms of Resveratrol: A Narrative Review. Foods. 2020 Mar 14;9(3):340.

544 Dudley J, Das S, Mukherjee S, and Das DK. Resvera-trol, a unique phytoalexin present in red wine, deliverseither survival signal or death signal to the ischemicmyocardium depending on dose.JNutrBiochem2009; 20: 443–452.

545 Weiskirchen S, Weiskirchen R. Resveratrol: How Much Wine Do You Have to Drink to Stay Healthy? Adv Nutr. 2016 Jul 15;7(4):706-18.

546 Corpas R, Griñán-Ferré C, Rodríguez-Farré E, Pallàs M, Sanfeliu C. Resveratrol Induces Brain Resilience Against Alzheimer Neurodegeneration Through Proteostasis Enhancement. Mol Neurobiol. 2019 Feb;56(2):1502-1516.

547 Cicero AFG, Ruscica M, Banach M. Resveratrol and cognitive decline: a clinician perspective. Arch Med Sci. 2019 Jul;15(4):936-943.

548 Koushki M, Amiri-Dashatan N, Ahmadi N, Abbaszadeh HA, Rezaei-Tavirani M. Resveratrol: A miraculous natural compound for diseases treatment. Food Sci Nutr. 2018 Oct 26;6(8):2473-2490.

549 Burns J, Yokota T, Ashihara H, Lean ME, Crozier A. Plant foods and herbal sources of resveratrol. J Agric Food Chem. 2002 May 22;50(11):3337-40.

550 Beekwilder J, Wolswinkel R, Jonker H, Hall R, de Vos CH, Bovy A. Production of resveratrol in recombinant microorganisms. Appl Environ Microbiol. 2006 Aug;72(8):5670-2.

551 Sergides C, Chirilă M, Silvestro L, Pitta D, Pittas A. Bioavailability and safety study of resveratrol 500 mg tablets in healthy male and female volunteers. Exp Ther Med. 2016 Jan;11(1):164-170.

552 Meng X, Zhou J, Zhao CN, Gan RY, Li HB. Health Benefits and Molecular Mechanisms of Resveratrol: A Narrative Review. Foods. 2020 Mar 14;9(3):340.

553 Meng X, Zhou J, Zhao CN, Gan RY, Li HB. Health Benefits and Molecular Mechanisms of Resveratrol: A Narrative Review. Foods. 2020 Mar 14;9(3):340.

554 Shaito A, Posadino AM, Younes N, Hasan H, Halabi S, Alhababi D, Al-Mohannadi A, Abdel-Rahman WM, Eid AH, Nasrallah GK, Pintus G. Potential Adverse Effects of Resveratrol: A Literature Review. Int J Mol Sci. 2020 Mar 18;21(6):2084.

555 Mattson MP. Hormesis defined. Ageing Res Rev. 2008 Jan;7(1):1-7.

556 Mattson MP. Hormesis defined. Ageing Res Rev. 2008 Jan;7(1):1-7.

557 Calabrese EJ, Mattson MP, Calabrese V. Resveratrol commonly displays hormesis: occurrence and biomedical significance. Hum Exp Toxicol. 2010 Dec;29(12):980-1015.

558 de la Lastra CA, Villegas I. Resveratrol as an antioxidant and pro-oxidant agent: mechanisms and clinical implications. Biochem Soc Trans. 2007 Nov;35(Pt 5):1156-60.

559 Salehi B, Mishra AP, Nigam M, Sener B, Kilic M, Sharifi-Rad M, Fokou PVT, Martins N, Sharifi-Rad J. Resveratrol: A Double-Edged Sword in Health Benefits. Biomedicines. 2018 Sep 9;6(3):91.

560 Dudley, J., Das, S., Mukherjee, S., & Das, D. K. (2009). Resveratrol, a unique phytoalexin present in red wine, delivers either survival signal or death signal to the ischemic myocardium depending on dose.

561 Patel KR, Scott E, Brown VA, Gescher AJ, Steward WP, Brown K. Clinical trials of resveratrol. Ann N Y Acad Sci 2011;1215:161–9.

562 https://www.ted.com/talks/rod_phillips_a_brief_history_of_alcohol?language=en

563 Rumgay H, Shield K, Charvat H, Ferrari P, Sornpaisarn B, Obot I, Islami F, Lemmens VEPP, Rehm J, Soerjomataram I. Global burden of cancer in 2020 attributable to alcohol consumption: a population-based study. Lancet Oncol. 2021 Aug;22(8):1071-1080.

564 Rumgay H, Murphy N, Ferrari P, Soerjomataram I. Alcohol and Cancer: Epidemiology and Biological Mechanisms. Nutrients. 2021 Sep 11;13(9):3173.

565 https://www.cato.org/commentary/alcohol-caffeine-created-civilization#:~:text=Palm%20wine%2C%20still%20popular%20in,and%20non%E2%80%90%E2%80%8Bnomadic%20civilization.

566 Pauwels EKJ, Volterrani D. Coffee Consumption and Cancer Risk: An Assessment of the Health Implications Based on Recent Knowledge. Med Princ Pract. 2021;30(5):401-411.

567 https://www.who.int/europe/news/item/04-01-2023-no-level-of-alcohol-cons umption-is-safe-for-our-health

568 Daviet R, Aydogan G, Jagannathan K, Spilka N, Koellinger PD, Kranzler HR, Nave G, Wetherill RR. Associations between alcohol consumption and gray and white matter volumes in the UK Biobank. Nat Commun. 2022 Mar 4;13(1):1175.

569 Prickett CD, Lister E, Collins M, Trevithick-Sutton CC, Hirst M, Vinson JA, Noble E, Trevithick JR. Alcohol: Friend or Foe? Alcoholic Beverage Hormesis for Cataract and Atherosclerosis is Related to Plasma Antioxidant Activity. Nonlinearity Biol Toxicol Med. 2004 Oct;2(4):353-70.

570 Krenz M, Korthuis RJ. Moderate ethanol ingestion and cardiovascular protection: from epidemiologic associations to cellular mechanisms. J Mol Cell Cardiol. 2012 Jan;52(1):93-104.

571 Cui M, Li F, Gang X, Gao Y, Xiao X, Wang G, Liu Y, Wang G. Association of alcohol consumption with all-cause mortality, new-onset stroke, and coronary heart disease in patients with abnormal glucose metabolism-Findings from a 10-year follow-up of the REACTION study. J Diabetes. 2023 Apr;15(4):289-298.

572 Benedek M, Panzierer L, Jauk E, Neubauer AC. Creativity on tap? Effects of alcohol intoxication on creative cognition. Conscious Cogn. 2017 Nov;56:128-134.

573 McDonough KH. Antioxidant nutrients and alcohol. Toxicology. 2003 Jul 15;189(1-2):89-97.

574 Baglietto L, English DR, Gertig DM, Hopper JL, Giles GG. Does dietary folate intake modify effect of alcohol consumption on breast cancer risk? Prospective cohort study. BMJ. 2005 Oct 8;331(7520):807.

575 Martinez-Hurtado JL, Calo-Fernandez B, Vazquez-Padin J. Preventing and Mitigating Alcohol Toxicity: A Review on Protective Substances. Beverages. 2018; 4(2):39.

576 Schumacher B, Pothof J, Vijg J, Hoeijmakers JHJ. The central role of DNA damage in the ageing process. Nature. 2021;592(7856):695-703.

577 Knox, Malcolm (June 11, 2008). "The game's up: jurors playing Sudoku abort trial". The Sydney Morning Herald. Retrieved June 11, 2008.

578 Souders, Dustin J. and Boot, Walter R. and Blocker, Kenneth and Vitale, Thomas and Roque, Nelson A. and Charness, Neil. Evidence for Narrow Transfer after Short-Term Cognitive Training in Older Adults. Frontiers in Aging Neuroscience. 2017;9. https://www.frontiersin.org/articles/10.3389/fnagi.2017.00041

579 Naidu, E., Gabriel, S., Wildschut, T., & Sedikides, C. (2023). Reliving the Good

Old Days: Nostalgia Increases Psychological Wellbeing Through Collective Effervescence. Social Psychological and Personality Science, 0(0).

I'LL TAKE IMMORTALITY PLEASE.

580 https://www.businessinsider.com/billionaires-who-want-to-live-forever-2015-9

581 https://www.businessinsider.com/billionaires-who-want-to-live-forever-2015-9

582 https://www.cnbc.com/2022/04/11/elon-musk-on-avoiding-longevity-research-i-am-not-afraid-of-dying.html

583 https://www.republicworld.com/world-news/rest-of-the-world-news/cant-think-of-a-worse-curse-elon-musk-on-immortality-as-world-population-tops-8-bn-articleshow.html

584 https://www.businessinsider.com/neil-degrasse-tysons-answer-to-what-if-we-could-live-forever-will-change-how-you-think-about-time-2017-6#:~:text=The%20urgency%20of%20accomplishment.,Because%20we%20always%20have%20tomorrow.

585 Cave, Stephen. Immortality: The Quest to Live Forever and How It Drives Civilization (2012). New York: Crown

586 Michel de Montaigne: The Complete Essays. https://www.gutenberg.org/ebooks/3600

587 Williams, B. (1973a), 'The Makropoulos Case: Reflections on the Tedium of Immortality', in Problems of the Self: Philosophical Papers 1956–1972. Cambridge: Cambridge University Press

588 Fischer, J. M. (2009), 'Why Immortality is Not So Bad', in Our Stories: Essays on Life, Death, and Free Will. Oxford: Oxford University Press

589 Levy BR, Slade MD, Kunkel SR, Kasl SV. Longevity increased by positive self-perceptions of aging. J Pers Soc Psychol. 2002 Aug;83(2):261-70.

590 Bhatia-Dey N, Kanherkar RR, Stair SE, Makarev EO, Csoka AB. Cellular Senescence as the Causal Nexus of Aging. Front Genet. 2016 Feb 12;7:13.

591 Hiyama E, Hiyama K. Telomere and telomerase in stem cells. Br J Cancer. 2007 Apr 10;96(7):1020-4.

592 Hayflick L, Moorhead PS (1961). "The serial cultivation of human diploid cell strains". Exp Cell Res. 25 (3): 585–621.

593 Duesberg P, McCormack A. Immortality of cancers: a consequence of inherent karyotypic variations and selections for autonomy. Cell Cycle. 2013 Mar

1;12(5):783-802.

594 Sell S. On the stem cell origin of cancer. Am J Pathol. 2010 Jun;176(6):2584-494.

595 https://www.smithsonianmag.com/science-nature/henrietta-lacks-immortal-ce lls-6421299/

596 https://www.nature.com/articles/d41586-020-02494-z

597 https://en.wikipedia.org/wiki/HeLa

598 Skloot, Rebecca (2010). The Immortal Life of Henrietta Lacks. New York: Crown/Random House. ISBN 978-1-4000-5217-2.

599 Martínez DE (May 1998). "Mortality patterns suggest lack of senescence in hydra". Experimental Gerontology. 33 (3): 217–25.

600 Schaible R, Sussman M, Kramer BH. Aging and potential for self-renewal: hydra living in the age of aging - a mini-review. Gerontology. 2014;60(6):548-56.

601 https://www.lifespan.io/news/is-immortality-possible/?utm_source=google&ut m_medium=cpc&utm_campaign=16570202286&utm_content=&utm_term=wh at%20animals%20are%20immortal&gclid=CjwKCAjww7KmBhAyEiwA5-PUSo zG6aH5_qAK9SoI1CCNs3Sd0Sl6VyNRJVVchzDTDUmwORUEIrkL5xoCUjk QAvD_BwE

602 Stenvinkel P, Shiels PG. Long-lived animals with negligible senescence: clues for ageing research. Biochem Soc Trans. 2019 Aug 30;47(4):1157-1164.

603 Valenzano DR, Terzibasi E, Genade T, Cattaneo A, Domenici L, Cellerino A. Resveratrol prolongs lifespan and retards the onset of age-related markers in a short-lived vertebrate. Curr Biol. 2006;16:296- 300.

604 Smith P, Willemsen D, Popkes M, Metge F, Gandiwa E, Reichard M, et al. Regulation of life span by the gut microbiota in the short-lived African turquoise killifish. Elife. 2017;6:e27014.

605 Lee CH, Steiner T, Petrof EO, Smieja M, Roscoe D, Nematallah A, Weese JS, Collins S, Moayyedi P, Crowther M, Ropeleski MJ, Jayaratne P, Higgins D, Li Y, Rau NV, Kim PT. Frozen vs fresh fecal microbiota transplantation and clinical resolution of diarrhea in patients with recurrent Clostridium difficile infection: a randomized clinical trial. JAMA. 2016;315:142–149.

606 https://www.healthcarepackaging.com/quick-hits/article/22860465/fda-approv es-first-fecal-transplant-pill#:~:text=The%20pill%2C%20called%20%22SER%2D, to%20help%20prevent%20recurrent%20C.

607 Feuerstadt P, Louie TJ, Lashner B, Wang EEL, Diao L, Bryant JA, Sims M, Kraft CS, Cohen SH, Berenson CS, Korman LY, Ford CB, Litcofsky KD, Lombardo MJ, Wortman JR, Wu H, Auniņš JG, McChalicher CWJ, Winkler JA, McGovern BH,

Trucksis M, Henn MR, von Moltke L. SER-109, an Oral Microbiome Therapy for Recurrent *Clostridioides difficile* Infection. N Engl J Med. 2022 Jan 20;386(3):220-229.

608 Amor C, Feucht J, Leibold J, Ho YJ, Zhu C, Alonso-Curbelo D, Mansilla-Soto J, Boyer JA, Li X, Giavridis T, Kulick A, Houlihan S, Peerschke E, Friedman SL, Ponomarev V, Piersigilli A, Sadelain M, Lowe SW. Senolytic CAR T cells reverse senescence-associated pathologies. Nature. 2020 Jul;583(7814):127-132.

609 Jogalekar MP, Rajendran RL, Khan F, Dmello C, Gangadaran P, Ahn BC. CAR T-Cell-Based gene therapy for cancers: new perspectives, challenges, and clinical developments. Front Immunol. 2022 Jul 22;13:925985.

610 https://www.nhm.ac.uk/discover/immortal-jellyfish-secret-to-cheating-death.html#:~:text=The%20hydrozoan%20Turritopsis%20dohrnii%2C%20an,been%20dubbed%20the%20immortal%20jellyfish.

611 https://www.batepapocomnetuno.com/post/small-jellyfish-and-the-secret-to-eternal-life

612 Kubota S. (2011). Repeating rejuvenation in Turritopsis, an immortal hydrozoan (Cnidaria, Hydrozoa). Biogeography 13: 101–103.

613 Shen CN, Burke ZD, Tosh D. Transdifferentiation, metaplasia and tissue regeneration. Organogenesis. 2004 Oct;1(2):36-44.

614 Takahashi, K.; Yamanaka, S. (2006). "Induction of Pluripotent Stem Cells from Mouse Embryonic and Adult Fibroblast Cultures by Defined Factors". Cell. 126 (4): 663–76.

615 Takahashi, K.; Tanabe, K.; Ohnuki, M.; Narita, M.; Ichisaka, T.; Tomoda, K.; Yamanaka, S. (2007). "Induction of Pluripotent Stem Cells from Adult Human Fibroblasts by Defined Factors". Cell. 131 (5): 861–872.

616 Lensch MW, Mummery CL. From stealing fire to cellular reprogramming: a scientific history leading to the 2012 Nobel Prize. Stem Cell Reports. 2013 Jun 4;1(1):5-17.

617 Abad M, Mosteiro L, Pantoja C, Cañamero M, Rayon T, Ors I, Graña O, Megías D, Domínguez O, Martínez D, Manzanares M, Ortega S, Serrano M. Reprogramming in vivo produces teratomas and iPS cells with totipotency features. Nature. 2013 Oct 17;502(7471):340-5.

618 Gene Therapy Mediated Partial Reprogramming Extends Lifespan and Reverses Age-Related Changes in Aged Mice. Carolina Cano Macip, Rokib Hasan, Victoria Hoznek, Jihyun Kim, Louis Metzger IV, Saumil Sethna, Noah Davidsohn bioRxiv 2023.01.04.522507; doi: https://doi.org/10.1101/2023.01.04.522507

619 Yang JH, Hayano M, Griffin PT, Amorim JA, Bonkowski MS, Apostolides JK, Salfati EL, Blanchette M, Munding EM, Bhakta M, Chew YC, Guo W, Yang X, Maybury-Lewis S, Tian X, Ross JM, Coppotelli G, Meer MV, Rogers-Hammond R, Vera DL, Lu YR, Pippin JW, Creswell ML, Dou Z, Xu C, Mitchell SJ, Das A, O'Connell BL, Thakur S, Kane AE, Su Q, Mohri Y, Nishimura EK, Schaevitz L, Garg N, Balta AM, Rego MA, Gregory-Ksander M, Jakobs TC, Zhong L, Wakimoto H, El Andari J, Grimm D, Mostoslavsky R, Wagers AJ, Tsubota K, Bonasera SJ, Palmeira CM, Seidman JG, Seidman CE, Wolf NS, Kreiling JA, Sedivy JM, Murphy GF, Green RE, Garcia BA, Berger SL, Oberdoerffer P, Shankland SJ, Gladyshev VN, Ksander BR, Pfenning AR, Rajman LA, Sinclair DA. Loss of epigenetic information as a cause of mammalian aging. Cell. 2023 Jan 19;186(2):305-326.

620 https://www.technologyreview.com/2021/09/04/1034364/altos-labs-silicon-valleys-jeff-bezos-milner-bet-living-forever/

621 https://www.ft.com/content/60d9271c-ae0a-4d44-8b11-956cd2e484a9

622 https://www.ft.com/content/60d9271c-ae0a-4d44-8b11-956cd2e484a9

623 https://www.cbsnews.com/news/richest-americans-are-more-likely-to-live-longer-than-those-lower-down-the-ladder/

624 Davis, John. New Methuselahs: The Ethics of Life Extension. 2018. Cambridge: The MIT Press.

625 Linden, Ingemar Patrick. The Case Against Death. 2022. Cambridge: The MIT Press.

626 https://www.ft.com/content/60d9271c-ae0a-4d44-8b11-956cd2e484a9

YOU MIGHT WANT A DEATH PLAN

627 Lee SH, Lee TW, Ju S, Yoo JW, Lee SJ, Cho YJ, Jeong YY, Lee JD, Kim HC. Outcomes of very elderly (≥ 80 years) critical-ill patients in a medical intensive care unit of a tertiary hospital in Korea. Korean J Intern Med. 2017 Jul;32(4):675-681.

628 Guillon, A., Laurent, E., Godillon, L. et al. Long-term mortality of elderly patients after intensive care unit admission for COVID-19. Intensive Care Med 47, 710–712 (2021).

629 Guillon A, Hermetet C, Barker KA, Jouan Y, Gaborit C, Ehrmann S, Le Manach Y, Dequin PF, Grammatico-Guillon L. Long-term survival of elderly patients after intensive care unit admission for acute respiratory infection: a population-based, propensity score-matched cohort study. Crit Care. 2020 Jun 29;24(1):384.

630 Nahm, M., Greyson, B. Kelly, E. and Harroldsson, E. (2011)Terminal Lucidity: A Review and a Case Collection. Archives of Gerontology and Geriatrics. 55,138-142.

631 Levett DZH, Grimmett C. Psychological factors, prehabilitation and surgical outcomes: evidence and future directions. Anaesthesia. 2019 Jan;74 Suppl 1:36-42.

632 Cohen, S. (2004). Social Relationships and Health. American Psychologist, 59(8), 676–684.

633 Leach, John. Survival Psychology. (1994) London: Palgrave Macmillan.

634 Bukhtoiarov OV, Arkhangel'skiĭ AE. [Psychogenic death in oncology: validation, pathogenesis, development patterns and prophylactic potential]. Vopr Onkol. 2006;52(6):708-15.

635 Cannon WB. Bodily Changes in Pain, Hunger, Fear and Rage. New York, NY: D. Appleton & Company; 1915.

636 https://www.simplypsychology.org/fight-flight-freeze-fawn.html

637 Leach J. 'Give-up-itis' revisited: Neuropathology of extremis. Med Hypotheses. 2018 Nov;120:14-21.

638 Bures, Frank. Inside psychogenic death, the phenomenon of "thinking" yourself to death. Dec 2021.
       https://www.salon.com/2021/12/31/psychogenic/

639 Gawande, Atul. (2017). Being Mortal: Medicine and What Matters in the End. London: Picador.

640 https://en.wikipedia.org/wiki/Assisted_suicide_in_the_United_States

641 https://en.wikipedia.org/wiki/Assisted_suicide

642 OREGON DEATH WITH DIGNITY ACT: 2015 DATA SUMMARY" (PDF). Oregon.gov. Oregon Health Authority. Retrieved 4 October 2016.

643 https://www.opb.org/article/2022/03/31/what-oregons-death-with-dignity-set tlement-means-for-terminally-ill-patients-from-out-of-state/#:~:text=Oregon% 20is%20now%20the%20first,law%20to%20end%20their%20lives.

644 Pham HH, Lerner BH. In the patient's best interest? Revisiting sexual autonomy and sterilization of the developmentally disabled. West J Med. 2001 Oct;175(4):280-3.

CONCLUSION

645 Dass Ram. Be Here Now. (1971). San Cristobal: Lama Foundation.